REMEMBERING PINOCHET'S CHILE

✻

A book in the series

LATIN AMERICA OTHERWISE: LANGUAGES, EMPIRES, NATIONS

Series editors:

Walter D. Mignolo, Duke University

Irene Silverblatt, Duke University

Sonia Saldívar-Hull, University of California, Los Angeles

LATIN AMERICA OTHERWISE: LANGUAGES, EMPIRES, NATIONS
is a critical series. It aims to explore the emergence and consequences of concepts
used to define "Latin America" while at the same time exploring the broad interplay of political, economic, and cultural practices that have shaped Latin American
worlds. Latin America, at the crossroads of competing imperial designs and local
responses, has been construed as a geocultural and geopolitical entity since the
nineteenth century. This series provides a starting point to redefine Latin America
as a configuration of political, linguistic, cultural, and economic intersections that
demands a continuous reappraisal of the role of the Americas in history, and of the
ongoing process of globalization and the relocation of people and cultures that have
characterized Latin America's experience. *Latin America Otherwise: Languages,
Empires, Nations* is a forum that confronts established geocultural constructions,
that rethinks area studies and disciplinary boundaries, that assesses convictions
of the academy and of public policy, and that, correspondingly, demands that the
practices through which we produce knowledge and understanding about and from
Latin America be subject to rigorous and critical scrutiny.

September 11 brought terror to Chile when General Augusto Pinochet, in 1973, led a coup to overthrow the country's elected president, Salvador Allende. With the backing of the United States, Pinochet used the machinery of state to intimidate Chile's citizenry and unspeakable acts of state violence—torture and murder —became life's daily fare. Steve Stern here asks piercing questions of historical memory—how those who suffered as well as those who caused such inhuman suffering recalled those terrible times.

Steve Stern has written an extraordinary trilogy, "The Memory Box of Pinochet's Chile," devoted to those years and how they were understood by participants in the horrors. The first book, *Remembering Pinochet's Chile: On the Eve of London 1998*, tackles interpretive questions raised by "memory" itself. Stern takes advantage of a turning point in Chilean history—when Pinochet, sought by a Spanish magistrate for crimes against humanity, was placed under house arrest outside London for more than a year and was later indicted by a Chilean court after returning to his homeland. This was a moment when the complications and competitions of "memory" surfaced with a vengeance. In *Remembering Pinochet's Chile*, Stern presents a typology of prisms through which historical memories of a chilling, but indelible, moment were sorted out, conjoined, and opposed to one another. With humanity and compassion, Stern introduces us to the conflicting and overlapping structures of meaning through which that history is filtered—along with the sometimes intersecting, sometimes clashing visions they project. *Remembering Pinochet's Chile* forces us to reconsider—to see "otherwise"—that tortured history and the memories that, in the end, give it life.

STEVE J. STERN

❊

Remembering Pinochet's Chile

On the Eve of London 1998

BOOK ONE OF THE TRILOGY: *The Memory Box of Pinochet's Chile*

Duke University Press   Durham & London 2006

© 2006 Duke University Press

All rights reserved

Printed in the United States of America

on acid-free paper

Designed by C. H. Westmoreland

Typeset in Scala by Keystone Typesetting, Inc.

Library of Congress Cataloging-in-Publication

Data appear on the last printed page of

this book.

First hardcover edition © 2004 Duke University Press

Para mi tan querida Florencia,

mi chilenita de corazón,

corazón sin fronteras . . .

Contents

ACKNOWLEDGMENTS   xi

MAPS   xvi

Introduction to the Trilogy: The Memory Box
of Pinochet's Chile   xix

Introduction to Book One: Remembering
Pinochet's Chile   1

Chapter 1
Heroic Memory: Ruin into Salvation   7
AFTERWORD Childhood Holidays, Childhood Salvation   35

Chapter 2
Dissident Memory: Rupture, Persecution, Awakening   39
AFTERWORD The Lore of Goodness and Remorse   68

Chapter 3
Indifferent Memory: Closing the Box on the Past   88
AFTERWORD The Accident: Temptations of Silence   102

Chapter 4
From Loose Memory to Emblematic Memory:
Knots on the Social Body   104
AFTERWORD Memory Tomb of the Unknown Soldier   134

CONCLUSION: Memories and Silences of the Heart   143

ABBREVIATIONS USED IN NOTES AND ESSAY ON SOURCES   155

NOTES   157

ESSAY ON SOURCES   215

INDEX   237

Acknowledgments

✳

If the measure of one's riches is people—the help and friendship one receives from others—I am one of the richest persons on earth. I have so many people to thank for making this project possible, and for improving how it turned out.

In Chile, the numbers of people who helped are so many I cannot list them all. I am deeply grateful to every person who consented to an interview, a conversation, or an argument; to the people who provided documents from their personal archives; to the staffs of the archives, documentation centers, and libraries; to the human rights activists and the victim-survivors who inspired and challenged me. My colleagues at Facultad Latinoamericana de Ciencias Sociales (FLACSO)–Chile provided an office base, intellectual exchanges, and contacts; a library and network of expert transcribers of interview tapes; and a supportive human environment. I owe particular thanks to Claudio Fuentes, José Olavarría, and Marisa Weinstein for support, intellectual advice, sharing of research, and, in Marisa's case, research assistance; to Magaly Ortíz for organizing a network of people, including herself, to produce interview transcripts; to María Inés Bravo for her amazing FLACSO library and ability to find materials; to Enrique Correa and Francisco Rojas for institutional support; and, most especially, to Alicia Frohmann and Teresa Valdés, for their intellectual engagement and suggestions, their generosity with useful contacts, and their personal affection and friendship. Alicia's help extended from everyday discussions in her office at FLACSO, to comments and critical suggestions after reading a first draft of the first and third books of the trilogy. Teresa worked through ideas at almost every stage of the way, generously shared contacts and her Mujeres Por La Vida archive, and offered a helpful critique of an early formulation of ideas. At the Fundación de Documentación y Archivo de la Vicaría de la Solidaridad, the most important memory and human rights archive and library in Chile, I owe a special thanks to three amazing women who offered warmth, knowledge, and access to their documentary treasure: Carmen Garretón, María Paz Vergara, and Mariana Cáceres. I owe similar thanks to Teresa Rubio, a dear friend and dedicated bibliographer and custodian of documents at the Fundación Salvador Allende, and to my close friend Helen Hughes, photographer extraordinaire, for sharing her photojournalism collection and reproduction of numerous photographs in Books Two and Three of this trilogy.

Among my other colleagues and friends in Chile whose intellectual guidance and personal support meant more than they may know, I thank Roberta Bacic, Mario Garcés, my cousin Gastón Gómez Bernales, Elizabeth Lira, Pedro Matta, Juan O'Brien, Anne Perotin and Alex Wilde, Julio Pinto and Verónica Valdivia Ortiz de Zárate, Alfredo Riquelme, Claudio Rolle, Gonzalo Rovira, Sol Serrano, María Elena Valenzuela, Augusto Varas, Pilar Videla and her family, and José Zalaquett. Sol Serrano was a model colleague and warm friend. She shared her astute historical mind, her experiences and social contacts, materials from her library, her interpretations and disagreements. Sol and Pepe Zalaquett also demonstrated extraordinary generosity by reading and critiquing the entire first draft of the trilogy.

Among the busy public figures who made time for interviews and discussion, I must especially thank the late Sola Sierra, President of the Association of Relatives of the Disappeared (Agrupación de Familiares de Detenidos-Desaparecidos), and former Chilean President Patricio Aylwin Azócar. I did not see eye to eye with either on every point, nor did they agree with one another on every point. But precisely for that reason, each taught me a great deal and each proved generous, direct, and inspiring.

A number of persons anchored in varied countries and disciplinary perspectives enriched my learning process. After the initial stage of research, it was my privilege to work as a collaborating faculty member on a Social Science Research Council (SSRC) project to train and mentor young Latin American intellectuals—from Argentina, Brazil, Chile, Paraguay, Peru, and Uruguay—on issues of memory, repression, and democratization. The inspired idea behind the project was to build a critical mass of transnationally networked young intellectuals able to research and reflect rigorously on the wave of violent military dictatorships, and attendant memory struggles and legacies, that had shaped Brazil and Southern Cone countries in recent times, and on related memory issues that emerged in the wake of the Shining Path war period in Peru. Involvement in this work enhanced my thought process, intellectual exchange networks, and feedback enormously. I wish to thank Elizabeth Jelin, the Argentine faculty director of the project; Eric Hershberg, the SSRC organizer and codirector of the project; Carlos

Iván Degregori, who took on a codirecting role as Peruvian experiences were integrated into the project; and the fellows and other faculty collaborators, especially Susana Kaufman, who worked during one or another phase of the project.

I also wish to thank my colleagues in the University of Wisconsin Legacies of Authoritarianism study circle, especially Leigh Payne and Louis Bickford, Ksenija Bilbija, Al McCoy, Cynthia Milton, and Thongchai Winichakul, for opportunities for comparative and interdisciplinary thinking on memory issues. Additional Wisconsin colleagues who offered helpful insights, encouragement, suggestions, and critiques included Florence Bernault, Alda Blanco, Stanley Kutler, Gerda Lerner, the late George Mosse, Francisco Scarano, Thomas Skidmore (now at Brown University), and Joseph Thome. I wish to thank, too, various colleagues and students who heard talks, engaged the issues, and offered suggestions at international meetings and workshops in Buenos Aires, Cape Town, London, Lucila del Mar (Argentina), Montevideo, Piriápolis (Uruguay), and Santiago; in Latin American Studies Association panels in the United States; and in lectures and seminars at various U.S. universities. Finally, I must thank two of the leading senior historians of Chile, Paul Drake and Peter Winn, for warm encouragement and valuable ideas during various phases of the project, and the graduate students at the University of Wisconsin, for the intellectual energy and insight they bring into our learning community and its seminars on violence and memory.

I received indispensable material assistance. I thank the Fulbright-Hays Faculty Research Abroad Program, the Social Science Research Council, and the University of Wisconsin at Madison for generous grants without which this project could not have happened. I also thank Nancy Appelbaum, Claudio Barrientos, Gavin Sacks, and Marisa Weinstein for valuable research assistance and good cheer in various phases of the project; and Onno Brouwer and Marieka Brouwer of the Cartographic Laboratory of the University of Wisconsin at Madison, for production of the maps, accompanied by expert technical and aesthetic counsel.

My editor at Duke University Press, Valerie Millholland, has been a source of wisdom throughout this project. Valerie helped clarify a host of intellectual, practical, and aesthetic issues, and the particular demands of a trilogy project. Her astute professional advice, her understanding of the human issues at stake, and her enthusiasm for the project have added up to an extraordinary experience and a valued friendship. I am deeply grateful, also, to the many people at the Press who brought the project to fruition and to my patient and skilled copy editor, Sonya Manes.

Two anonymous readers for Duke University Press offered meticulous and thoughtful advice in response to the first draft of the trilogy. A third reader offered equally pertinent advice on a subsequent draft. I thank them, along with Chilean readers Alicia Frohmann, Sol Serrano, and José Zalaquett, for taking the time to review and critique the manuscript. I have not responded successfully to every point or suggestion, but my readers saved me from specific mistakes and offered ideas and insights that helped me improve the larger analysis. I accept full responsibility for the shortcomings that remain despite their best efforts.

Finally, I must also thank my family. The large Chilean family I acquired by marriage to Florencia Mallon offered affection, friendship, contacts, and experiences. My deepest thanks to *mis tías y tíos* Tenca and the late Roberto, Celina and Gastón, Alfredo and Smyrna, and Nieves; *mis primos* Polencho and Gabriela, Diego, Gastón and Tita, Pablo and Sol, Ignacio and Alejandra, Chimina and Gonzalo; my parents-in-law Nacha and Dick, with whom we enjoyed a wonderful family reunion in Chile; my nieces and nephews who scampered around during family gatherings; and my own children, Ramón and Rafa, for navigating an international life and its challenges together, supporting the idea of the project, and reminding me of what is enduring and important. My own large U.S.-based family of siblings and parents also provided important support, and I must especially thank my mother, Adel Weisz Rosenzweig Stern. Mom, in a sense you raised me to write this trilogy. The treasured stories of life in Hungary with my grandparents and aunts and uncles, the fears and nightmares of Auschwitz and Buchenwald you also shared despite your desire not to do so, the spoken and unspoken memories and anxieties that permeated our lives, the fierce love and closeness we always experienced, these kindled a fire. Someday, I would have to confront and write about the most challenging and paradoxical aspects of twentieth-century history—the way modern times brought forth a horrifying human capacity to organize, and implement systematically, political projects of mind-bending absoluteness, violence, destructiveness, and hatred; and the way modernity *also* brought forth an amazing human capacity to build or reassert values of universal caring, dignity, rights, and solidarity, even in trying and terrifying times.

I dedicate this trilogy to my brilliant colleague and beloved partner for life, Florencia E. Mallon. The intellectual ideas and information and support you contributed to this work were fundamental, yet they constitute only a modest fraction of the many reasons for a thank you and a dedication. Our journey together has been a wondrous gift. May the journey never end.

1. Chile in the Pinochet Era.

This map shows major cities, towns, and sites of memory struggle mentioned in the trilogy text. It excludes the Juan Fernández Islands, Easter Island, and Chilean Antarctic territory. For a more detailed geography of places and memory sites in central and southern regions, see map 2 (opposite). *Cartographic Laboratory, University of Wisconsin, Madison.*

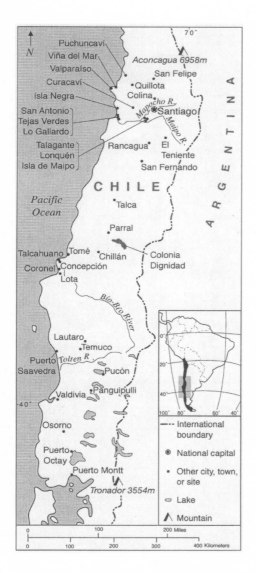

2. Central and Southern Chile in the Pinochet Era.
This map shows cities, towns, and sites of memory struggle mentioned in the trilogy text, and corresponding to central and southern regions (Regions V through X and the Metropolitan Region). *Cartographic Laboratory, University of Wisconsin, Madison.*

Introduction to
the Trilogy

※

The Memory Box of Pinochet's Chile

This trilogy, The Memory Box of Pinochet's Chile, studies how Chileans have struggled to define the meaning of a collective trauma: the military action of 11 September 1973, when a junta composed of Augusto Pinochet and three other generals toppled the elected socialist government of Salvador Allende, and the massive political violence unleashed against perceived enemies and critics of the new regime.

The time frame under analysis corresponds to Pinochet's period as a major figure in public life—from 1973, when he stepped into rule as the army's commanding general in the new military junta, to 2001, when a Chilean court ruling on his health released him from jeopardy in criminal proceedings but completed his marginalization from public life. Many of the tensions and dilemmas analyzed for the 1990–2001 postdictatorship period, however, continued to shape national life and power after 2001. In this sense, "Pinochet's Chile" and its attendant memory struggles have remained a strong legacy, even as the person of Pinochet has receded.

The crisis of 1973 and the violence of the new order generated a contentious memory question in Chilean life. The memory question proved central to the remaking of Chilean politics and culture, first under the military regime that ruled until 1990, and subsequently under a democracy shadowed by legacies of dictatorship and a still-powerful military. As a result, the study of memory cannot be disentangled from an account of wider political, economic, and cultural contexts. Indeed, the making of memory offers a useful new lens on the general course of Chilean history in the last quarter of the twentieth century. To my knowledge, although excellent studies have established a reliable chronicle of basic political and economic events (some of them related to collective memory themes) under the rule of Pinochet, there still does not exist an account that systematically traces the long process of making and disputing memory by distinct social actors within a deeply divided society, across the periods of dictatorship and democratic transition.

The memory question is not only a major subject in its own right; its history opens up the underexplored "hearts and minds" aspect of the dictatorship experience. We often see the history and legacy of recent dictatorships in South America, especially Chile, in terms of several now-obvious and well-analyzed aspects: the facts of brute force and repression, and the attending spread of fear; the imposition of neoliberal economic policy, and the corresponding dismantling of statist approaches to social welfare and economic development; the rise of a depoliticized technocratic culture, within and beyond the state, and its consequences for social movements and political activism; and the political pacts and continuing power of militaries that conditioned transitions and the quality of democracies in South America in the 1980s and 1990s. These are crucial themes (and many were not at first obvious). A superb social science literature has emerged over the years to analyze them—a key early wave on "bureaucratic authoritarianism" led by Guillermo O'Donnell among others, followed by more recent waves on transitions and democratization. This literature has also illuminated relationships between modernity, technocracy, and state terror—that is, South America's version of a central disturbing issue of twentieth-century world history, posed forcefully by reflections on the Holocaust, and reinforced by regimes of terror and mass atrocity that arose in various world regions after World War II.[1]

The history of "memory" enables us to see an additional aspect of Chilean life that is subtle yet central: the making and unmaking of political and cultural legitimacy, notwithstanding violent rule by terror. In the struggle for hearts and minds in Chile, the memory question became strategic—politically, morally, existentially—both during and after dictatorship. In this way "memory," which by the 1980s crystallized as a key cultural idea, code word, and battleground, casts fresh light on the entire era of dictatorship and constrained democracy from the 1970s through the 1990s. Its study complements the fine scholarly analyses that have given more attention to the facts of force and imposition than to the making of subjectivity and legitimacy within an era of force. Indeed, the lens of memory struggle invites us to move beyond rigid conceptual dichotomy between a top-down perspective oriented to elite engineering, and a bottom-up perspective that sees its obverse: suppression, punctuated by outbursts of protest. In this scheme, the moments of protest render visible the frustration, desperation, organizing, and resilience that often have an underground or marginalized aspect in conditions of repressive dictatorship or constrained democracy.

Tracing the history of memory struggles invites us to consider not only the genuine gap and tensions between top-down and bottom-up perspectives but also more subtle interactive dynamics within a history of violence and repression. We see efforts of persuasion from above to shore up or expand a social base from below, not simply to solidify support and concentrate power from above; grassroots efforts to seek influence among, split off, or pressure the elites of state, church, and political parties, not simply to organize networks, influence, and protest among subaltern groups and underdogs; specific collaborations in media, human rights, cultural, or political projects that yield both tension and synergy among actors in distinct "locations" in the social hierarchy, from respectable or powerful niches in state, church, and professional institutions, to precarious or stigmatized standing as street activists, victim-survivors, the poor and unemployed, and alleged subversives. Memory projects—to record and define the reality of the Allende era and its culminating crisis of 1973, to record and define the reality of military rule and its human rights drama—ended up becoming central to the logic by which people sought and won legitimacy in a politically divided and socially heterogeneous society that experienced a great turn and trauma.[2]

The repression in Pinochet's Chile was large in scale and layered in its implementation. In a country of only 10 million people in 1973, individually proved cases of death or disappearance by state agents (or persons in their hire) amount to about 3,000; torture victims run in the dozens of thousands; documented political arrests exceed 82,000; the exile flow amounts to about 200,000. These are lower-end figures, suitable for a rock-bottom baseline. Even using a conservative methodology, a reasonable estimated toll for deaths and disappearances by state agents is 3,500–4,500, for political detentions 150,000–200,000. Some credible torture estimates surpass the 100,000 threshold, some credible exile estimates reach 400,000.[3]

The experience of a state turning violently against a portion of its own citizenry is always dramatic. In a society of Chile's size, these figures translate into pervasiveness. A majority of families, including supporters and sympathizers of the military regime, had a relative, a friend, or an acquaintance touched by one or another form of repression. Just as important, from political and cultural points of view, Pinochet's Chile pioneered a new technique of repression in the Latin American context: systematic "disappear-ance" of people. After the point of abduction, people vanished in a cloud of secrecy, denial, and misinformation by the state. Also important was cul-tural shock. Many Chileans believed such violence by the state—beyond margins set by legal procedure and human decency—to be an impossibility. Fundamentally, their society was too civilized, too law abiding, too demo-cratic. In 1973, many victims voluntarily turned themselves in when they appeared on arrest lists.[4]

The Chilean story of memory struggle over the meanings and truths of a violent collective shock is part of a larger story of "dirty war" dictatorships in South America. During the 1960s and 1970s, at the height of the Cold War, ideas of social justice and revolution sparked significant sympathy and so-cial mobilization. Urban shantytowns were populated by poor laborers, street sellers, and migrants in search of a better life. Many rural regions evinced systems of land tenure, technology, and social abuse that seemed anachronistic as well as violent and unjust. Educated youths and progres-sive middle-class sectors saw in the young Cuban revolution either an in-spiring example or a wake-up call that argued for deep reforms. Presidents of influential countries such as Brazil and Chile announced agrarian reform —an idea whose political time had finally arrived. On the fringes of estab-lished politics, some middle-class youths began to form guerrilla groups, hoping to produce a revolution through sheer audacity.

Not surprisingly, proponents of deep change—whether they considered themselves "reformers" or "revolutionaries"—ran up against entrenched opposition, fear, and polarization. The obvious antagonists included the socially privileged under the status quo, that is, wealthy families and social circles under fire in the new age of reform, middle-class sectors who either identified with conservative social values or were frightened by possible upheaval, and notable landowning families and their local intermediaries in rural regions facing agrarian reform. There were unexpected antagonists, too, including persons of modest means and backgrounds. Some poor and lower middle-class residents of urban shantytowns, for example, proved nervous and interested in order as they saw polarization unfold, were du-bious about the viability of grand reforms, or had aligned themselves on one side or another of the political squabbles among competing reformers and revolutionaries.[5]

Most important for the political and cultural future, however, the antagonists included militaries whose doctrines of national security, consistent with the ideology of the Cold War, came to define the internal enemy as the fundamental enemy of the nation. In this line of thinking, the whole way of understanding politics that had arisen in Latin America was a cancerous evil. The problem went beyond that of achieving transitory relief by toppling a government if it went too far in threatening the military forces' institutional cohesion or interests, or if it went too far in upsetting the status quo, mobilizing the downtrodden, tolerating self-styled revolutionaries or guerrillas, or sparking economic crisis or social disorder. The "political class" of elites who worked the body politic had become addicted to demagoguery, and civil society included too many people addicted to the idea of organizing politically to end injustice. The result was fertile ground for the spread of Marxism and subversion that would destroy society from within.

As military regimes displaced civilian ones, they defined a mission more ambitious than transitory relief from an untenable administration. They would create a new order. The new military regimes would conduct a "dirty war" to root out subversives and their sympathizers once and for all, to frighten and depoliticize society at large, to lay the foundation for a technocratic public life. To a greater or lesser degree, such regimes spread over much of South America—Brazil in 1964 (with notable "hardening" in 1968), Bolivia in 1971, Chile and Uruguay in 1973, and Argentina in 1976. Paraguay, ruled by General Alfredo Stroessner since 1954, followed a distinct political dynamic but aligned itself with the transnational aspect of the new scheme—"Operation Condor," a program of secret police cooperation across South American borders. To a greater or lesser degree, all these regimes also generated contentious struggles over "memory"—truth, justice, meaning.[6]

The Chilean version of struggles over collective memory is worth telling in its own right. It is a dramatic story, filled with heroism and disappointment on matters of life and death. It is a story of moral consciousness, as human beings attempted to understand and to convince compatriots of the meaning of a great and unfinished trauma and its ethical and political implications. It is a story that lends itself to serious historical research, because it has unfolded over a long stretch of time, because survivors and witnesses are still alive, and because it generated substantial and diverse documentary trails. Indeed, this trilogy draws on three streams of sources: written documents—archival, published, and, more recently, electronic— that constitute the traditional heart of historical research; audio and visual traces of the past, in television and video archives, photojournalism, radio transcripts, and sound recordings; and oral history, including formal semi-structured interviews, less formal interviews and exchanges, and field notes from participant-observation experiences and focus groups. The "Essay on Sources" offers a more technical guide to these sources, as well as a reflection on oral history method and debates.

The Chilean version of the memory question is also worth telling because of its international significance. For better or worse, the long and narrow strip of western South America we call Chile has constituted an influential symbol in world culture in the last half century. As the model "Alliance for Progress" country of the 1960s, it constituted the Kennedy and Johnson administrations' best example of a Latin American society that could stop "another Cuba" through democratic social reforms assisted by the United States. When Salvador Allende was elected president in 1970, his project—an electoral road to socialism and justice in a Third World society—exerted almost irresistible symbolism. The blending of a Western-style electoral political culture with socialist idealism and economic policies had obvious resonance in Western Europe and its labor-oriented parties, and it provoked extreme hostility from the Nixon administration. The David-versus-Goliath aspect of relations between Chile and the United States proved compelling across the conventional fault lines of international politics. Allende's Chile drew sympathetic attention not only among radicals, social democrats, and solidarity-minded activists in the West but also in the Soviet bloc countries and in the "Non-aligned Movement" then influential in the Third World and the United Nations. Chile, a small country determined to achieve social justice by democratic means, against odds set by a monstrous power spreading death and destruction in Vietnam, stood as the beleaguered yet proud symbol of a wider yearning.

After 1973, Chile continued to occupy a large symbolic place in world culture. For critics and admirers alike, the new regime became a kind of laboratory, an example of early neoliberalism in Latin America and its power to transform economic life. Most of all and most controversially, Pinochet and the Chile he created became icons of the "dirty war" dictatorships spreading over South America. For many, Pinochet was also the icon of U.S. government (or Nixon-Kissinger) complicity with evil in the name of anti-Communism.

In short, the symbolic power of Augusto Pinochet's Chile crossed national borders. For the world human rights movement, as Kathryn Sikkink has shown, Chile's 1973 crisis and violence constituted a turning point. It marked a "before" and "after" by galvanizing new memberships in human rights organizations such as Amnesty International; by sparking new organizations, such as Washington Office on Latin America; by spreading "human rights" as an international vocabulary and common sense—a public concern voiced in transnational networks from the United Nations, to churches and nongovernmental organizations including solidarity groups, to influential media and political leaders including the U.S. Congress. The symbolism of Pinochet and Chile's 1973 crisis proved more than a short-lived blip. For many (including baby boomers in Europe and the United States, who became politically and culturally influential in the 1990s) it had been a defining moment of moral growth and awareness. The symbolism was reactivated in October 1998, when London police detained Pinochet by request of a Spanish judge investigating crimes against humanity. It has been reinforced by the precedent set by his arrest for international human rights law.[7]

What has given memory of Chile's 1973 crisis and the violence it unleashed such compelling value? As a story in its own right, and as a symbol beyond its borders? The answers are many, and they include the value of work undertaken by many Chileans in exile—to mobilize international solidarity, to work professionally on themes of human rights, to build circuits of political dialogue, with Europeans and North Americans as well as among themselves, about the meaning of the Chilean experience. Among many valid reasons, however, one cuts to the core. Chile is Latin America's example of the "German problem." The Holocaust and the Nazi experience bequeathed to contemporary culture a profoundly troubling question. How does a country capable of amazing achievement in the realm of science or culture also turn out to harbor amazing capacity for barbarism? Can one reconcile—or better, disentangle—the Germany that produced and appreciated Beethoven and Wagner from the Germany that produced and appreciated Hitler and Goebbels?

In the case of Latin America, tragic historical patterns and international cultural prejudices may incline the foreign citizen-observer to view violent repression and the overthrow of elected civilian governments as in some way "expected"—part of Latin America's "normal" course of history. After all, Latin America has not been notable for the resilience of democratic institutions, nor for hesitation about using strong-arm methods of political rule.

In the case of Chile, however, both Chileans and outsiders believed in a myth of exceptionalism. Chile was, like other Latin American societies, afflicted by great social needs and great social conflicts. But it was also a land of political and cultural sophistication. Its poets (Gabriela Mistral, Pablo Neruda) won Nobel Prizes. Its Marxist and non-Marxist leaders were veterans of a parliamentary tradition resonant with Western Europe. Its intellectuals worked out respected new approaches to international economics with the United Nations Economic Commission on Latin America. Its soldiers understood not to intervene in the political arrangements of civilians. In Chile, social mobilization and turbulence could be reconciled with the rule of law and competitive elections. The political system was democratic and resilient. Over time it had incorporated once-marginalized social sectors—the urban middle class, workers, women, peasants, and the urban poor. Its leaders and polemicists knew how to retreat into the conserving world of gentleman politicians, where cultural refinement could be appreciated, a drink or a joke could be shared, the heat of verbal excess and battle pushed aside for another day. In this clublike atmosphere, personal confidences were reestablished to navigate the next round of conflict and negotiation. Compared to other Latin American countries, military intervention was rare and had not happened since the early 1930s. Chile's "amazing achievement," in the Latin American context, was precisely its resilient democratic constitutionalism.

Not only did the myth of democratic resilience finally break apart under the stresses of the 1960s and early 1970s. The country also descended into a world of brutality beyond the imaginable, at least in a Chilean urban or middle-class context. The assumed core of Chile, civilized and democratic and incapable of trampling law or basic human decency, would not resurface for a very long time. What happened after the military takeover of 11 September 1973 was more shocking than the takeover itself.[8]

Beyond the argument that a history of memory offers insight into the "hearts and minds" drama, still present and unfinished, of Pinochet's Chile, a brief statement of how I specifically approach memory—what I am arguing against, what I am arguing for—may be useful. Two influential ideas hover over discussions of memory in Chile. The first invokes the dichotomy of memory against forgetting (*olvido*). In essence, memory struggles are struggles against oblivion. This dichotomy, of course, is pervasive in many studies of collective memory in many parts of the world and not without reason. The dialectic of memory versus forgetting is an inescapable dynamic, perceived as such by social actors in the heat of their struggles. In regimes of secrecy and misinformation, the sense of fighting oblivion, especially in the human rights community, is powerful and legitimate. In recent years, influential criticism of the postdictatorship society of the 1990s has invoked the dichotomy of remembering against forgetting to characterize Chile as a culture of oblivion, marked by a tremendous compulsion to forget the past and the uncomfortable. A second influential idea, related to the first, is that of the Faustian bargain. In this idea, amnesia occurs because the middle classes and the wealthy, as beneficiaries of economic prosperity created by the military regime, developed the habit of denial or looking the other way on matters of state violence. They accept moral complacency as the price of economic comfort—the Faustian bargain that seals "forgetting."[9]

The interpretation in this trilogy argues against these ideas. The dissent is partial; I do not wish to throw out the baby with the bathwater. At various points in the analysis, I too invoke the dialectic of memory versus forgetting and attend to the influence of economic well-being in political and cultural inclination to forget. The problem with the memory-against-forgetting dichotomy, and the related idea of a Faustian bargain, is not that they are "wrong" or "untrue" in the simple sense. It is that they are insufficient— profoundly incomplete and in some ways misleading.

What I am arguing *for* is study of contentious memory as a process of competing selective remembrances, ways of giving meaning to and drawing legitimacy from human experience. The memory-against-forgetting dichotomy is too narrow and restrictive; it tends to align one set of actors with memory and another with forgetting. In the approach I have taken, the social actors behind distinct frameworks are seeking to define that which is truthful and meaningful about a great collective trauma. They are necessarily selective as they give shape to memory, and they may all see themselves as struggling, at one point or another, against the oblivion propagated by their antagonists.

Historicizing memory in this way blurs an old conceptual distinction, given a new twist by the distinguished memory scholar Pierre Nora, between "history" as a profession or science purporting to preserve or reconstruct the unremembered or poorly remembered past; and "memory" as a subjective, often emotionally charged and flawed, awareness of a still-present past that emerges within a community environment of identity and experience. Insofar as the historian must take up memory struggles and frameworks as a theme for investigation in its own right—as a set of relationships, conflicts, motivations, and ideas that *shaped* history—the distinction begins to break down. The point of oral history research becomes not only to establish the factual truth or falsehood of events in a memory story told by an informant but also to understand what social truths or processes led people to tell their stories the way they do, in recognizable patterns. When examining the history of violent "limit experiences," moreover, the historian cannot escape the vexing problems of representation, interpretation, and "capacity to know" that attach to great atrocities. Conventional narrative strategies and analytical languages seem inadequate; professional history itself seems inadequate—one more "memory story" among others.[10]

The metaphor I find useful—to picture memory as competing selective remembrances to give meaning to, and find legitimacy within, a devastating community experience—is that of a giant, collectively built memory box. The memory chest is foundational to the community, not marginal; it sits in the living room, not in the attic. It contains several competing scripted albums, each of them works in progress that seek to define and give shape to a crucial turning point in life, much as a family album may script a wedding or a birth, an illness or a death, a crisis or a success. The box also contains "lore" and loose memories, that is, the stray photos and mini-albums that seem important to remember but do not necessarily fit easily in the larger scripts. The memory chest is a precious box to which people are drawn, to which they add or rearrange pictures and scripts, and about which they quarrel and even scuffle. This trilogy asks how Chileans built and struggled over the "memory box of Pinochet's Chile," understood as the holder of truths about a traumatic turning point in their collective lives.

When considering the consequences of such memory struggles for politics, culture, and democratization, I argue that Chile arrived at a culture of "memory impasse," more complex than a culture of oblivion, by the mid-to-late 1990s. The idea of a culture of forgetting, facilitated by Faustian complacency, is useful up to a point, but it simplifies the Chilean path of memory struggles and distorts the cultural dynamics in play. The problem turned out to be more subtle and in some ways more horrifying. On the one hand, forgetting itself included a conscious component—political and cultural decisions to "close the memory box," whether to save the political skin of those implicated by "dirty" memory, or in frustration because memory politics proved so intractable and debilitating. It is this conscious component of "remembering to forget" that is often invoked when human rights activists cite a famous phrase by Mario Benedetti, "oblivion is filled with memory." On the other hand, memory of horror and rupture also proved so unforgettable or "obstinate," and so important to the social actors and politics of partial redemocratization in the 1990s, that it could not really be buried in oblivion.[11]

What emerged instead was impasse. Cultural belief by a majority in the truth of cruel human rupture and persecution under dictatorship, and in the moral urgency of justice, unfolded alongside political belief that Pinochet, the military, and their social base of supporters and sympathizers remained too strong for Chile to take logical "next steps" along the road of truth and justice. The result was not so much a culture of forgetting, as a culture that oscillated—as if caught in moral schizophrenia—between prudence and convulsion. To an extent, this was a "moving impasse." Specific points of friction in the politics of truth, justice, and memory changed; the immobilizing balance of power did not simply remain frozen. But travel to logical "next steps" in memory work proved exceedingly slow and arduous, and the process often turned back, as in a circle, to a reencounter with impasse between majority desire and minority power.

The impasse has unraveled partially since 1998. It remains an open question—a possible focal point of future struggles—whether memory impasse will prove so enduring and debilitating that it will eventually yield, for new generations in the twenty-first century, a culture of oblivion.

A brief guide to organization may prove useful. I have designed the trilogy to function at two levels. On the one hand, the trio may be viewed as an integrated three-volume work. The books unfold in a sequence that builds a cumulative, multifaceted history of—and argument about—the Pinochet era, the memory struggles it unleashed, and its legacy for Chilean democracy since 1990. On the other hand, each volume stands on its own and has a distinct focus and purpose. Each has its own short introduction (which incorporates in schematic form any indispensable background from preceding volumes) and its own conclusions. Each reproduces, as a courtesy to readers of any one book who wish to understand its place within the larger project and its premises, this General Introduction and the Essay on Sources.

Book One, *Remembering Pinochet's Chile: On the Eve of London 1998,* is a short introductory volume written especially for general readers and students. It uses select human stories to present key themes and memory frameworks, historical background crossing the 1973 divide, and conceptual tools helpful for analyzing memory as a historical process. Its main purpose, however, is to put human faces on the major frameworks of memory—including those friendly to military rule—that came to be influential in Chile, while also providing a feel for memory lore and experiences silenced or marginalized by such frameworks. The "ethnographic present" of the book, the most "literary" and experimental of the three, is the profoundly divided Chile of 1996–97, when memory impasse seemed both powerful and insuperable. Pinochet's 1998 London arrest, the partial unraveling of memory impasse and immunity from justice in 1998–2001—these would have seemed fantasies beyond the realm of the possible.

Subsequent volumes undertake the historical analysis proper of memory struggles as they unfolded in time. Book Two, *Battling for Hearts and Minds: Memory Struggles in Pinochet's Chile, 1973–1988,* traces the memory drama under dictatorship. It shows how official and counterofficial memory frameworks emerged in the 1970s, and expressed not only raw power but also brave moral struggle—remarkable precisely because power was so concentrated—centered on the question of human rights. It proceeds to show how dissident memory, at first the realm of beleaguered "voices in the wilderness," turned into mass experience and symbols that energized protest in the 1980s and set the stage for Pinochet's defeat in a plebiscite to ratify his rule in October 1988.

Pinochet's 1988 defeat did not lead to a one-sided redrawing of power but rather to a volatile transitional environment—tense blends of desire, initiative, constraint, and imposition. The most explosive fuel in this combustible mix was precisely the politics of memory, truth, and justice. Book Three, *Reckoning with Pinochet: The Memory Question in Democratic Chile, 1989–2001,* explores the memory-related initiatives and retreats, the tensions and saber rattling, the impasse of power versus desire, that shaped the new democracy and its coming to terms with "Pinochet's Chile." For readers of the entire trilogy, Book Three completes the circle by bringing us back to the point of frustrating impasse, now traced as historical process, that served as an "ethnographic present" in Book One. But Book Three also spirals out from there—by taking us into the realm of accelerated and unexpected unravelings of impasse and taboo after 1998, and into historical conclusions about memory and the times of radical evil that are, paradoxically, both hopeful and sobering.

An unusual feature of these books' organization of chapters requires comment. Each main chapter of a book is followed by an Afterword, intended as a complement that enriches, extends, or unsettles the analysis in the main chapter. At the extreme, an "unsettling" Afterword questions—draws limits on the validity of—a main chapter. Each book's numbering system links main chapters and corresponding Afterwords explicitly (the chapter sequence is *not* 1, 2, 3 . . . but rather 1, Afterword, 2, Afterword, 3, Afterword . . .). In an age of Internet reading, such lateral links may not seem unfamiliar. But my purpose here has little to do with the Internet or postmodern tastes. On the one hand, I have searched for an aesthetic—moving forward in the argument while taking some glances back—that seems well suited to the theme of memory. On the other hand, the Afterword method also draws out useful substantive points. At some stages, it sharpens awareness of contradiction and fissure by creating counterpoint—for example, between a lens focused on changes in the adult world of memory politics and culture, and one trained on the memory world of youth.

Above all, I am aware that in books about remembrance, which pervades human consciousness and belongs to everyone, something important is lost in the analytical selectivity that necessarily governs chapters about main national patterns or trends. The Afterwords allow the revealing offbeat story, rumor, or joke that circulates underground; the incident or bit of memory folklore that is pertinent yet poor of fit with a grander scheme; the provincial setting overwhelmed by a national story centered in Santiago, to step to the fore and influence overall texture and interpretation more forcefully. They are a way of saying that in cultures of repression and impasse, it is the apparently marginal or insignificant that sometimes captures the deeper meaning of a shocking experience.

A history of memory struggles is a quest, always exploratory and unfinished, to understand the subjectivity of a society over time. At bottom, this trilogy is a quest to find *Chile profundo*—or better, the various Chiles profundos—that experienced a searing and violent upheaval. Sometimes we find "deep Chile" in a chapter about the nation's main story. Sometimes, Chile profundo exists at the edges of the main story.

Introduction to
Book One

※

Remembering Pinochet's Chile

On the eve of 1998, the year of General Augusto Pinochet's shocking arrest in London by request of a Spanish judge charging crimes against humanity, Chileans lived in a world of intimate memory impasse. Not only had the memory question—how to remember the origins, violence, and legacy of Pinochet's rule—proved strategic in Chilean politics and culture since the 1970s. Not only had divisiveness over memory often translated into sensations of impasse—majority desire frustrated by minority power and by Pinochet's ongoing role as army commander in chief—when Chileans sought to take logical "next steps" on the road to truth, justice, and human rights in the democracy of the 1990s. (Pinochet was army commander until March 1998, when he retired from active military duty and became lifetime senator under rules of the Constitution written under his dictatorship. As army commander he cast a shadow—an eight-year warning and constraint, built into the culture of transitional democracy—as the potential ultimate enforcer of his own legacy.) For many citizens and social actors, memory also had an intimate aspect. It spoke to heart, identity, and loyalty. It gave meaning to formative life experience or rupture; it reactivated key moments of moral awakening or political growth. Memory could also place under fire colossal political errors and human failings, especially indifference to atrocity.

Many Chileans on all political sides, it turned out, had lived the "national" experience of Pinochet's Chile as a time that marked them personally and profoundly. They established dialogues between "loose" or personal memories, and "emblematic" frameworks that imparted meaning and integrated personal remembrance into collective remembrance. The intimate aspect of memory struggles and impasse had several sources: the intense politicization and mobilization of Chilean society in the years culminating in the crisis of 1973; the massive scale of the repression and reordering of life that ensued after 11 September 1973; the sheer duration of the dictatorship and struggles for and against it. Seventeen long years of dictatorship, from 1973 to 1990, had turned the crisis of 1973 and the violent Pinochet era into a repeatedly personal, formative, and polemical experience. It was not only young adults and youth who came of age during the 1960s and early 1970s —the tumultuous era of "reform versus revolution"—who experienced the 1973 crisis as a time of personal crisis, rupture, or liberation. Nor was it only their elders—adults who navigated the upswell of rural-to-urban migration, social mobilization and labor politics, expanded electorates and intensified multiparty competition in the 1950s and 1960s—who also experienced the turn to military rule as personal and decisive. It was also youngsters who came of age during or just before the early to mid-1980s, when Chile turned toward mass protest against the dictatorship and repression again surged, for whom the memory question was at once personally searing and collectively urgent.[1]

This book brings readers into the Chilean world of intimate memory impasse on the eve of the London arrest. It operates in an "ethnographic present" of 1996–97, when Chile was profoundly divided on the memory question and impasse could seem endless—powerful, permanent, intractable. It brings us face to face with the drama of living with divided memory of violent state-sponsored atrocity, a condition of life all too familiar in the world of the late twentieth and early twenty-first centuries. It brings us face to face, too, with one of the great recurring dilemmas of our times: how to forge a true and just reckoning with the traumatic recent past, when politically organized raw power and violence wrecked assumptions of social limits and human normalcy, that can somehow reaffirm our faith in humanity, society, and peaceable coexistence. The task is not eased when the reality of democratic transitions or rebirths includes substantial continuing power not only by former direct perpetrators of atrocity, but also by a social base that identified or sympathized with the outgoing or defeated regime.

This book uses select human stories—life experiences and memories of individuals from varied walks of life—to introduce the major frameworks that came to be influential in Chilean memory culture and debate, and that enabled people to build bridges between personal and collective experience. It also uses select stories of individuals to provide a feel for memory lore and experiences that are powerful and important, and to an extent circulate socially, yet prove marginalized or silenced by major memory frameworks.

My central purpose is to offer a human portrait of Chile's memory division and drama on the eve of the London arrest, in a manner respectful of the paradox of humanity embedded within an inhuman experience. (Pinochet's London arrest both hastened and symbolized a turn in the culture of memory impasse, but that is another story for another volume.) For this reason, I resort in this volume to a somewhat experimental approach. On the one hand, I seek to provide essential analytical material the reader will need to understand better a human portrait of Chile's contentious memory question: historical background that illuminates the crisis of 1973, the violence of dictatorship, and distinct reactions to it; main memory frameworks built by Chileans to give meaning to the upheavals of their lives and nation, to struggle in defense of human life and integrity, and to legitimize or delegitimize military rule; conceptual tools or theory useful to understand the *process* of creating contending memory frameworks, nourished by dialogues of the personal and the public. On the other hand, rather than provide a conventional segregated chapter at the outset on "historical background" or on "theory," before probing specific human memory stories, lore, and experience, I seek to harness the power and insight of individual stories as a pathway toward useful historical context and theory. Thus key aspects of historical background are woven into several chapter stories on individual lives, in layers that build a feel for relevant background and context and for shifting definitions of the "relevant" according to one's social or class background, one's political, familial, or regional experience, or one's memory framework. Theory, for its part, is presented here not as an abstract point of departure but as a culmination (chapter 4). By building on the foundation laid by human stories, the conceptual discussion will make more sense and seem less abstract.

Two additional notes on the theoretical chapter (chapter 4) and its Afterword are in order. First, the theoretical language is my own, even as my debt to the burgeoning scholarship on memory is enormous (and acknowledged in the endnotes). Rather than apply mechanically languages or concepts rooted in other historical experiences, I have found it more helpful to use such scholarship as inspiration—as a source of basic questions, insights, and approaches—while remaining free to adapt and build a conceptual language suitable to the Chilean case. Striking such a balance has been crucial for me. Otherwise, one slips into too uncritical or even misleading usage of concepts that, however insightful and useful, are also drawn from significantly distinct historical and cultural contexts.

For example, I have learned from James Young's superb scholarship on Europe and the Holocaust that monuments can and do call forth multiple contending memory-truths and, eventually, antimemory monuments or countermonuments. Yet, while drawing on Young's insights on the power of specific memory places and monuments to convene or concentrate struggles, I also needed to forge my own more flexible language of "memory knots" for several reasons: The physical monument aspect of memory work on twentieth-century disaster was not nearly as developed in the Chilean case, in the time frame examined here, as in Europe in the late twentieth century. Also, events and anniversaries in time proved far more important than fixed place or monument in galvanizing memory work and struggles in Chile, for at least fifteen years after 1973. Finally, "antimemory," as a memory project or sensibility expressive of a new generation and challenging earlier modes of memorialization, could not yet "arrive," as a serious artistic-cultural agenda, in the first quarter-century of memory struggles over the Pinochet era.[2]

Similarly, I have benefited from Pierre Nora's stimulating insight about the connection between the cultural death of living memory and the freezing of memory into sites of preservation. Indeed, his point may eventually prove telling for Chile in the twenty-first century. But Nora's theoretical language and somewhat rigid dichotomy between living environments of memory (*milieux de mémoire*) and preserved sites or realms of memory (*lieux de mémoire*) serve poorly for Chile in the first quarter-century after 1973. His intellectual and theoretical energy focuses mainly on lieux de mémoire and their functions after the death of living memory. But even if one fully accepted his dichotomy and reasoning, the Chilean case examined here would be, in his terms, more a study of living milieux de mémoire—a problematic fit.[3]

Under such circumstances, I found it more practical to forge my own conceptual language, as a kind of theory-building discussion based on research in Chile, while doing so in a way that resonates with useful insights in the superb memory scholarship on other regions and experiences, and in the exciting scholarship recently emerging in Latin America.[4] My main purpose in the conceptual chapter is to outline the processes that generate dialogue between personal memory and collective memory frameworks of searing and violent upheaval, and that generate struggles over culture and politics through the building of "emblematic" memory frameworks that resonate widely in society.

The second special note pertains to the Afterword to chapter 4 that immediately follows, and the function of the Afterwords as a whole. Precisely because my theory-building chapter focuses on the making of emblematic memory frameworks, it raises a crucial follow-up question. What drops out of main memory frameworks? Put another way, What is silenced by analytical concepts or approaches used to understand the building of main memory frameworks? How important, in human as well as political and cultural terms, is that which drops out of main frameworks and struggles to hegemonize collective memory? In short, the conceptual culmination to this book's human portrait of divided memory seems to demand a look at the underside, that is, a bringing to the fore of that which remains silenced by the course of memory struggles over devastating times of atrocity. The final Afterword redresses the balance in the most powerful way possible—not through abstractions that are useful and have their purpose but are also somewhat removed from specific human experiences, but by telling one individual's dramatic story. It culminates the implicit argument running through all the Afterwords. All focus, in a kind of counterpoint to main chapters, on temptations and dynamics of silence—the lore whose "fit" with main memory frameworks is problematic, the persons who have reason to turn away from memory, the voices marginal or suffocated within a culture of memory struggle and memory impasse.

The conclusion to this book integrates the human portraits and the conceptual discussion, the main chapters and the Afterwords, into a larger reflection on memory, struggle, and silence. During and after the times of atrocity, the making of all three happens at once. Social actors create an entangled weave of remembrance, conflict, and taboo.

Chapter 1

⁂

Heroic Memory: Ruin into Salvation

One person's criminal is another person's hero. To appreciate the memory question in Chile, on the eve of General Augusto Pinochet's October 1998 detention in London, requires that we understand the Chileans who saw Pinochet as a hero as well as those who condemned him as a criminal. Pinochet's detention responded to an extradition request by a Spanish judge pursuing crimes against humanity covered by international law. For some Chileans, the arrest proved an apt culmination of the previous quarter century. For others, it violated history.

After eight years of democratic rule that included credible revelations of human rights violations by a blue-ribbon truth commission and by national media outlets, a substantial minority of Chileans—about two of five—continued to remember the military overthrow of the elected government of Salvador Allende in 1973 as a rescue mission.[1] Military intervention saved their families and their nation from a disaster and set Chile on the road to good health. This sense of salvation also framed the meaning of political violence under military rule, between 1973 and 1990.

Doña Elena F.'s experience, as told to me in 1996, introduces one of the major ways people recalled their personal stories and linked them to a sense of collective remembrance. Her story connects to one of several treasured scripts, or albums, in the memory box of Pinochet's Chile. Her experience also serves as an initial vehicle to present historical background on the crisis of society and politics that convulsed Chile by 1973.

Twenty-three years later, Doña Elena still thought back on 11 September 1973 as the best day of her life.[2] Early that morning, "we turned on the radio, the jets flew up over here [and] when we learned that all the Armed Forces were united, I think it was the happiest day of my life." Doña Elena and her husband, Hugo, lived in an apartment near Cerro Santa Lucía, the historic hill (the Spanish conquistadors led by Pedro de Valdivia encamped there) that overlooks downtown Santiago. Later that morning, when the air force made good on its threat to bomb the presidential palace of La Moneda, the Hawker Hunter jets swooped right by the hill and Doña Elena's building. Doña Elena and Hugo had climbed up to the rooftop, where they feted the passing jets with cheers and champagne.

And why not? For Doña Elena, the bombing put an end to a period of trauma and marked the beginning of salvation. Life in Chile had begun its turn toward disaster with the election of Christian Democrat Eduardo Frei Montalva in 1964. The Christian Democrats had promised a "Revolution in Liberty," inspired by Catholic social doctrine. A progressive communitarianism would steer Chilean society away from the materialistic evils of capitalism and Communism, thereby fostering social justice and class harmony without violating democratic liberty and political pluralism.[3]

Frei won the presidency because the Chilean Old Regime had become untenable by the early 1960s and because social discontent had found genuine electoral expression in Chile's vibrant multiparty politics. In 1938, the Communist Party and the Socialist Party participated in the victorious Popular Front coalition, led by the centrist Radical Party and President Pedro Aguirre Cerda. The Popular Front experience channeled the Left and Chile's rather militant working-class politics into a framework of electoral organizing and state populism. In this framework, state interventionism would accelerate industrialization, through protectionist tariffs that promoted import substitution and through price and credit policies that subsidized Chilean manufacturing. The state would also redistribute resources into health, housing, labor, consumer, and pension programs designed to improve the standard of living of the working classes and the poor. Within ten years, the strategy of reform through participation in Center-led coalitions had fallen apart. Center-Right opposition to the labor militance and agrarian organizing promoted by the Left, along with political rivalry between Socialists and Communists and the charged ideological chasm opened up by the Cold War, imposed insuperable strains. In 1948, the Radical administration of President Gabriel González Videla implemented a purge against the Communist Party. Legally dissolved as a valid political party, its members were banned from legal participation in the labor movement and its leaders shipped off to internal exile—"relegation" districts—in the provinces.

The failure of a Center-Left strategy did not steer the Left away from strategies that channeled social need and mobilization toward electoral paths. Instead, the Left—especially its emerging leader, Socialist Salvador

Allende Gossens—sought to build a Left-led electoral coalition that would promote a more aggressive social reformism, responsive to social discontent and an expanding electorate. Aguirre Cerda had named Allende, then a dynamic young doctor and Socialist congressman, his minister of health. The lesson Allende drew from his parliamentary and Popular Front experiences in the 1930s and 1940s was that social reform required an alliance of the exploited laboring classes with progressive middle-class sectors, but under different political conditions. Coalition politics would become a more effective instrument of change if led from the Left rather than the Center, and if the Socialist and Communist Parties muted their rivalry in the interests of Left unity.

In the 1950s, Allende and the Left began to test this new approach. Allende broadened the appeal of radical Left ideas by advocating national expropriation of the U.S.-owned copper mines that constituted the lifeblood of the Chilean economy. Politically, the miserable living and working conditions of Chilean workers were at once a social justice question and a national sovereignty question. Allende ran as the joint candidate of the Socialists and the Communists (notwithstanding the outlaw status of the latter in 1952) in the presidential elections of 1952 and 1958. Left organizers sought to extend their political base from established strongholds in mining camps and urban working-class communities, into the countryside and the new urban shantytowns (*callampas*) that sprang up when the poor invaded land and sought assistance to build affordable housing and a basic infrastructure of water, transport, energy, and health services.[4]

The strategy almost won Allende the presidency in 1958. As the elections approached, two legal reforms heightened competition and expanded the electorate. Outgoing President Carlos Ibáñez del Campo, who had run in 1952 on an antipolitics campaign that promised to clean up the mess caused by the political parties and the intrigues of the González Videla period, fulfilled a pledge to lift the Law for the Permanent Defense of Democracy that had outlawed the Communist Party. A 1958 electoral reform also replaced separate ballots by political parties—a mechanism enabling owners of rural estates to control votes by peasant tenants—with a secret and unified ballot and compulsory voting. (An earlier reform, extension of the vote to women in 1949, had brought fewer benefits to the Left because Allende fared better among men than women.) The election results dramatically shifted the political landscape. Allende, candidate of the Left coalition known as the FRAP (Popular Action Front), lost to Jorge Alessandri, leader of the Right coalition of the Liberal and Conservative Parties. In the five-way race, Alessandri carried nearly a third of the vote. But Allende lost by a shockingly slim margin—fewer than 34,000 (2.7 percent) among the over 1.2 million votes cast.[5]

Just as important, the new political competitiveness generated a more vital and reform-minded Center. The 1958 elections had marked the appearance of the Christian Democrats, led by Eduardo Frei Montalva, as a centrist party that disdained the Old Regime for its tolerance of social misery, the Radical Party for its manipulativeness and absence of vision, and the Left for its ties to materialistic Communism and atheism. Inspired by Catholic social doctrine and labor activism in the countryside, the Christian Democrats promoted a vision of alternative reform and emerged as the dominant force in the political Center by winning a fifth of the presidential vote (the Radicals garnered a sixth). After the elections, Christian Democrats competed intensely with the Left to gain the loyalties of rural laborers, urban shantytown dwellers, and trade unionists.

The Left's near victory in the 1958 presidential elections, the social mobilizations and reform demands supported by both the Center and the Left, the decline of the Right to a congressional minority of less than a third (insufficient to veto legislation) after the 1961 parliamentary elections, passage of an additional electoral reform expanding the electorate in 1962: all added up to an Old Regime on the defensive. By 1964, a third (34.3 percent) of the national population registered to vote; in 1946, only a ninth (11.2 percent) had registered to vote. By 1964 as well, Chile's several decades of state-induced industrialization, and the growing service sector associated with modernizing economies and rural-to-urban migration, created expanding populations of voters receptive to the politics of populist assistance and social reform. Indeed, Chile made the turn to an urban majority faster than most Latin American countries. Some 60 percent lived in urban locales of over 20,000 inhabitants, about 40 percent in cities over 100,000, and some 30 percent in metropolitan Santiago. The population of greater Santiago doubled to nearly 2 million between 1940 and 1960, approaching 3 million by 1970. By 1964, the literacy rate for Chileans at least fifteen years old had climbed past 85 percent. Chile's labor force had developed substantial industrial and service sectors. Nearly 771,000 laborers (30.3 percent of the national labor force) worked in mining, industry, construction, or utilities; within this proletarian grouping, the industrial sector (478,000) was largest. Commerce and services together accounted for 942,000 (37.0 percent), and transport added nearly 144,000 laborers (5.6 percent). While the labor force in agriculture was still large (681,000), its declining national share (26.7 percent) reflected the transition to a more modern configuration of work, residence, and politics. Trade union membership, hardly any of it in agriculture in 1964, had reached over 270,000.[6]

Even the countryside, however, moved toward a new era of political effervescence. Here was the heart of aristocratic culture and the political Right, organized as a coherent interest group (Sociedad Nacional de Agricultura, or National Agricultural Society) that had established an important national radio station, Radio Agricultura. The countryside had been deemed off limits to serious political competition in the older electoral system. The prohibition was enforced through repeated government and landowner repression of rural unionization efforts since the 1930s. Rural labor, in fact, had borne the brunt of the effort to reconcile Chile's state subsidies of agricultural and industrial interests on the one hand, and policies that sought to limit inflation of urban consumer prices on the other. During the 1940s and 1950s, the cumulative effect cut real wages for rural laborers by about 50 percent. For those who did not migrate to the cities or did not find favored personal treatment from their *patrones* (a *patrón* is a master or landowner-boss), a harsh deterioration of material life coincided with emerging discourses about Catholic moral responsibility, political justice, and rural economic backwardness. Along with new electoral rules, these new languages of public life redefined political possibility. Even the Alessandri administration—dependent on a congressional alliance with the Radicals to offset the FRAP, under pressure to implement moderate anti-Communist reform envisioned by President John F. Kennedy's Alliance for Progress—could not block passage of a modest agrarian reform in 1962.[7]

Just as significant, as the 1964 presidential elections approached, Frei and the Christian Democrats seemed the only alternative to socialist reform. To stop Salvador Allende, again the candidate of the FRAP leftist coalition, the Right held its nose, dissolved its own electoral coalition, and threw its support to Frei. Boosted by this expanded base, as well as media and political campaign funds channeled surreptitiously into the elections by the U.S. Central Intelligence Agency (CIA), Frei won an outright majority (55.5 percent) of the vote.[8]

For Doña Elena and her family, Frei's election marked the turn toward trauma. Their ordered world began to come apart and turn upside down. Like many a family of good lineage and good manners, Doña Elena had been building a life marked by a firm sense of social place and unpretentious good taste. The good wood furniture, decorative silver plates, paintings of significant persons and picturesque landscapes, and historical and family artifacts that fill Doña Elena's apartment are arranged not as a flashy show of nouveau riche wealth designed to impress the visitor, but as a low-key expression of the good taste that comes with dignified social belonging. Doña Elena and her husband Hugo belonged to "declining aristocracy" (*aristocracia venida a menos*), a familiar and influential sector of society in Chile (and much of Latin America) during the mid-twentieth century. Even when income sank to a respectable middle-class level, their social circles and values joined them to upper- and upper middle-class families who could claim superior social standing—through inheritance of significant property and social networks; descent from good aristocratic stock; or marriage into networks of notable descent, property, and friendship. Such families built their sense of social order and place in the countryside as well as the city. Doña Elena and some cousins had inherited a rather unprofitable *fundo* (landed estate) in the Center-South. Her brother Andrés had been educated as an agronomist and administered haciendas further south, near Temuco, and other cousins owned a fundo in a central valley province near Santiago. Although Doña Elena and Hugo made their living in the city—he worked as a finance lawyer; she worked for a time in a clothing store—the rituals of social place and belonging included trips to the rural fundos. There, peasant tenants (*inquilinos*) worked the wheat and cattle properties, kept up the homes, and served the visiting patrones and their guests during relaxing meals followed by social and family conversation. The inquilinos might also occasionally ask for advice or help on personal matters.[9]

What separated families of high social standing from their more grasping counterparts—whether economically precarious strata among middle-class families, or culturally clumsy versions of the nouveau riche—was precisely their connection to the rural milieu and rituals that traditionally undergirded elite status. Access to this milieu, or the desire to become a part of it, provided a significant social base for cultural conservatism in Chile.

For Doña Elena and Hugo, President Alessandri represented all that was right about the Old Regime. During his six-year term (1958–1964), they repeatedly reminded me, Alessandri combined political conservatism with personal unpretentiousness. He did not need to put on airs. He greeted people in the streets as he walked his dog or walked to work at La Moneda Palace. There he sought to scale back government economic interventionism and to fend off political organizing in the countryside.

Frei's election upended the fundamental conservatism of Chile's democracy. Whatever their anti-Communist views, the Christian Democrats had forged their own militant vision of social reform and democratization. However much Frei sought not socialism but a modernized and more humane capitalism, balanced by a Catholic communitarian ethic and supported by forward-looking entrepreneurs and middle-class sectors, the Christian Democrats had committed themselves to political competition with the Left for new bases among the socially downtrodden in the countryside and urban shantytowns. As a result, Frei's government promoted not only a program of "Chileanization" of the U.S.-owned copper industry, and not only social assistance, housing, and public health programs in the shantytowns and working-class communities. In 1967, the government and Congress also passed a more thorough agrarian reform that sought to expropriate the inefficiently exploited landed estates of Chile's central and southern provinces, and to reorganize them into agrarian cooperative settlements (asentamientos) that would transform servile peasant tenants and laborers into agrarian proprietors. At the time, Chile's landed estate system, especially in the central valley provinces near Santiago and in the southern frontier provinces where Mapuche Indian peoples had finally been conquered in the 1880s, was oriented mainly toward wheat and cattle production. The labor system still relied substantially on a servile peasant tenant system, in which resident inquilinos worked the lands of their patrones in exchange for use rights supplemented by modest pay or goods in kind. Technologically, many fundos relied on production methods inherited from the late nineteenth century and the early twentieth, rather than adopting the intensive inputs, scientific management techniques, and capitalization associated with more modern agriculture and ranching.[10]

The most graphic social upheavals occurred in the countryside, the milieu so fundamental to the sense of social well-being and place that defined the lives of the wealthy, and of those middle-class families that identified with the respectability of the rural regime—because they came from good stock or married into it, had inherited or bought rural property, or had kin working in rural supervisory positions. For such persons, the prereform countryside could seem almost idyllic. "Andrés . . . my older brother, was an agronomist linked with the Catholic University and all his life he worked in the

South, on large haciendas where he was administrator. Such lovely areas, agricultural, very pretty . . . near Temuco . . . from which he had to leave because there came along the famous agrarian reform of Mr. Frei."

What especially irked Doña Elena and the family was the capriciousness they saw in the agrarian reform—and which they remembered in social conversation.[11] The family lore told of a reform directed against political enemies while exempting political clients, applied without regard for the state's declared interest in expropriating inefficient haciendas in need of modernization, and promoting conflict that undermined the once good relationships that had held between the inquilinos and their patrones and administrators.

> DOÑA ELENA: Well, in Frei's time there arose the *toma* [land invasion], so to speak, . . . the expropriation of the properties wherever they wanted, of course they expropriated nothing from people who were their supporters. They would say they were expropriating the badly run fundos, a claim which was absolutely not true: this hacienda where [my brother] Andrés worked won a prize, one year, for the best harvest in the Ninth Region. Nonetheless it was expropriated.
> AUTHOR: Was it a wheat-producing fundo?
> DOÑA ELENA: Wheat and cattle . . . it didn't have a dairy. . . . Well, the lands passed over to the people who were working [them]; they asked my brother . . . to stay on and manage their lands a while. Andrés went and worked them for a time. But what I'm getting at is how arbitrary was the way that they carried out agrarian reform in this country, sowing hate in the country-side against the patrones.

Arbitrariness also prevailed in the case of the fundo Doña Elena and some cousins inherited from their grandmother. Precisely because the fundo was inefficient—theoretically, therefore, a good candidate for reform—the Christian Democrats decided *not* to expropriate it. But first they overturned the rules of good order and manners. "The Christian Democrats arrived there . . . they would enter the fundo, look around, go in; they left the doors open, they would leave, do whatever they wanted. They didn't expropriate it because it was a nonirrigated fundo [*fundo de rulo*], not attractive from the point of view of production. . . . This was the period of Mr. Frei, . . . very awful in many ways."

When fundos were sufficiently modern and well run to be coveted by the agrarian activists, on the other hand, compensation bore little relation to economic reality. "Look, I have here very near Santiago . . . some cousins, who had a very beautiful fundo, from their mother, . . . but worked by their father, with very nice homes for the inquilinos, very pretty homes they had. . . . They took [from my relatives] a large portion of the fundo and paid them with agrarian bonds over X years—an absurdity, nothing to do with true remuneration."

In some instances, the disorder even destroyed the will to live. Doña Elena's lore includes the story of a relative, patriarch of a large family including three handicapped children, who was forced to abandon his fundo and move to Santiago from one day to the next. He died shortly thereafter—not from hunger but from depression. "He had other means, he was not going to die of hunger, but that was his life, then, his work, everything."

For Doña Elena, however, it was Allende's election in 1970 that generalized the social disorder and brought Chile to the brink of catastrophic violence. Frei's presidency not only destroyed the tranquility and order of her world; it also failed to stop Chile's political march to the Left. The new government legitimized and unleashed expectations of social justice and economic growth that were unevenly met. By the end of Frei's term in 1970, his government had achieved only a modest increase (5 percent) in real per capita gross domestic product. It had expropriated some 1,300 rural fundos and turned rural trade unions into a political reality. Membership had soared from fewer than 2,000 persons in 1964 to over 114,000 in 1970. But the agrarian reform bureaucracy could not keep up with the pace of legal and extralegal seizures of property that created needs for credit, technical inputs and advice, and political protection, let alone satisfy peasants excluded from the redistributions. Frei's successes, moreover, raised the issue of the proverbial half-loaf. The government built 260,000 new housing units—an impressive figure, but well short of the announced target of 360,000 units. It cut the terrible infant mortality rate (102.9 per 1,000 births in 1964) notably, but infant death remained a crushing health burden in 1970 (79.0 per 1,000 births).

In retrospect, one could argue that these and other partial achievements— such as education and "popular promotion" programs—were the best one could expect in only six years, especially given the scale of the agrarian reform program, the country's small and internationally dependent copper economy, and a political system that mixed democratic rules of the game with ferocious political contentiousness between the Right, Center, and Left. In its historical time, however, this mixed record generated a frustration that echoed the critique expressed by the Left—a critique that interpreted unmet needs and expectations as consequences of Frei's failure to push for truly radical reform.

After all, in Chile as elsewhere in Latin America, the mid-to-late 1960s was an era when the political exhaustion of the Old Regime coincided with the idea that revolution was both necessary and possible. The mystique of the Cuban Revolution gave impetus to the idea that youthful rebels and activists could indeed produce a major rupture with an unjust status quo, even against the wishes of the United States, and that their revolution could open the door to a bright future. In this vision, the workers, peasants, urban poor, ethnoracial outcasts, and progressive sectors of youth and the middle and professional classes constituted the large social majority—the "pueblo" constantly marginalized and frustrated by Latin America's tragic and exploitative history but now on the verge of redemption. The mystique of revolution was both complement and rival to the revitalized Catholic social doctrine of the 1950s and 1960s, a period of political and theological experimentalism by priests, lay activists, and church authorities that would culminate in liberation theology and human rights activism in sectors of the church in the 1970s. The new political and religious currents lent legitimacy to the idea that Latin America required far more than tepid reformism. For the political Center as well as the Left, Latin America's road to a bright political future required a deep transformation—either thorough reform, or outright revolution. The terms of this debate, and its exposure of truly crushing social needs and injustices, pushed the Center toward Left ideas. The call of "reform versus revolution" defined the sensibilities of Center and Left youth who came of age as a political generation of leaders and grassroots activists in the 1960s.[12]

Chile fully participated in and contributed to this larger environment of Latin American politics. What distinguished Chilean political and cultural life was not the absence of the idea that the Old Regime was unsustainable and that major transformation, either deep reform or a revolution, was necessary and possible. Chile's uniqueness derived from the conjunction of such ideas and a history of social struggle, on the one hand, with a culture of resilient political democracy that included the Left, on the other. Since 1932, the Chilean political elite had managed to put aside nearly a decade of constitutional crises, unstable governments, and military coups. They had managed to abide by the presidential and congressional electoral system envisioned in the 1925 Constitution, and to draw the Left into electoral strategies and coalitions. As we have seen, this conservative and resilient democracy had its underside in the repression of agrarian organizing and the purges of Communists that came to the fore in the 1940s and 1950s. Nonetheless, since 1932 Chile had stood out in Latin America for a history of vigorous multiparty politics and electoral campaigns uninterrupted by military coups. The Chilean Left stood out for its experience and effectiveness in linking political struggle and mobilization with participation in a competitive multiparty democracy.

The critique that interpreted Frei's mixed record and Chile's frustration as evidence that the country needed far more than mild reformism therefore took many political channels, some of them familiar elsewhere in Latin America, others unique to Chile. On the one hand, by the end of Frei's term Chile had experienced the splintering of Center and Left parties, the flirtations with guerrilla politics and armed revolutionary utopias, and the direct grassroots actions familiar elsewhere. Radical Christian activists developed sympathies with the Left; a dissident branch of young, former Christian Democrats reorganized as the MAPU (Movimiento de Acción Popular Unitaria, Movement of Unified Popular Action), a party dedicated to grassroots direct action to advance social transformation. In the university cultures of Concepción and Santiago, and in the countryside between Concepción and Temuco, youthful admirers of Che Guevara and the Cuban Revolution disdained the electoral and reformist baggage of the Communist and Socialist Parties and organized the MIR (Movimiento de Izquierda Revolucionaria, Revolutionary Left Movement) as a revolutionary party committed to direct action and guerrilla organization. By 1969–70 MIRista direct actions included land invasions and well-publicized bank robberies. Significantly, the politics of extralegal grassroots activism was not limited to the Left. Christian Democratic as well as Left organizers, eager to build clienteles as well as respond to social need, supported rural and urban land invasions (in 1969–70 urban land invasions numbered 293, agrarian seizures 419). Grassroots actions such as these would presumably relieve injustice and pressure the Frei administration into greater responsiveness.

On the other hand, the unique vitality and inclusiveness of Chile's electoral system and political life also proved evident. Established Center and Left parties sought to shore up appeal to their Left flanks and to prepare for the 1970 presidential elections. The Christian Democrats nominated Radomiro Tomic, a leader of the party's Catholic left wing. Tomic ran on a platform of root and branch reform, including radical agrarian reform, quite similar to the program promised by the Left. The Socialist Party had appealed to its revolutionary Left branch by declaring, at its 1967 Party Congress, that it considered electoral politics only one instrument of political struggle and that over time political struggle would eventuate in armed struggle. Yet the Socialists' most important national leader, Salvador Allende, had built his career as the architect of a Left committed to electoral politics in the 1950s and 1960s, and the Socialists joined Allende's coalition, the Popular Unity (*Unidad Popular,* or UP), for the 1970 campaign. Allende, for his part, had managed to broaden the old FRAP and realize his dream of a Center-Left coalition to be led from the Left rather than the Center. The UP included not only the Socialist and Communist Parties but also the former Christian Democrats who broke away to form the MAPU, a reorganized Radical Party (the most conservative Radical factions split off), and two other small parties.

Just as important, Allende ran a campaign that proclaimed a goal of socialism and asserted that a revolutionary transition could unfold by electoral and constitutional means. Chile's unique political inheritance would enable a popular government—supported by an alliance of workers, peasants, the urban poor, and socially conscientious youth and middle classes—to use peaceful means toward great goals. The new government would work to end dependence on imperialist powers within a mixed economy concept, via nationalization of copper, banking, and other strategic sectors while preserving property rights for small business. It would boost the lives and dignity of laboring and poor people via deep agrarian reform, social services (housing, health, education, subsidized food), and redistribution of income toward labor. It would democratize society by mobilizing workers and the pueblo as persons of dignity and rights, whose yearnings shaped policy and had become the yearnings of a president.

Allende frightened the Right, but political conservatives such as Doña Elena could not contemplate a repeat of 1964, when they had backed the Christian Democrats to stop Allende. The Christian Democrats had themselves caused trauma by upending agrarian life and destroying respect for good order and property. Now they had nominated Tomic, a candidate as subversive to good order as Allende. Organized as the Partido Nacional for the elections, the Right brought back Doña Elena's favorite, ex-president Alessandri, as its candidate and expected he would win. Then the nightmare struck. The polarization and march toward the Left that had reframed Chilean politics and society limited the Right to its core vote, in a polity more or less evenly split among Right, Center, and Left. The elections held on 4 September 1970 inverted Allende's near miss in 1958. This time it was Alessandri who fell just short (34.9 percent of the vote, compared to Allende's 36.3 percent and Tomic's 27.8 percent). Two months of political intrigue to block the normal constitutional practice—congressional certification of the candidate with the most votes as president—culminated in a botched kidnapping attempt against the firmly Constitutionalist commander of the army, General René Schneider. The kidnappers killed Schneider. Revulsion over an assassination to thwart a democratic election set the stage for a pact with Christian Democrats: Allende agreed to a set of constitutional guarantees; Congress declared Allende the duly elected president.

Allende phrased the project of peaceful revolution through elections and constitutionalism as an expression of Chile's uniqueness. The Popular Unity government, went his maxim, would lead a revolution of *empanadas con vino tinto* (that is, of the red wine and small pies, stuffed with meat or other fillings, considered typical of Chilean cuisine). Precisely because it was so unprecedented and audacious within the Latin American and Cold War contexts, Allende's project acquired a powerful international mystique. Consider the potent juxtaposed symbols: a vibrant Western-style political democracy that elected a president who was a self-declared Marxist; a socialist project of revolution, formulated as programs using inherited law and proposed legislation to overcome the classic Third World problems of poverty, agrarian backwardness, social domination, and weak national sovereignty; a culture of youthful joy and idealism, manifest in "New Song" music and in giant street rallies festively proclaiming loyalty to a revolution of social justice against all odds; and the tough odds implied by the implacable hostility of President Richard Nixon's administration in the United States. The combination yielded a nearly irresistible symbolism. In biblical terms, Allende's drama was a replay of David versus Goliath. In political terms, Allende's experiment seemed a laboratory for new political possibilities. Indeed, the election and fate of a Marxist as a coalition president, in a European-style system of multiple parties and competitive elections, would hold importance for the discussions that culminated in the proclamation of a heterodox "Euro-Communism" suited to Western Europe. This emerging new approach to Left and Marxist politics, sharply distinct from orthodoxies anchored in the politics and history of the Soviet Union and Cold War, had found a living history example in a Third World laboratory called Chile.

The revolution of David versus Goliath, therefore, acquired a certain international cachet. In part, this derived from Allende's personal qualities. He spoke about the needs of common Chileans and the prospects of his own death in ways that projected loyalty to his cause, a genuineness of commitment to a revolution of politics and society that would favor workers and the poor. In face-to-face interactions, he exuded a disarming charm and sense of humor that built rapport with diverse interlocutors, who found themselves drawn into the magic of the performance—they emerged not quite knowing if they had been manipulated or convinced.[13] In speeches for an international audience, he demonstrated an astute capacity to interpret yearnings for a viable road to Third World revolution and nonalignment, and thereby generate badly needed international solidarity.

Allende put all these qualities on display and mobilized the power of the David-versus-Goliath idea during his famous address to the United Nations General Assembly on 4 December 1972. "I come from Chile, a small country," he began, "but where today any citizen is free to express himself however he wishes, with unrestricted cultural, religious, and ideological tolerance."[14] From this premise Allende built a powerful explication of a country that needed a revolution and had begun to forge it, democratically and peacefully; that held fast to its sovereign purpose despite imperialism and financial strangulation led by transnational corporations (especially ITT, or International Telephone and Telegraph, and Kennecott Copper Corporation, key players in Chile); that aligned itself with similar yearnings for liberation in other parts of the underdeveloped world; and that renewed its fortitude and confidence through the solidarity received round the world. For Europeans drawn toward socialist experimentation or renovation, for Europeans and U.S. citizens horrified by the Vietnam War and eager to support the right of Third World countries to chart paths free of imperial interventionism, for Third World nationalists, leftists, reformers, and youth who found their Old Regimes intolerable and searched for alternatives, Chile's experiment was more than intriguing. It was symbolic.

Within Chile, however, Allende's project was an embattled and controversial long shot. Many fine scholars have analyzed and debated the multiple forces that lengthened the odds against Allende's experiment and that turned his three years as president into a tragic saga, a kind of "chronicle of a coup foretold." Understandably, scholarly controversy surrounds many aspects of the story—from the assignment of relative responsibilities for the overall disaster of 1973 and for the specific turning points that brought Chile closer to the abyss between 1970 and 1973; to the balance struck between internal Chilean forces and external U.S. interventionism as causes of disaster; to the nature of Allende's project and its feasibility; to the debates about inevitability that often swirl around great historical ruptures.[15]

For purposes of this book, we need not reproduce the details of such debates and analyses. But we do need to pause to consider the many fronts on which the Allende project contended with battles serious enough to place the entire experiment at risk and to generate a sensation, by late 1972 and 1973, of a country spiraling out of control.

Consider six forces that placed governability at risk. First, Allende was a *minority* president committed to achieving radical change through legal and democratic channels. He faced implacable hostility from the Right, and enormous suspicion from the Center, yet took seriously his promise to bring to life a socialist revolution. Unable to build a working legislative alliance with the Christian Democrats, Allende resorted to technical legal devices to carry out much of his program. He invoked a provision of the Christian Democrats' own agrarian reform law that allowed state intervenors to take over management of rural properties that suffered a work stoppage. He also invoked a dormant 1932 law to intervene and requisition industries that failed to comply with technical price, supply, or hoarding provisions or that failed to produce key commodities at full capacity. Resort to legal technicalities is not an uncommon practice of minority presidents in a democracy. In a context of revolution and property transfer, however, such legal shortcuts generated enormous controversy—accusations of executive illegality, a hardening of political lines, and eventually, a set of unfavorable rulings by Chile's conservative court system.

As a practical matter, the legal devices encouraged de facto invasions of property and labor crises that culminated in state interventions. By December 1972, Allende's state had resorted to over 300 permanent interventions or requisitions, and it owned or administered over 200 industries. For the Right, the process implied that the revolution was real, not empty rhetoric. For the Center, it implied that Allende would push his revolution along even if he could not achieve a grand legislative alliance to set clear rules of the game for division of Chile's future property system between public, mixed, and private sectors.

Such circumstances meant that sooner or later the dominant factions in each camp—Allende's Left coalition, and the Right and Center opposition—ended up more interested in organizing to crush the other camp than to negotiate with it. As we shall see, by April 1973 a hardening impasse seemed to lend credence to hard-liners on the Right, Center, and Left who granted primacy to organizing civil society and the military for a "battle" too profound and intractable to be resolved through normal institutional and political negotiations, or through legal strategies.

Allende's status as a minority president committed to a revolution through constitutional means represented the most fundamental ("structural") problem for his ability to govern. Five additional forces, however, many of them related to this larger problem, bedeviled his ability to rule while unleashing a revolution. First, the U.S. foreign policy apparatus, led by President Richard Nixon and advisor Henry Kissinger, aimed to render the Allende government unworkable, Chilean society ungovernable. The key tools: drastic reductions of economic aid; trade obstacles that impeded acquisition of machinery, parts, and credits or made them more expensive; covert funding of opposition media and strike actions (especially the crippling truckers' strike of October 1972); and sympathetic political conversation with Allende's opponents including coup-oriented actors.

The Cold War fear evoked by Allende, of course, had preceded the Nixon-Kissinger period. In the wake of Allende's 1958 near miss and the Cuban Revolution in 1959–61, the United States had committed itself to economic aid strategies and political boosterism, including covert funding to benefit Frei in the 1964 elections, to build within Chile an alternative to Communist revolution. But Nixon and Kissinger insisted adamantly that an electoral road to a Marxian-led revolution should either be blocked or end in ruins. As Kissinger put it before the 1970 election, "I don't see why we need to stand by and watch a country go Communist due to the irresponsibility of its own people." Nixon was just as blunt when he met with CIA Director Richard Helms, eleven days after the 4 September election, to consider how to block Allende's ascension. Helms's notes recorded the key points: count on at least $10 million for covert action, use the "best men we have," keep the U.S. Embassy uninformed, and "make the economy scream." Once Allende came into office, the Soviet Union, led by Leonid Brezhnev, provided only modest material counterweight. Détente with the United States held priority. Especially when he needed it the most, after economic and political crisis sharpened late in 1972, Allende would receive mainly rhetorical solidarity.[16]

Second, the economic populism of Allende's government produced a classic trade-off: a short-term gain as real wage increases and redistribution increased purchasing power and mobilized excess production capacity, against a medium-run crisis as production bottlenecks and deficit spending —compounded by hoarding and sabotage by opponents, and mismanagement by government administrators—yielded scarcities, inflation, rationing, and black markets. By 1973, the scarcities led to long lines for rationed goods, the inflation rate soared into a triple-digit spiral, and real gross domestic product had begun to fall.[17]

Third, Allende was an embattled president within his own coalition, especially by 1972. The Popular Unity was anything but unified. Allende had emerged as its candidate more as a result of grassroots support and visibility than through popularity with leaders in his own Socialist Party. The coalition mixed "moderate" factions and leaders committed to Allende's vision of a democratic revolution through constitutional means, with *ultra* (maximalist) factions for whom the political battle over Chile's future would inexorably supersede legal channels. To assure his coalition allies that he would negotiate controversial issues rather than resolve them by fiat, and that he would distribute patronage equitably, Allende promised to clear major policy decisions with a committee of the Popular Unity's political parties. His hands partly tied, Allende tended to rely on his personal magic and parliamentary experience to bridge the coalition's internal divides, rather than renege on the consultation commitment or discipline and drum out the uncooperative. As Chile's political crisis became more intractable in August and September 1973, Allende's status as leader of a divided coalition government—supported more by the moderate line of the Communist Party than that of his own Socialist Party, led by maximalist Carlos Altamirano—complicated efforts to find a political solution. An effort to achieve an accord with Christian Democrats foundered (to be fair, by this point the Christian Democrats' leadership had also succumbed to an ultra oppositional stance), and Allende's decision to announce a plebiscite to resolve the crisis was postponed to 11 September.[18]

Fourth, Allende's project unleashed a revolution from below that complicated political engineering from above. As Peter Winn has brilliantly shown for the case of textile workers, Allende's victory yielded profound political and cultural experimentalism at the grass roots. Among some workers, the revolution opened the door to a transformed consciousness of the desirable and the possible, and also promoted political organizing designed to accelerate and deepen the pace of the revolution. Also, Allende's well-known disinclination to use repressive force—not even against political opponents, let alone the workers, peasants, or shantytown dwellers who supported him but exceeded the boundaries of political engineering—perhaps encouraged the de facto process whereby land invasions and factory shutdowns sparked technical interventions and requisitions that transferred property to state management or ownership. Confronted with crisis after crisis caused by the revolution from below, with which he sympathized despite the havoc it wreaked on political engineering, Allende resorted more to political theater, rebuke, negotiation, and stalling tactics than to outright refusals or repression.[19]

The same ambivalent sympathy and reluctance to repress marked Allende's stance toward youthful ultras in the MIR. The MIR encouraged direct action to speed up revolution at the grass roots, remained outside the Popular Unity coalition, and condemned reformists for failing to organize the people for the violent confrontation that would surely come. Allende rejected and condemned ultra politics, especially when it signified disloyalty by factions from within his own coalition. But he also displayed a certain paternal understanding and tolerance of many youthful MIRistas and maximalists. The radicalized youth were misguided younger relatives of the revolution who shared Allende's ultimate goals, even if they failed to understand Chile's political realities and possibilities. The generational paternalism was apt, since some MIRistas and other radicalized youth were indeed younger relatives—children, nieces, nephews—of prominent UP figures. The zone of tolerance opened up by Allende's reluctance to repress and his sympathy for youthful idealism meant that the Popular Unity government contended with a grassroots revolution from "below" and "outside," as well as within, the Popular Unity project.[20]

Fifth, the specter of violence and "disloyal opposition" haunted efforts to achieve lasting political accords. As we have seen, violence and disloyal opposition—that is, direct challenges to democratic constitutionalism as "rules of the political game"—had asserted themselves dramatically even at the start of the process. The assassination of General Schneider in 1970 made clear that some oppositional sectors would organize violent direct action to stop the Allende revolution. The sense of a "conspiracy in the shadows" did not fade, and it was not mere fantasy. Already by September 1971, the key business association SOFOFA (Society for Industrial Development, Sociedad de Fomento Fabril), began organizing a "structure of war"— in the words of its president, Orlando Sáenz—at a seminar in Viña del Mar. The group brought together key industrialists and leaders of the Right. It raised funds locally and abroad to finance the struggle; organized discreet conversation channels with military officers; set up an intelligence group and a media, propaganda, and street action campaign; and developed programs for a new government.

As polarization hardened in 1972, the sense of contending with a "disloyal opposition" problem rendered successful crisis negotiation by moderates more difficult, even when violence itself was not the main issue. When truckers went on strike in October 1972 against expansion of state enterprise in the transport industry, they enjoyed enthusiastic support from the hard-line National Party and the equally hard-line *gremialista* movement (the professional, student, and trade associations self-identified as "guilds" —that is, corporate groups ideologically committed to a society of non-politicized advancement of professional and group interests, at odds with the politicization of associational life under the Unidad Popular). They also turned out to have financial staying power (assisted by covert CIA support), and drew both small business owners and the Christian Democrats into support of a general strike. In short, the truckers represented more than an interest group of small business operators seeking a better economic deal. The key questions—and ambiguities—had turned political and entangled with the disloyal opposition problem. In a society experiencing a serious class struggle, were the truckers of October 1972 an interest group leading a coalition that pushed for a different political balance *within* democracy? Or were they instruments of a political conspiracy to paralyze Chile and crush its government by any means necessary? As important, by the end of 1972 was the "disloyal opposition" phenomenon no longer containable? Was it still mainly the work of sectors of the Right and business and landowner communities whose economic lockouts and sabotage, media propaganda, white guard patrols and retaking of property, conversations with military officers and foreign officials, and discreet encouragement of violent fringe Right groups stoked "chaos" and the idea of possible solution by military means? Or had it become dynamic and expansive, increasingly able to draw actors from the Center and even labor into giving up on democratic rules of the game or solutions?

Such questions nagged away. Their very nature undermined the assumptions—or necessary fictions—of good faith needed to mediate or resolve conflict with the political adversary.

From the perspective of the political opposition, of course, "disloyal government" was the main issue. The government favored or tolerated a dismantling of the rules of property and democratic politics as the opposition had lived and understood them. Sáenz's point to peers at the 1971 SOFOFA seminar was that already he had reached the "conclusion that the government of Allende was incompatible with Chile's liberty and the existence of private enterprise. The only way to avoid that end was to defeat it." They did not need much convincing.[21]

In the end, what rendered the problem of disloyal opposition so vexing was that it could not be disentangled from another dread: organized violence to achieve or impose political results. Once Allende was in office, there quickly emerged symbols on the Right and Left of groups who envisioned a revolutionary battle to decide Chile's future. The rhetoric of violence and the organized direct actions including street clashes by such groups as Patria y Libertad (Fatherland and Liberty) on the Right, and the MIR on the Left, took few lives, especially compared to the killings that emerged later under military rule. But the specter of violence, fueled by a pluralistic and sensationalist press, became a part of the political equation. As Chile's political crisis hardened in 1973—notwithstanding an economy careening out of control, in the congressional elections of March Allende's coalition won 43 percent of the vote, sufficient to block his impeachment— all sides deployed a rhetoric that suggested the possibility that a civil war might loom. The race was on either to prevent a violent confrontation or to prepare to win it. In this kind of atmosphere, the politics of achieving accords between Christian Democrats and the Popular Unity, between moderates and maximalists within the Popular Unity, and between Constitutionalists and interventionists within the military would prove exceptionally difficult.[22]

In short, Allende's revolution faced an uphill battle on many fronts. He was a minority president attempting radical change within a parliamentary democracy, a Third World leader under siege by the United States, an economic populist increasingly under squeeze, a political leader beholden to an internally divided coalition, a revolutionary who contended with an accelerating bottom-up revolution, a democrat who could not rein in the specter of violence and disloyal opposition. The retrospective view of obstacles is in a certain sense misleading. It is too unilateral. It slides over the political gifts and self-confidence that made it possible for Allende to bridge difficult divides and to tap the deeply felt desires for social dignity and inclusion that defined the political imagination of his times. (It also slides over that aspect of Chilean political culture that valued finding some sort of negotiated constitutional exit to crisis short of democratic collapse.) Since we know the disastrous outcome, we can fall into an overly fatalistic determinism, thereby overlooking the staying power of Allende's political magic and projecting backward the loss of control that defined the last months of his presidency. Late in 1972, even as polls indicated that Chileans perceived a "climate of violence," they also showed that economic hardship—not violence—was perceived as the fundamental political problem of Chile. Even on 11 September 1973, Allende's ability to steer face-to-face discussion and manipulate political scenarios in a direction of his choosing—his famed *muñeca* ("wrist," meaning capacity to maneuver, charm, and manipulate)—inspired fear on the part of the junta generals. When Allende suggested a meeting to resolve the crisis, they adamantly resolved to avoid the face-to-face discussion that might undermine their ultimatum. The same fear of Allende's muñeca probably also accounted for the determination to launch a coup before the president could announce a plebiscite to resolve the national political crisis.[23]

Nonetheless, by 1973 Chile was a country governed by a president who could not keep his own revolutionary house in order, let alone his opponents at bay. For better or worse, a revolution had been unleashed. With it came a rush of direct actions that redistributed property and power; economic struggles and reorganization that generated serious scarcities, inflation, and production bottlenecks; and a certain theater of violence oriented more to discursive performance and self-deception than to serious organization and embodied in heated street confrontations, political speeches, and media reports.[24] Eventually Allende lost control, and the country seemed on the brink of a catastrophe.

It is this sense of imminent catastrophe, embodied in specific family experiences, that defines Doña Elena's memory of 11 September.[25] Doña Elena remembers the transition from Frei to Allende as the time when political violence spiraled out of control and finally threatened to destroy family and friends. Not only did seizures of property become more rampant. Revolutionary activists given free rein by the government took property by force and prepared to seize power in a violent civil war. "Well, then Mr. Allende came along and now the thing got much worse, because they started up what they called the tomas. People would take the lands, they would take the industries, all this with impunity. But beyond all that, the guerrilla schools started up in Chile, there were who knows how many schools of guerrillas— of guerrillas, organized by the government. What for?"

When Doña Elena spoke, I knew that the oppositional news media under Allende and the officialist media under military rule had given extensive coverage to alleged threats of imminent violence and arms stockpiling by the Left. When I asked her whether political violence was exposed in the media, she said yes but quickly turned to personal knowledge—the family lore that gave specific meaning and credibility to her remembrance of violence.

> AUTHOR: And did the newspapers denounce it?
> DOÑA ELENA: They would denounce it, but they [the UP government and its backers] would say whatever other thing. Well. But I am going to talk to you about things I have known. This brother of mine [Andrés] in the South had an intimate friend, with a fundo he built up from scratch, in which fifty years ago [the 1940s] they would have to use a car from Temuco part of the way, put up in my brother's house, and they'd have to go on by horse and cart to their land.
>
> [They were] tremendously hardworking people, this owner built the main house—he built all the new homes of the inquilinos—well he raised up those lands far away that had been a bit abandoned.

In Doña Elena's memory, Andrés's friend, a real-life version of the young Esteban Trueba of Isabel Allende's *The House of the Spirits,* finally cracked under the strain of imminent violence. "In Allende's time they had to go around armed at night out of fear of a toma of the fundo, and the moment came [probably 1972] when a man so hard working, very intelligent . . . told my brother, 'Flaco [Skinny],' he told him, 'I'll sell you this fundo for whatever you can pay me, I'm leaving.'" Andrés turned down the offer, arguing he was too old to face up to such risks but said he would pass on the offer to his children. "And two sons of my brother bought the fundo . . . because they were willing to go around with carbine to the shoulder."

Doña Elena links such remembrances to other specific stories of people who fled to escape threats and intimidation. In her mind's eye, these specific histories corroborate the media reports under military rule that "Many foreigners came here . . . There were fifteen thousand extremists in Chile."

For Doña Elena, it does not matter much whether Allende himself favored violent revolution. Whatever his own ideas, he was too frivolous and irresponsible to control those on the Left who did advocate and organize violence. I asked her how she saw Allende personally. Was he a person who feigned belief in democratic institutions but actually favored revolutionary violence and assassination? Or was he an authentic democrat who could not control the extremist hard-liners within and outside his coalition? Her answer did not come easily. "It's really very difficult—I did not know him," she began.

> They say he was very charming with people . . . , but he was a man very fond of the good life, so all this love of fellow man, it was up to a point, no more. He was a politician who wanted at all costs to come into power and . . . [maybe] he would not agree with many [extremist] things—I think—but he was not capable of holding back the wave. He was something of a bon vivant [*un hombre bastante sibarita*], very taken with the fine things [of life].

In this vision, the military's decision to oust Allende and rule Chile saved Doña Elena's family and the country from a horrendous violent fate. When I asked Doña Elena how she thought back on the problem of human rights under military rule—the thousands of deaths and disappearances by the military and its agents, whose remembrance destroys claims that 11 September was a day of national salvation in other circles—she had little difficulty framing an answer.

> I have always seen it . . . in the following way. In a country in which there was practically a civil war, because, just in time, the *pronunciamiento* [the military takeover] was just in time but soldiers died, people were wounded. . . . Those people do not count in [talk about] human rights. Now then, the human rights of people on the edge of a war prepared by these people— what for? To get killed by one other—having gotten elected democratically, a president begins to accept that there are going to be these guerrillas. . . . That does not concern those who concern themselves now with human rights. None of that matters to them—how many deaths there would have been, what would have happened to the country if these people end up continuing in power.

In Doña Elena's mind, what must be remembered is that the cost in deaths would have been far worse had the military refrained from intervention. Terrible social situations often require severe remedial actions. By this standard, deaths were lamentable, but they constituted the social cost of setting the country right. In Chile, she said, the social cost was modest.

> I do not know any country in the world that escapes chaos and a state of war without producing deaths and without producing unfortunately some injustices, because the people who do this are not angels [and] naturally they commit errors. But I think that Chile has been the least within the [bounds

of] horror one sees in various countries. . . . I don't know, I am very tough in thinking that the country would have fallen into a horror of deaths, of greater hardships, of jailings—there were not more than a minor amount, with considerable harshness, of course.

When considering foreign criticism of Chile's human rights record, Doña Elena asked rhetorically whether other countries had not also made brutal decisions when faced with a wartime choice between ruin or salvation. "Look," she recalled telling a critical friend, "when the United States used the atomic bomb, did anyone know how many deaths there were and the effects and what happened? Nobody. Well, they are things that have to be done, it's very hard, it's terrible, but this did not come about because of desires by the military people. The military men at first did not want to do anything, but [people] put pressure on them and they became aware, [even] Frei himself."

In Doña Elena's mind, the whole country—even Frei—had come to its senses by September 1973 and asked the military to save Chile. Only the Left, which was mixed up with international guerrillas and organizations, remained outside this consensus. It was this national sentiment, and the pressure it imposed on the military, that made the action of 11 September not a *golpe de estado* (coup d'état) but a pronunciamiento (declaration on behalf of society).

Let us acknowledge the obvious. Remembrances such as these can make the blood boil. When we consider the memories presented in chapter 2 and its Afterword, and the political and cultural uses of memory, we appreciate the many reasons for this reaction. Memory as salvation became part of a process of intense struggles over truth and misinformation. Moreover, memory as salvation changed over time. In the 1970s, many of its proponents simply denied the reality of secret executions, abductions leading to permanent disappearances, and torture sessions perpetrated by agents of the state. According to Doña Elena's relatives, she too denied the reality of such allegations in the 1970s. It would not be until the 1990s, when Chilean politics made a democratic turn and a truth commission and follow-up panel painstakingly documented the military state's organization and cover-up of several thousand deaths and permanent disappearances, that the proponents of memory as salvation grudgingly conceded the reality of these events. (Torture still remained a delicate topic, outside the realm of such concessions.) Under the new circumstances, proponents of memory as salvation, perhaps voicing what many of them thought more discreetly before the 1990s, began conceding the reality of the deaths and disappearances while contextualizing them as a modest social cost. A cost had to be paid to repair the ruin and turn back the catastrophe of imminent civil war caused by the Left and politicians.

Finally, and perhaps most important, the direct perpetrators of "radical evil" (to use the Kantian formulation adapted by Hannah Arendt and, more recently, Carlos Santiago Nino) used memory as salvation, and the denials of human rights violations embedded in early versions of such memories, to cover up the state's violence and to legitimize their political project.[26] That project turned out to include policide, an effort to destroy root and branch—permanently—the ways of doing and thinking politics that had come to characterize Chile by the 1960s.[27]

Policide meant building a regime of systematic violence and fear so that the old ways of understanding, organizing, and practicing politics could be annihilated and replaced by technocratic and authoritarian governance. In Chile, the old democratic ways had built politics on a foundation of organized social mobilization, competition, and conflict. This foundation was accompanied by a culture of fiercely contending political parties, endemic institutional rivalry between the legislative and executive branches of government, rhetorical appeals and promises by professional politicians to voting constituencies, and populist redistributive and subsidy programs that secured the loyalty of key groups. For the advocates of policide, the old ways blocked economic advance and ultimately led to an irresponsible politics of revolution (whether the "revolution in liberty" of the Christian Democrats or the socialist revolution of the Popular Unity) that brought disorder and ruin to Chile. Eventually, as the new regime moved past its ad hoc and almost purely "reactive" phase, the "foundational" dimension of its project would come into clearer focus. The new project envisioned a future shaped by economic neoliberalism, political authoritarianism, and technocratic decision making. It sought to grant the new scheme durability by institutionalizing it in a new Constitution and guaranteeing it in the personal rule of Augusto Pinochet.[28]

The details of this transformational project need not detain us here. For our purposes, what is important is that policide served as the precondition for building the new order and implied a "war" to destroy the old ways. Through its new secret police as well as the established armed forces and police, the state would identify and locate dissident political leaders or activists, kill or exile them (some would also be killed in exile), use torture to convert some dissidents into informants or collaborators, penetrate and dismantle any nascent capacities for organized criticism or protest, and implement a culture of fear and violence. This culture was embodied in individualized abductions, political cleansings of key institutions such as schools and universities, and massive sweeps of targeted neighborhoods to search homes and arrest suspects. Danger and violence would be so pervasive and intimidating that potential critics would presumably be frightened into apathy, a kind of active rejection of political knowledge and concern as legitimate activity.[29]

In short, the historical uses of memory as salvation, especially its uses by the perpetrators of radical evil to hide violent persecution and frighten citizens from questioning it, render such remembrances profoundly offensive and outrageous for anyone who identifies with the persecuted. Given that my own political values lean toward the Left, and given my sensibilities as a Jewish child of Holocaust survivors, the identification with the persecuted comes readily. I sit uneasily with remembrance as salvation. I confess that I do not care to understand *too* well the direct perpetrators of radical evil, and that at some level they exceed my capacity to understand. Yet as a historian undertaking a study of the ways memory issues played themselves out over time in Chile, I have a responsibility to include, in my quest for critical social analysis and understanding, the social base of people who supported military rule and who remember it as a time of personal and national salvation. That social base was not limited only to persons of privileged social descent in the middle and upper classes of Chilean society.[30] And as we shall see in the specific case of Doña Elena, remembrance as salvation does not preclude concern with morality or ethical responsibility.

Doña Elena's sense of moral order is not limited to the firm sense of good rule and manners, much of it founded in traditional rural society, described earlier. Profoundly Catholic, she had also built a piece of her life and sense of self around the idea of religious responsibility to help the less fortunate. At the time Doña Elena and I spoke in 1996 and 1997, her family knew her as the one who had been going out to the *poblaciones* (neighborhoods of urban poor people, often with a background as shantytowns that began with land invasions and flimsy housing) once a week ever since they could remember. Doña Elena began these trips as a young woman (twenty-something years old) in the 1950s, under the auspices of priests who organized lay groups to survey poor neighborhoods, size up their needs, and distribute food. During President Alessandri's time, she worked in a Centro de Madres (Mothers Center) that gathered the women for talks and instruction in sewing, and set up a cooperative with donated sewing machines. Over the years, Doña Elena kept up this sort of social work. For a time under military rule, when the Secretariat of Women (Secretaría de la Mujer) reinvigorated voluntary female tutelage and charity work and linked it to patriotic instruction and exhortations of poor women, Doña Elena became a paid social worker. But paid or unpaid, on her own or in conjunction with the state or church, Doña Elena kept up her contacts in the poblaciones. Once a week, at the time we spoke, Doña Elena continued to gather up usable remnants from people she knows—the old clothes of friends, factory discards of cloth, blankets, or mattresses, the occasional small home appliance that might still have use—and went out to a *población* to distribute goods to the needy and worthy, or to help someone find a job or solve a problem.

Doña Elena's good works fall within a traditionalist concept, paternal and conservative, of Catholic charity. They reaffirm her sense of honorable social standing in a vertically ordered society. Notwithstanding its Catholic inspiration, from time to time her work in the poblaciones has intertwined with conservative social assistance and political indoctrination programs run by the state. The work has focused on ameliorating the lot of the individual poor, rather than questioning, in the manner common in more progressive sectors of the Catholic Church in the 1950s and 1960s, the social conditions that produced poverty in the first place. In this sense, it has ratified the status quo—the structure of social relationships and hierarchies—while doing good works for individuals. Whatever these limitations, however, Doña Elena's work—a record of caring that has outlasted the vicissitudes of politics and to which she does not draw special attention—contributes to the sense of moral constancy that she brings to conversation and remembrance. It is as if her life activities affirm calmly, almost between the lines, to any critic who cares to listen: "Do not confuse us, the Pinochet loyalists, with monsters. The foreign critics and the human rights activists are wrong about us. We who supported the military's salvation of the country are responsible people. We are good Catholics who work to improve the lot of the less fortunate."[31]

The world of conservative middle-class and Catholic morality, as well as conservative arrangements of property, fell apart in the 1960s and early 1970s. For Doña Elena, the trauma occurred in the Frei-Allende years—

before 11 September 1973, not after. After we talked, Doña Elena pulled out a historical artifact of the era, a double-album record published by Radio Agricultura in 1973 to document the historic day of Chile's salvation. We decided to listen to the record. The well-known military correspondent and commentator of Radio Agricultura, Werner Arias Aeschlimann, provided some retrospective narration. Most of the record, however, reproduced the broadcast on the historic eleventh by Radio Agricultura—the downtown street reporting, the military announcements and decrees, the martial music, the drama of the ultimatum to Allende to surrender or face bombardment of La Moneda Palace. In the background one heard the sounds of sporadic gunfire and most dramatically, the screeching roar of the Hawker Hunter combat jets that Doña Elena and Hugo had feted when the jets swooped by to bomb La Moneda. Doña Elena settled her tall body into a rocking chair to listen. As she took in and reactivated the emotion and drama of "the happiest day of my life," she seemed to drift into another dimension. Eventually her eyes welled up and a few tears of joy rolled down her cheeks.

Later, when the climactic moment had passed and Hugo arrived for a late lunch, she would announce—cheerily and almost impishly—that parts of the record were sheer propaganda. No, he protested, every bit of it was true.

AFTERWORD

Childhood Holidays, Childhood Salvation

Doña Elena came of age, as a person passing into adult status with a conservative civic and moral consciousness, in the 1950s. She brings the experience of a grown-up person into a discussion of upheaval during the Frei-Allende period, and into the way she frames the meaning of 11 September 1973. Although she is not a person eager to discuss politics, she also displays no hesitation in explaining and defending the role of military rule in recent Chilean history. Not every person who frames military rule as a time of salvation, however, puts forth a narrative of adult experience. Nor does every such person explain memory as salvation with as much gusto.

I immediately liked Gabriela, the young schoolteacher with an open face, round and freckled and friendly. She displayed a warm style with the children, smiling and sensitive. She seemed a good match for a school self-defined as educationally enlightened and progressive. This was a school that saw itself as unusually attuned to the child's total personal development—aesthetic and social, intellectual and physical—into an autonomously thinking citizen of the world. This was a school unusually committed to religious nonsectarianism and to the tolerance and cross-cultural contact needed to live wisely and successfully in today's world. Gabriela mixed warmth and caring into that enlightened pedagogical philosophy.

Then came the hard part. As often happened in conversations with Chileans, Gabriela asked why I had come to Chile. When I told her about my research on memories of the 1973 crisis and political violence under military rule, the conversation turned toward her childhood.[1]

Gabriela was only eight years old in 1973. She could call up only a few memory fragments in 1996. Unlike Doña Elena, she could not put forth a personally based coherent account of Chilean life during the Frei-Allende period. As with Doña Elena, however, fear of violence and an idea of salvation provided meaning to her memory fragments.

On the one hand, Gabriela remembered the extra holidays from school. The various strikes and shutdowns of public transport led to unscheduled cancellations. This aspect of the Allende period added fun, even an element of adventure, to life. Gabriela and her friends enjoyed unexpected vacations and playtime!

Eventually, however, the disorder of the Allende years injected a profound fear into her childhood. Gabriela's family lived in Las Condes, part of metropolitan Santiago's *barrio alto* ("upper district"), a sector dominated by upper middle-class and wealthy Chileans in the 1990s. The attractions that fuel high property values in Las Condes are obvious to any visitor. Its location near the foothills of the snowcapped mountains northeast of Santiago provides spectacular vistas during winter, afternoon breezes and nightly chills that break the heat during summer. In the 1960s and early 1970s, however, the class character of Las Condes was more mixed. Although prosperous families of the middle class and the elite dominated the area, Las Condes was a zone of relatively recent urban expansion. Its people included migrants of modest social origins, its land use pattern still included truck gardening. Land values were uneven. Neighborhoods included areas with laboring and migratory folk who worked in domestic and garden service, construction projects, shops, or other nearby jobs. In the Frei-Allende era, this situation meant that some parts of Las Condes included the kinds of modest people and communities who sought to invade unused or under-utilized lands, redistribute power and property, and press the state for social services.

Gabriela was too young to understand the political aspect of such tensions. She cannot assess to what extent her parents' fears were based on rumor and exaggeration, to what extent on knowledge of a genuine threat. She simply remembers that at a certain point, fear took over her life. An invasion (toma) of the neighborhood seemed imminent. Her parents thought it might yield a violent street confrontation to evict them and their neighbors from their homes. Her father decided to ship Gabriela, her younger sister, and her mother to his mother-in-law's house, in a safer and more centrally located Santiago neighborhood. He would remain behind to defend the family's house from violence and invasion. The family separation and Gabriela's fear for her father would have to continue indefinitely, until some sort of resolution were achieved.

For Gabriela, military intervention on 11 September provided the resolution. The fear dissolved, and the family could reunite. Order returned. In-deed, in the 1980s the military government would implement a removal-and-resettlement plan that eradicated pockets of troublesome poor people and squatter settlements from various barrio alto zones of Metropolitan Santiago, and resettled them in poblaciones in the southern and north-western peripheries of greater Santiago. The new human geography of Santiago installed a starker segregation by social class.[2]

Of course, Gabriela's childhood fears and sense of relief cannot be di-vorced from her family's respectable class standing and conservative political inclinations. Her "personal memory" of fear is also "group memory," fash-ioned from narrative and explanation of frightening events by parents and family elders to a child over the years. In this sense, her recollection sits well with the observation of Maurice Halbwachs, the pioneer of scholarly thought on collective memory, that even the most intimate personal memory takes shape within a social process that frames remembrance and identity.[3]

Equally important, from a social point of view, is an obvious contrast with victims of military rule. Under military rule, children of the persecuted—families whose parents, other elders, or adolescent youth experienced gen-uine house raids, along with detention, torture, exile, clandestinity, execu-tion, or secret disappearance—suffered a much more tangible and extreme nightmare.

Gabriela acknowledged the obvious but preferred not to dwell on it. Unlike Doña Elena, she resisted discussion of human rights violations and political violence after 11 September. A caring person with those around her, she did not want to justify human rights violations, not even as a regrettable social cost of Chile's salvation. She did not want to get drawn into a potentially contentious discussion of political problems. The human rights theme seemed beyond solution ("there is no solution"), and politics seemed be-yond the realm of meaningful conversation. The human rights theme was an embarrassing and painful subject to be pushed aside, perhaps consigned to a willful amnesia. More to her liking was her role as a warm teacher interested in the human and intellectual development of children.

Gabriela resisted entrapment in political discussions of memory, and she consigned uncomfortable themes to the margins of consciousness. She avoided a provocatively melodramatic tone when depicting her own past. None of these adaptations to a culture of contending memories, however, diminished her clarity about the meaning of 11 September in her own life. Like Doña Elena, Gabriela remembered the date as a personal and familial salvation. In microcosm, she understood the urgency of a national rescue mission. A child who had begun by enjoying the extra school holidays of a turbulent period ended up terrified that she would lose her father. For better or worse, the events of 11 September brought profound relief.

Chapter 2

❋

Dissident Memory:
Rupture, Persecution, Awakening

Doña Elena remembers military intervention in 1973 and the subsequent political violence as a rescue story, a tale of personal and collective salvation from a terrible disaster. Memory as salvation, however, is but one of several principal ways that people recall their stories and build a bridge to Chile's collective story.

This chapter presents two additional forms of remembrance: memory as rupture, profoundly brutal and still unresolved; and memory as persecution and awakening. These ways of remembering are allied scripts, complementary to one another and associated with "dissident" sensibilities during the military period. (The irony, consistent with the mentality of a Cold War crusade against Communism and the political reality of dictatorship, was that critical memory was "dissident," even if anchored in a wide social base and eventually, majority support.) The dissident memory frameworks compete with heroic scripts of national salvation for primacy of place within the memory box of Pinochet's Chile. They also bring to the fore additional background on the historical crisis of society and politics that engulfed Chile by the early 1970s.

MEMORY AS RUPTURE

Señora Herminda Morales lives in La Legua, a población south of downtown Santiago that got its start as a shantytown in the late 1940s and 1950s and acquired a certain fame for working-class militance and Communist Party organizing.[1] In 1952 Señora Herminda and her husband, Ernesto, migrants from provinces south of Santiago, began to build a family life and political life in La Legua. Ernesto, a construction worker and member of the Young Communists (La Juventud Comunista), soon threw himself into the struggles for the electric lighting, streets and sidewalks, and potable water essential to a young shantytown community. He proved active, as well, in trade union politics. Over the 1950s and 1960s Señora Herminda balanced her activity between domestic work as a young mother caring for her children, life as an occasional textile worker and trade unionist, and participation in the marches, demonstrations, and presidential campaign rallies for Salvador Allende that defined La Legua's emerging public culture. Ernesto used the skills he learned in the construction trades to build their house bit by bit, in the manner common to shantytown communities all over Latin America. To this day, the homes in their neighborhood range from small and deteriorating wooden shacks, testament to the precariousness of life and income in the poblaciones, to houses whose larger size, solid masonry, and structural soundness are testament to the hard work, persistence, family income pooling, and struggles for social services that could yield—at least for some old-time families from the 1950s and 1960s—a dignified working-class life and a lower middle-income living standard.

Señora Herminda and Ernesto live with their children and grandchildren in one of the sizable and solid houses. A large room dominates the public space inside their home. A refrigerator sits in the corner of the section used for dining, while an old sofa marks off the living room section. The constant running and jabbering of young grandchildren, firmly and repeatedly reminded to keep their voices down so that adult conversation can proceed, adds a touch of informal vitality and chaos to the ambience.

From a marriage that left her widowed at the age of twenty-two, Señora Herminda brought two children, including Gerardo, into her life with Ernesto. Born in 1948, Gerardo won a scholarship to study accounting after his primary school years, but epilepsy problems cut short his studies. Gerardo found white-collar work in construction and made a name for himself as a dynamic young labor union delegate. During the Popular Unity period he organized food supplies for working-class vacation communities (*balnearios populares*) on the Pacific Coast near Santiago. In 1973 he was elected to the National Congress of the CUT (Central Unica de Trabajadores), the unified labor union federation more or less aligned with the Socialist and Communist Parties since its creation in the 1950s. Like so many others in his community and trade union subculture, Gerardo had grown up a Communist. After their marriage in 1952, Señora Herminda and Ernesto would raise eight additional children—"because in that time there was no birth control."

Their first child together, born in 1953, was Ernesto, or as Señora Herminda prefers to call him, Ernestito (little Ernesto). Little Ernesto was special. Señora Herminda had to leave him at the nursery room of the textile factory, where she worked the 7:00 A.M. shift. The experience suggested a life in which children would grow up destined from birth to become factory peons. This motivated Señora Herminda "to struggle to educate my son, so that he wouldn't have to go around lugging boxes and being bossed." Ernestito studied electromechanics at an industrial school and worked at Chile's telephone company, but in 1973 he enrolled in the University of Chile's Education and Philosophy School. A good athlete, he made the university's soccer team. Like his brother, Ernestito had grown up in a subculture of political and social struggle. He joined the Young Communists, served on local shantytown committees, and attended the national Young Communists Congress of 1972.

Señora Herminda remembers Ernestito as a peacemaker. During Allende's last half-year, when right-wing gangs from Patria y Libertad tried to undermine the Unidad Popular by provoking violent street confrontations, and when angry Left youth or ultras obliged the Right by taking the bait, it was her Ernestito who sought to calm people down. "He didn't like for people to fight when Fatherland and Liberty went to pick fights at the University," she recalled. An example stood out. "Once he was coming [home] with some music records. He tells [me] that he left the records on a green field . . . he had gone over to separate some youths of Fatherland and Liberty and the Communist Party who were fighting. . . . There they were fighting, [and he said], 'No, look you're making problems for the government, one shouldn't fight and one shouldn't be making these scandals.' " When he got home, he suddenly remembered—"Ay, the records"—and went back to look for them on the field. In those tense times, Ernestito hewed to the Communist Party's moderate line and loyalty to Allende. He would explain to his mother, "one shouldn't fight, one should scream [demonstrate], not make problems for the government."

Señora Herminda thinks of her two older sons, Gerardo and Ernestito, as boys more mature than their years. "They were people who wanted a better society, for our country, for children, . . . I call them old youths [jóvenes viejos] because they thought that way and did things, thought about the future." Indeed, Ernestito had confided his plans to help his parents finance the education of his younger brothers and sisters.

More than her words, it was Señora Herminda's face that expressed remembrance as a profound and unresolved shattering. As we spoke, the upper half of her face was all tears—the eyes continually glistening and running over as she recalled the missing presence of Gerardo and Ernestito. The bottom half of her face was all smiles, as if the act of recall were a warm embrace.

That contradictory face conveyed remembrance as rupture—Chileans use the cultural metaphor of an open wound, an awful hurt that fails to heal—more powerfully than words on a transcript. So did Señora Herminda's way of speaking and feeling. She had a penchant for jumping from event to event with only a rough attentiveness to an interviewer's questions, as if reentering the shock caused by a time beyond time. In this time beyond time, chronologically distant events seem to have just happened. As Señora Herminda remarked at one point, "twenty years it's been and it seems just like yesterday."

Gerardo and Ernestito are among the persons permanently disappeared by the state. The basic outlines of the story, investigated and confirmed by Chile's Truth and Reconciliation Commission under a democratic government in 1990, are fairly clear.[2] On Sunday, 16 September 1973, military and police forces conducted a systematic sweep and break-in of homes (*allana-miento*) in La Legua. As tanks, trucks, jeeps, and helicopters cordoned off and kept watch over Señora Herminda's neighborhood, armed squads went from house to house to find and imprison the young men, most of whom ended up with thousands of other prisoners in the National Stadium. Such sweeps leading to break-ins and detentions occurred in various working-class and poor neighborhoods in Santiago, but prisoners from La Legua may have experienced especially ferocious handling because theirs was one of the few areas that had put up some armed resistance on the eleventh. Six *carabineros* (police) died in the shootings; Catholic youths organized by Father Luis Borremans to care for wounded civilians were arrested and accused of running a clandestine health clinic for subversives.[3] When the junta lifted the curfew for a few hours on the thirteenth, Señora Herminda fled with her younger children to another house. Gerardo, Ernestito, and their younger brother Vladimir—only fifteen years old—stayed on in La Legua with their father. The elder Ernesto left to join his wife on Saturday the fifteenth, but Gerardo and Vladimir got caught in the next day's round-up of the neighborhood's young males.

In a declaration under oath taken six years later, Vladimir recalled being beaten and briefly losing consciousness during his initial arrest, his transport in an air force bus to the gymnasium at the El Bosque Aviation School on the sixteenth, and finally his trip to the National Stadium on the seventeenth. Beatings and execution threats were part of the routine. An interrogation about events in La Legua on the eleventh did not happen until 5 October. One beating stood out in Vladimir's mind—the blows by carabineros upon arrival at the stadium included a rifle butt to the face that knocked out his front teeth. But at least the boys survived. Vladimir and Gerardo were freed on 8 October.[4]

The worst came later. The family left Santiago and on 28 October settled down with relatives in San Juan de Lo Gallardo, a small town on the Maipo River near the port of San Antonio—and near the army's Military Engineers Regiment at Tejas Verdes. The elder Ernesto found work laying drain pipes at a petrochemical company and supplemented it with labor in January on a neighbor's wheat harvest. Vladimir joined the family in the provinces and worked in the wheat fields with his father. But the older boys, Gerardo and Ernestito, decided to stay on in Santiago, where they thought they were needed for solidarity with the persecuted, and probably, for keeping the Party alive for another day—a time when conditions might permit resistance. Señora Herminda remembers trying to convince them to flee Santiago. "One cannot lie to history," she said. "The kids stayed [in La Legua], they didn't listen to us. . . . I would cry and tell them to leave with us." She could not persuade them. "They said, 'No, Mama, because we're going to help those we can, because just like you're in need and hurting there are many mothers in the same situation and we are going to help,' and Ernestito told me, 'if we have to fight we are going to fight, one must do something.' " The elder Ernesto sent the boys money to help them out, and the boys visited during the Christmas and New Year's holiday.

The idea of helping out in Santiago, and waiting for a time when resistance might be possible, was consistent with political understandings Gerardo and Ernestito had learned in the Communist Party. During August and September 1973, when Chile's crisis spun out of control, the Communist Party had taken a moderate Left line. It provided the most consistent Left support to Allende in his effort to achieve a political solution through an accord with Christian Democrats, and in his idea of a plebiscite to resolve the crisis—at the risk of splitting the Unidad Popular coalition as well as losing the election. In September, the Communist Party also indicated its willingness, in view of the political emergency, to release Allende from his obligation to clear major policy decisions with the Unidad Popular parties.

Political moderation, however, did not necessarily imply an unwillingness to contemplate resistance to an attempted military coup. On the contrary, many Allendistas and Left activists, including Communists, believed that if Allende could not find a political solution, the last best hope for defense of the Constitutional government lay in civilian resistance to an attempted coup. The resistance would presumably buy time and strengthen the resolve of Constitutionalist factions in the army. The splits in the military might then thwart the takeover.

Consistent with this idea, on 11 September, Gerardo and Ernestito joined a march of *pobladores* (residents of poblaciones) in La Legua urging people to defend themselves in the event of a military sweep and allanamiento of homes in the neighborhood. As the march proceeded, the group encountered a column of armed workers on the way to the textile plant SUMAR Polyester to see if some sort of resistance could be organized. According to a witness, a bus of carabineros suddenly appeared and fired shots on the crowd. The fire was returned (probably from the armed workers column), a policeman was wounded, and a surreal sequence followed. Carabineros waved a white flag from their bus, the firing stopped, and the vehicle headed off toward Barros Luco Hospital.[5]

Although "resistance" on the eleventh proved naive and unworkable, the shocking scale and severity of the violence during and soon afterward created a host of emergencies. In the first month alone, the new regime arrested about 45,000 persons.[6] Solidarity was required to help families of prisoners, to hide and find embassies for those who might be persecuted, to keep political identities alive, to wait for a time when resistance or protest might prove viable. One result was a mentality of desperation—the idea that "one must do something." As we shall see, the military intelligence services would play upon this idea in La Legua.

Late at night on 24 January or 25 January 1974, Gerardo and Ernestito visited unexpectedly.[7] The report issued by the Truth and Reconciliation Commission summarizes what happened next.[8]

> They came to the house of their parents in [San Juan de] Lo Gallardo . . . the two brothers with about twelve heavily armed people. They said they came to liberate the prisoners at Tejas Verdes. The brothers looked nervous. The next morning they left. Nonetheless, some of those who had brought the brothers returned and detained the father . . . and a younger brother [Vladimir], who were taken to Tejas Verdes, [where they were] severely tortured and released after being disappeared for 42 days.

When Vladimir and his father were taken away, the armed band continued talking up the idea of "liberating" Tejas Verdes while asking about people in La Legua. But the ruse was obvious and lasted only a short while. Vladimir and his father were soon blindfolded and on their way to Tejas Verdes.[9]

At the time, Tejas Verdes, under the authority of Army Colonel Manuel Contreras, had been transformed into a concentration camp run by Contreras and the secret police, drawn in large part from the army, that would come to be known as the DINA (Dirección de Inteligencia Nacional, or National Intelligence Directorate). The DINA would not be officially created until June 1974, but the Truth and Reconciliation Commission's research demonstrated the existence of an active and well-organized "DINA group," anchored at the Military Academy (Escuela Militar) in Santiago and at Tejas Verdes since 11 September, possibly earlier in the case of Tejas Verdes and Colonel Contreras.[10]

In December and January, the DINA developed a scheme to round up Communist and Socialist militants in La Legua. Agents of the DINA would "recruit" their targets for a project to "liberate" political prisoners, many of them from La Legua, at Tejas Verdes. It is impossible to know with certainty if Gerardo and Ernestito—desperate to "do something"—were initially fooled by the ploy. Agents of the DINA typically used crude cover stories when they first took a prisoner from a house to a vehicle; the coercive aspect was either obvious from the start or not long in coming. One youth from La Legua, Jorge Poblete, was "recruited" in January with a threat that he would be killed if he refused to collaborate.

Three points *can* be made, however, with greater certainty. First, La Legua's political prisoners were often tortured first at Londres 38, a DINA-run house in downtown Santiago, before their transfer to Tejas Verdes. Second, Jorge Poblete later testified that he spoke with Gerardo and Ernestito in the downstairs common room for prisoners at Londres 38, on 28 or 29 January, but that they were no longer present when Poblete returned from his torture session upstairs. Third, Margarita Durán, also a prisoner at Londres 38, testified that during her torture session on or shortly after 30 January, one of three agents in the directing group threatened that if she refused to cooperate, they would kill her as they had killed Gerardo and Ernestito. Because of a flare-up of tachycardia (racing heartbeat), her hood was temporarily removed during the session and she saw the agents who sat behind a desk in command of the torture session. The agent who had spoken, known as "Esteban," had an Argentine accent but eluded a more specific identification.

The other two she identified as Marcelo Moren Brito and Colonel (later General) Manuel Contreras.[11]

The Truth and Reconciliation Commission concluded unanimously that the DINA permanently "disappeared" Gerardo and Ernestito and that their last known location was the Tejas Verdes concentration camp.[12] Its method was meticulous: careful analysis of the multiple witness accounts, as well as the circumstances of state tracking, detention, and torture that fell on others in the family and on Gerardo's girlfriend, also detained at Tejas Verdes. All rendered unavoidable not only that the DINA agents disappeared Gerardo and Ernestito but that "the version offered by the political authority of the time, which held that the brothers were not detained, must be rejected."

Lack of specific information on the destiny of Gerardo and Ernestito makes it impossible to say precisely what happened to them at Londres 38 and at Tejas Verdes. But we do know, from the hair-raising diary of Hernán Valdés, a prisoner at Tejas Verdes in February and March 1974, that living conditions were primitive and cruel and that the prisoners' regimen included, aside from initial beatings and in some instances simulated executions, the terror of learning if one was on the day's list of prisoners selected for "interrogation." To judge from Valdés, the sessions included beatings, electric shock to various body parts including genitals, and verbal abuse, along with pressure to satisfy one's tormentors by providing real or invented information about "subversives."[13]

In addition, the family's search for Gerardo and Ernestito, with assistance from the Santiago Catholic Church's Vicaría de la Solidaridad (Vicariate of Solidarity) in the 1970s, led the elder Ernesto and Vladimir to recount their own harrowing experiences under oath. The initial torture of the elder Ernesto included a beating and electric shocks, accompanied by questions about people and politics in La Legua, about his son Gerardo, and about an alleged hidden arms supply near Tejas Verdes. Later there were fruitless digging sessions to unearth supposed arms near the mouth of the Maipo River, accompanied in at least one instance by a threatened execution at the riverbank. Vladimir remembered similar sessions and, in addition, a session of beatings while being hung in a cell. (To this day he walks with some difficulty and has limited movement in his left arm.) He also remembered sessions that played on his mind—"since they would alternate verbal abuse and application of current with soothing words and offers of drink to relieve the intense thirst."[14]

Given the survivor testimonies about Londres 38 and Tejas Verdes during the Chilean summer of 1974, it is difficult to escape the conclusion that Gerardo and Ernestito were cruelly tortured before their final disposition.

The files on Gerardo and Ernestito in the Truth and Reconciliation Commission archives, the case files in the archive of the Vicariate of Solidarity, and the mental archive of Señora Herminda all record an experience of desperate and unending rupture. A search without resolution took Señora Herminda and her family to every institution that might help find or free her children—the Comité Pro-Paz (Pro-Peace Committee), quickly formed by religious leaders of various faiths to deal with Chile's human rights emergencies during 1973–75; the Vicaría de la Solidaridad, set up by Santiago's Archbishop in 1976 to continue the work of the recently dissolved Pro-Peace Committee; the International Red Cross; the Ministry of the Interior; the National Arrests Secretariat (SENDET, Secretaría Ejecutiva Nacional de Detenidos); the emigration police; various hospitals, clinics, and jails; the medical office in charge of cadavers (Instituto Médico Legal); and the civilian and military courts. The number of inquiries is staggering. The constant official answer was that the state knew nothing about the fate of Gerardo and Ernestito and that aside from Gerardo's temporary imprisonment at the National Stadium, the authorities had not even arrested them.[15]

Given this experience, the establishment of a credible and rigorous truth commission by the state marked a tremendously important moment for Señora Herminda. In 1990, sixteen years into the disappearance and string of denials, Chile finally had a democratic government. President Patricio Aylwin Azócar appointed the National Truth and Reconciliation Commission (Comisión Nacional de Verdad y Reconciliación, known informally as the Rettig Commission after its president, Raúl Rettig Guissen). The Commission set out to investigate each case of alleged human rights violations leading to death or disappearance. Señora Herminda's remembrance of an early step in the Truth Commission process underscores her experience of military rule as a profoundly ruinous and unresolved rupture—the fight to continue believing that she might yet find her children, the dizzying consciousness that the time had really arrived for an official reckoning with the truth of her experience.

AUTHOR: You testified, I would imagine, before the Commission?
SEÑORA HERMINDA: Yes, we had to give testimony, of course the testi-

monies were very hard, because one remembers everything . . . one returns to live what one lived. . . .

One day I went alone, because one had to go to talk to get the hour and all that [i.e., to set appointments for testimonies by relatives to the Commission].

And when I entered, I remember, . . . there were some large tables in some large rooms, and I went in and to a man they gave some papers like this [Señora Herminda gestures the exchange], and everything went blurry for me and the ground went shaky on me—because I thought that for my sons, they were also going to give me some papers one day, like that, and they were not going to return the children. And I fell to the side [lost her balance] like this and a young woman [*señorita*] came over and said, "What happened to you, Señora?" And she took me inside and later, once it had passed, they began to attend [to my appointment] and gave me the hour on the day [we had to] go.

It would go too far to imply that memory as rupture always and inexorably reduces people to victims only, to fragile beings unable to function in ordinary everyday life or to mobilize a powerful inner resolve. On the contrary. Señora Herminda's search for answers took her into new forms of struggle, relationships, and inner determination. She met other people, mainly women, in search of disappeared relatives. She found comprehension and collective strategies of struggle in the Association of Relatives of the Detained and Disappeared (Agrupación de Familiares de Detenidos-Desaparecidos, or AFDD, hereinafter, Agrupación). With other members of the Agrupación and human rights activists, she sometimes joined in dramatic civil disobedience actions, while taking care to avoid arrest so that she could care for her younger children. She also challenged ambivalence and fear within her own family. She once commented to Vladimir that she had to stand up "because I am going for the children . . . and if your Dad gets mad it doesn't matter."

Señora Herminda belongs to a generation, a social class, and an urban subculture that saw collective struggle and solidarity as healthy and necessary to overcome injustice and achieve worthy ends. As Elizabeth Jelin and Susana Kaufman have implied in a brilliant essay on the many "layers" of memory, the life course of some generational cohorts may include formative moments of remembrance that precede the time of the great trauma, collective and personal, that generates new memory struggles.[16] These foundational times or moments may wield a decisive influence on the ways people organize their memories of the great trauma.

In our interview, Señora Herminda emphasized not only the rupture of her life but the importance of loyalty and organization in the service of a larger good. Just as Doña Elena's narrative of ruin followed by salvation draws on formative experiences in the 1950s to establish the true dimensions of good order and the nature of the disaster that nearly overtook Chile, so it is that Señora Herminda's experience of shantytown and labor union struggles in the 1950s and 1960s frames the meaning of a later disaster and the positive values that she draws from her family's history. "Man has the right to think, to struggle, to struggle for a more just society," she observed. It is on that basis that she remembers Gerardo and Ernestito as good people —"they were not terrorists, they were not bad people, but rather they were people who wanted a better society." It is on that basis, too, that she often sought to lift up the depressed spirits of her husband.

> I tell my husband, that they should build a monument to him while he is alive, because he was always a father, he attended to his mother until she died, he raised the nephews who were with the *abuelita* ["little grandma," the affectionate diminutive form in Spanish] . . . a super good man, he fought for the población [i.e., La Legua]. . . . He has got that thing about helping; he is a social activist [*luchador social*], in the trade union he gave all his free time, to the construction union.

Señora Herminda was delighted when, after seventeen years of relative silence and withdrawal, her husband finally resumed speaking out in public and began to move toward a more involved political life, starting at a public anniversary ceremony in honor of their children and the disappeared. "It does him good because he had been awfully ruined; . . . now he goes around rejuvenated." Speaking out, struggling, and talking gave him more resilience—even enabled him, at the end of a workday, to come home "telling jokes and things [that] are good for living together."

Not only does Señora Herminda remember the military period as the time that brought a deep and continuing rupture, a cruel wound that fails to heal, to her life. She has also reorganized much of her life around the idea of memory and rupture—the struggle to honor and maintain the memory of her missing sons. As remembered people who really existed, they must be found, if only to give them a decent burial. This struggle and the social involvement it brings may be viewed as a source of resilience, meaning, and energy, especially when her life is compared with those whose experience of memory as rupture is more solitary.[17]

But the struggle also takes its toll and it can produce contradictory ambiguities. On the day we spoke, 11 September 1996, Señora Herminda, now sixty-six years old, almost succumbed to cumulative fatigue. Early in the morning she had decided not to join that year's march from downtown Santiago to the National Cemetery to protest the period of military rule, demand full truth and justice, and honor the dead and disappeared. At the last minute, her sense of loyalty to her children, to the families of the other dead and disappeared, and to her comrades and friends in the Agrupación prevailed. She walked the long march and contended with the tear gas heaved into the crowd at the cemetery's Memorial to the Dead and Disappeared. The same sense of loyalty probably explained the energy she found for our interview in the late afternoon and early evening, at the end of a long and exhausting day.

The toll of memory as rupture, however, goes beyond fatigue and beyond the strain of a face caught perpetually between tears and smiles. Notwithstanding her loyalty to Gerardo and Ernestito, Señora Herminda has also experienced contradictions as a mother. To honor Gerardo and Ernestito, she has usually put up large pictures of them in the living room section of the main room in her house. But the photos were not on the wall when we spoke. She had had to remove them because one of her children, exiled in Argentina for many years, had fallen ill and the pictures made him more nervous. He was still upset that he had not been able to help his brothers. As a mother of living and present children, Señora Herminda has from time to time taken down the pictures. As a mother of missing children, she has from time to time put them back up. In the early years, "when the youngest girls were around, I would remove the photos because they would pass the time looking and crying, because they were their brothers' real pets [muy regalonas de ellos]." In time, Señora Herminda's daughters grew accustomed to living with their brothers Gerardo and Ernestito prominently remembered on the living room wall. The ups and downs of the pictures, like the contrast between the upper and lower portions of Señora Herminda's face, express the meaning of memory as a profound and unresolved rupture.

Before our interview ended, Señora Herminda gave me a gift: two large poster photos of Gerardo and Ernestito. They are the photos she has carried high on a stick and pinned on her chest in demonstrations over the years.

MEMORY AS PERSECUTION AND AWAKENING

Like Doña Elena and Señora Herminda, Violeta E. is of the generation, well into middle age or recently beyond it (between late forties and middle sixties in 1996–97), that experienced the Frei-Allende period as young adults.[18] But here the resemblance stops. If the class backgrounds and social experiences of Doña Elena and Señora Herminda are polar opposites within the pathways of Chilean life, Violeta's trajectory flows out of a more middling social layer and experience. Unlike Doña Elena, Violeta does not descend from high social stock. Her housing and living standard are too modest to place her in the urban consumption levels and vacation circuits, let alone the social circles, of prosperous upper middle-class professionals and wealthy elites. Nor does her political lineage flow from the Right or Center-Right. Unlike Señora Herminda, Violeta does not descend from the tradition of migrants and laborers who built a working-class shantytown community, anchored in a Left-oriented electoral culture and in a strong trade union movement and the Communist Party.

Violeta and her eight sisters and a brother built their young adult lives as part of Chile's expanding middle class and lower middle class between the late 1950s and early 1970s. As they made the transition into young adulthood, they sustained themselves as white-collar workers, secretaries, and functionaries in respectable positions with state agencies, Catholic Church organizations, political parties, universities and schools, and the like. The family's politics reflected both the emergence of the Christian Democrats as Chile's dynamic new political force in the Center, and the debates about politics, Christian reform, and social transformation that moved some Christian Democrats toward the Left. Most of Violeta's siblings identified with the Christian Democracy throughout the Frei-Allende period. Tita, the sister who over the years provided much of the moral center in the family— who helped organize care for aging parents and inherited the home that continues to serve as a nodal point for family meals, visits, and information exchange—was firmly aligned with the Christian Democrats. Indeed, Tita's

¿DONDE ESTAN?

ERNESTO GUILLERMO SALAMANCA MORALES
22 años.
Estudiante Filosofía Pedagógico U. de Chile
Detenido y Desaparecido el 25 de enero de 1974 por la DINA.

1. Señora Herminda's photograph of Ernestito, one of her disappeared children. She wears the photograph pinned to her clothing and displays it on a poster-banner she carries during demonstrations. Gift to author from Herminda Morales.

¿ DONDE ESTAN ?

GERARDO ISMAEL RUBILAR MORALES
26 años.
Consejero nacional Departamento Juvenil C.U.T.
Detenido y Desaparecido el 25 de enero de 1974 por la DINA.

2. Señora Herminda's photograph of Gerardo, one of her disappeared children. She wears the photograph pinned to her clothing and displays it on a poster-banner she carries during demonstrations. Gift to author from Herminda Morales.

husband worked with Frei's agrarian reform in the South and viewed Allende's version of reform as chaotic and irresponsible.

Violeta and three sisters, however, felt drawn to the Left. By 1970 Violeta and a sister joined the MAPU, the new political party that split off from the Christian Democrats and joined Allende's Unidad Popular coalition. Violeta and her husband, Ricardo, lived in a población west of downtown Santiago whose working-class and lower middle-class composition, and whose location near the militant Left población of Villa Francia, made for considerable political competition among Left and Center parties. By Allende's election, Violeta and Ricardo had four young children whom they raised on two incomes. Like many Chilean middle-class families, they had the assistance of a maid who helped with child care. Violeta worked as a secretary in the Social Work School of Catholic University, while Ricardo worked in the postal and telegraph service. Both identified with the politics of the Christian Left.[19] Violeta, more verbal and intellectual, had more of the party activist in her and in 1971 left the university to work as a secretary in Allende's Economics Ministry. In Villa Francia, Violeta and Ricardo took part in a Christian lay community that discussed the heated politics of the period.

Violeta remembers vividly the conflictive quality of life, as persons struggled about how and whether to bring about a socialist revolution to benefit the dispossessed and about the specific twists and turns of the political agony that took hold in 1972–73. The conflicts seemed to invade almost every sphere—work, the neighborhood, the political party (in 1973 the MAPU split into "moderate" and "ultra" factions), the family. As tension between the Christian Democrat and Left branches of the family deepened, shared times and spaces grew more difficult. "We began to live [like] people together-apart [*juntos separados*], . . . one practically could not touch on controversial subjects, . . . in reality practically everything one might raise . . . crossed with the political. Socially, it implied misunderstandings, confrontations, debates." Disagreements were passionate and stubborn, stoked by awareness that the stakes were so high. "And not only [was there disagreement], we were in a time in which we were all so very intolerant [*muy poco tolerantes*], because I think that on both sides we felt we were right." The same sorts of tensions were played out at work and in the neighborhood. " When I went to work in the Ministry there were career people who were not at all pro-Allendista, on the contrary, so that provoked moments of confrontation."

After the military takeover on 11 September, however, it was the cumulative effect of tensions in neighborhood life that caused the most concern. Would people who opposed Allende act on their resentments or fears of neighbor-hood Left activists? Would they identify people as subversives to be arrested by the new government? After the new government's initial takeover and arrests of high officials and political leaders, and the initial sweeps of pobla-ciones such as La Legua, the authorities announced on radios and television, and in newspapers and street posters, that citizens could help save the country from violent leftists and their hidden arms by identifying suspects.[20] "There was a call to denounce people [to the authorities], and there was a very strong thing against the Left; they were all accused of being Communists without knowing very much about what being Communist meant." In par-ticular, patriotic citizens were asked to "denounce any strange movement, any suspicious thing in the barrios, that might mean knowledge about arms." Given the new government's fear campaign, the cumulative effect of a period of political conflict, and Violeta's status as a MAPU militant and a vocal participant in a Christian lay community, she and Ricardo wondered whether Violeta might be targeted by anti-Allendista neighbors in the pobla-ción—whether out of fear or hatred.

The nightmare struck in October but not in the way Violeta and Ricardo had imagined. At least one neighbor had indeed denounced the couple as "sus-picious," but it was Ricardo—not Violeta—whom the soldiers would take away for three days. Aside from the general stigma that accrued to Violeta and Ricardo as leftists, an additional aspect was surreal, almost comical. In 1973 the couple and other Left activists in the barrio had formed a political discussion group whose members also built a cooperative pooling and dis-tribution network to acquire basic foodstuffs—to cope with the long lines of the rationing system, the high prices of the black market, and the political hostility of food vendors. The food itself was humble—"black noodles, the kind that I think now they give to dogs, beans, but oh the worst"—but it would have to do. The eleventh of September was the day when Ricardo and Violeta were supposed to go to take their portion of the pooled food, but the events and curfew of the day prevented circulation. Later that week, when people were allowed to leave their homes a few hours, Ricardo and Violeta went "to get our food because we had kids, and since we were carrying bundles—not that they were big things—people swore that we were trans-porting arms." Of course, soldiers might have come for them and people might have "denounced" them even in the absence of an alleged specific observation of arms.

Had political enemies in the neighborhood looked for any pretext to vent resentment or hate by "denouncing" people such as Violeta and Ricardo? Or, I asked, was the accusation made in good faith? Violeta could not know for sure about her own specific case, but her inclination was not to assume the worst. Some pobladores, she thought, truly believed they had been saved from a terrible fate. "I think that many people did not act in bad faith. Think of it: they did not act in bad faith but because they believed that we [people on the Left] really had weapons." Given the economic hardships (including food anxieties) and the sense of chaos that took hold by August and September 1973—"you didn't know what would happen from one moment to the next. . . . It was a country truly in convulsion"—some people in the población wanted to believe the worst was over. This attitude, she thought, especially influenced persons who did not have much political experience. They assumed that the new government acted in good faith and had solutions, and "they believed the propaganda" about dangerous leftists who had to be identified and denounced.

Ricardo and a number of other prisoners were taken away for three days to the animal corral complex (known today as FISA) in Cerrillos, in southern Santiago, that normally served as a trading fair for cattle and horses. In Violeta's mind the Catholic Church may well have saved Ricardo's life. Violeta sought help from Bishop Fernando Ariztía, a progressive auxiliary bishop of the Santiago Archdiocese who had known and ministered to the family. In addition, one of the prisoners was a former priest, a circumstance that perhaps gave the Church, especially Cardinal Raúl Silva Henríquez of the Santiago Archdiocese, an additional institutional claim in his discussions with the authorities. The efforts of Ariztía, Silva Henríquez, and others led to a fairly speedy release.

But Ricardo came home "destroyed." It was not the physical beatings that left the worst marks. It was the mental torture. " The worst of all is what they did to them at night, simulated execution by shooting. That was very dramatic, just tremendous. For years he could not—he could not recover and for years he thought they would come to arrest him, that they could do it to him again." Nights were rough. "He did not sleep at night. He always thought they were going to come for him. Any noise woke him up."

In many ways the real drama of Violeta's memory begins after Ricardo's persecution. For as Violeta and Ricardo awakened to the truly brutal character of the dictatorship—for themselves and for others—they would have to cope not only with the specific brutality and fear inflicted on their family. They would also have to decide what to do about the call of Christian and political conscience. Ricardo's supervisor in the postal service took an understanding view. In the absence of incriminating paperwork from the authorities, he approved Ricardo's return to work after his brief "illness." Given Ricardo's inner torment, it was clear that he could not get involved in direct work to support human rights.

But what about Violeta? She lacked a job, and the human rights emergencies of the country were tremendous. Religious leaders of various faiths, including Ariztía and Silva Henríquez, had formed the ecumenical Pro-Peace Committee, mentioned earlier, to attend to the emergencies. (The Comité Pro-Paz's formal name was Comité de Cooperación para la Paz en Chile, or Committee of Cooperation for Peace in Chile.) The ad hoc work mushroomed: Prisoners needed to be tracked. Appeals to the authorities needed to be made. Legal petitions and documents had to be written. Families required psychological and pastoral support, legal-institutional guidance, and economic help. Persons in imminent danger needed to find discreet ways to find refuge in a foreign embassy compound and leave the country. Communications and record keeping had to be organized. The Pro-Peace Committee became a natural point of confluence, moreover, for persons from the MAPU and other Christian-Left trajectories, and Bishop Ariztía was its copresident.[21]

When the Pro-Peace Committee asked Violeta in December whether she had a job and might want to work with them, she and Ricardo faced a dilemma. Ricardo's fears of a new nightmare and his need for personal support were real. The work might expose Violeta to conflicts with military rulers who had proved they would stop at nothing. To lose Violeta to an arrest or worse would devastate him. "Ricardo was truly terrified, Ricardo did not want me to work [there]. . . . He would say, 'You left the frying pan for the fire' [tú saliste del fuego para caer a las llamas]." The couple was not naive about the possible consequences of such work. "We already knew of the existence of the Peace Committee . . . that it was helping all the people who had problems. And think of it, that I, well apart from the decrees, apart from the news and seeing that the military had [control of] everything here . . . well with all [our] political reflection, we knew what it could mean." In the end, Violeta accepted the job. Ricardo found the decision difficult, although he understood the reasons for it and took some comfort from the fact that Bishop Ariztía worked with Violeta and the group.

Violeta's memory resembles a journey in which the persecution of others constantly tests her own values and strength. It is a journey of continuous encounters—with truth, with people, with herself. The early years of solidarity work with the Pro-Peace Committee and its successor organization, the Vicaría de la Solidaridad, exposed one to the dramas of persecution but also awakened one's own identity and values.

On the one hand, one confronted the brutal reality masked by the veneer of order and official news. The protective shield of the Catholic Church and the welcome given to the persecuted inspired confidence, "and somehow word [of the Pro-Peace Committee] went around because one person would tell another where [the person] could go." This meant continuous direct exposure to the truth of systematic and widespread persecution, especially the perpetual anguish and searching by relatives for persons detained and disappeared by the military or police. The intensity of this work became especially clear when Violeta recalled the discovery of human remains, through information passed discreetly to the Church and the Vicaría, in the abandoned lime oven of Lonquén in December 1978. The cadavers of the peasants matched up with persons whose cases had been taken up by the Pro-Peace Committee and the Vicaría. They constituted the first "hard" proof of the truth of permanent disappearances that broke into the public domain—and a devastating confrontation with the reality that at least some of the disappeared had indeed been killed.[22]

When we turned to the topic of Lonquén, Violeta's body language took a restless and almost writhing turn. She continually squeezed her hands hard and pulled at her nails. Perhaps this was because she recalled not only the impact of the news and the subsequent struggles to identify and bury the remains, but also what had happened *before* the discovery. The shattering aspect was evident not only in body language but also in her difficulty of finding the right words to explain. "Well, the time of Lonquén was a terrible time, because, well, . . . we had been seeing the constant pilgrimage of the relatives who kept going to—Look, they would live in the Vicariate of Solidarity, the relatives who came from the pueblos near Santiago, that were peasant families, they would pass entire day after day seeing what could be found out."

Especially in the early ad hoc phase of the Pro-Peace Committee in 1974, before awareness had fully set in about the long-term nature of the new regime and its continuous renewals of six-month states of legal exception, and before experience and institutionalization by the Vicaría created a more systematized approach, one by-product of such work was the danger of reaching "a point of saturation." One might simply become overwhelmed by the drama and scale of the persecution. In an extreme case, a foreign nun "who attended to the people who had to find asylum" lost her emotional balance and had to leave the country to recover her health. In less extreme cases, the persecution became a kind of obsession. " There came a point in which we all turned totally repetitive. In other words we could not let go; we could not stop talking about the subject."

An additional by-product was the knowledge that religious protection had its limits. Successful or insistent advocacy of human rights could provoke a reaction. Indeed, toward the end of 1975, tensions between the Pro-Peace Committee and the government came to a head. Lutheran Bishop Helmut Frenz, copresident of the Pro-Peace Committee, was expelled from the country and a number of persons on the staff were arrested, including José Zalaquett, the head of the legal section. Zalaquett would later be expelled as well.[23]

But there was another side to the coin. The times of persecution were also times of a more positive awakening—a strengthening of one's social commitments, a reawakening and validation of one's identity and values. Violeta recalls ways of coping and affirming life, sometimes including both the staff and victims of persecution, that went beyond a mere amelioration of the shocks of solidarity work. In the early Pro-Peace Committee days,

> For mental sanity we had the possibility of doing a kind of therapy. At lunch or snack time we would sing. All the staff got together, and somehow we maintained history a bit, the past history. Because, what did we sing? We would sing the songs . . . [of] the Popular Unity, not the combative songs but rather the folkloric songs, which meant a lot to us [nos decían mucho], the songs of Víctor Jara or those of Violeta Parra or whomever. But think of it, how it served to cleanse us of all the drama we were listening to all day long, and [the singing] also helped the people [who were victims] . . . Somehow people felt as if [they were] relaxed, one felt that it was not as hard.

In Violeta's mind, the therapeutic aspect went beyond the cleansing change of pace and the sense of community created by group song. Discreet singing of the more lyrical "New Song" tunes of the 1960s and early 1970s recaptured the idealism of an earlier time and its youth generation, affirming hope that all was not lost. "So, amidst everything that was being suffered, somehow something was being conserved. . . . We would sing discreetly [softly], and that was a way to bolster the people too, like [saying] 'Look, something still remains, a piece of who we are [de lo nuestro] continues. They cannot take everything away from us,' something like that."

Violeta recalled such aspects with a mix of affection and level-headedness. I had prompted her by asking how people coped with the drama of attending continuously to persecution. She was sophisticated enough to be self-conscious about the danger of nostalgic idealization, and indeed added, "I don't think I'm idealizing it, you know, because with time one idealizes things a bit." She was also experienced enough to be aware that the improvised "learning as you go" that characterized the early Pro-Peace Committee years had to give way to more institutionalized professional procedures, in view of the scale and urgency of the work.

Nonetheless, even as she remembers the crisis of 1973 and the subsequent violence as a time when persecution put one's values to a grueling test, and even as she draws distance from nostalgic idealization, Violeta also remembers the period as a time of inspiration. The solidarity work itself created a human meeting ground of hope and affirmation. Some such moments came when human rights activists worked with residents of various poblaciones to invent solutions to severe needs—community food pots (ollas comunes), microenterprise work projects, health clinics, women's weaving groups whose folkloric tapestries (arpilleras) commented on everyday life and problems, short-term recreation camps for young children.[24] Not only did such projects remove one temporarily from the grinding work of attending to the most extreme cases of direct violence. They also built faith in people and popular creativity and problem solving. "I think that what saved us from falling sick . . . was this chain of solidarity that permitted one to go on searching alternatives for solutions together with the people, because the idea[s] were not just ours, it was the people themselves. . . . It was a period of great creativity."

Living between hurt and hope, persecution and affirmation, is a draining undertaking that can bring frustration and restlessness. The mental torture that had been inflicted on Ricardo, the work at the Pro-Peace Committee and the Vicaría, a close friendship with a family in the población who lost children to the persecution in the 1980s—all these inscribed the violence of Chile's collective life onto Violeta's personal and intimate life. The staying power of the dictatorship also made difficult the complacency of supposing that Violeta had found the one true path, expressive of her values *and* adequate for the human rights problems at hand. Beyond a certain point in time, it became obvious that only replacement of the dictatorship by a democracy could solve such problems. Violeta found no comfortable harbor in her journey of growth and commitment. The only anchors were a deepening sense of Christian values, blended with the social justice ideals of the Left; a deepening affirmation of the value of human life and of attending to the suffering of others; and a strong commitment to one's children and family.

Violeta does not cast herself as a hero who found or created a solution, but as a person for whom solidarity work was a journey of human encounters. The Vicaría had been "an important space for encounter, encounter in every sense, because you really felt trust, [with which] you lost your fear when you were there." But circumstances changed. By the end of the 1970s the institutional consolidation of the dictatorship became obvious, and the Vicaría underwent a complex period of changing leadership styles and internal self-questioning.[25]

Violeta was part of this process. Her remembrance of the 1980s focuses on the restless, continuing quest for effective ways to end the period of dictatorship and persecution, and the ways this quest generated new family anxieties. In the early 1980s, she left the Vicaría a few years in order to work more "politically" in the world of alternative video and education projects organized by Ictus, an important theater group that established forums, through a network of churches and human rights organizations, for watching and discussing videos about Chilean life. She worked with a volunteer medical clinic and housed some French doctors from Médicos del Mundo (Doctors without Borders) who served the health needs of the población and treated the wounded in the cycle of street protests and repression that rocked Chile between 1983 and 1986. For a time, Violeta participated in an audacious civil disobedience group (Movimiento contra la Tortura "Sebastián Acevedo"). The militant human rights priests and other members of the group used sudden street actions—with little prior notice to the group members, for security reasons—to catch attention and thereby raise consciousness and outrage about torture. Through sit-ins accompanied by spirited shouts and songs, they identified torture sites, stopped traffic and pedestrian routines, and either dispersed rapidly or faced the arrival of police and water cannon trucks. After a time, Violeta worked again with the Vicaría.

Violeta's journey in the 1980s reactivated fear and provoked new awakenings. One was a self-knowledge that came to include honesty about her own limitations. After two or three civil disobedience actions with the antitorture group, she found that she could not continue. She admitted to herself—and to the group—that the tension and fear were too overwhelming. Another awakening focused on fears related to her children, now in late adolescence and early adulthood. Like many others in the youth generation of the 1980s, Violeta's children participated in the waves of street protests that met with repression, and they sometimes criticized their elders for timidity or ineffectiveness. Ricardo and Violeta took pride in their children's values and audacity. Violeta also found rewarding spaces of collaboration with some of them in volunteer service—in popular education forums, a health clinic, and recreational camps for young children. But Violeta and Ricardo also discovered an ironic ambivalence about the path of their children, autonomous beings living their own version of a life between persecution and awakening, and therefore susceptible to arrest or injury in the street protests.

The restless experimentation of the 1980s produced, as well, a process of political reflection and encounter. The cycle of street protest and violent repression faded after 1986. Attention turned to the impending plebiscite of 1988, mandated by the 1980 Constitution, as a path that might provide a possible exit from the dictatorship and a reckoning with the human rights reality and social needs of the country. Among the difficult and controversial aspects of this strategy—including whether it would prove viable or simply legitimize continuing rule of the military regime—was the question of political reconciliation between the Center and the Left around the ideas of democracy, human rights, and social equity.[26]

The divide between the Center and Left in Chilean society was familial and emotional as well as political and intellectual. It was the division that had split Violeta's family into a Christian Democrat branch and a Left branch. It was a division with several archaeological layers—from the breach and recriminations between the Center and the Left during the Frei-Allende years and in the immediate aftermath of September 1973; to controversies in the mid-to-late 1980s about the place of the Communist Party, which had moved toward an armed struggle concept of toppling the military regime; to the politics of electoral alliances and democratic transition. Indeed, the emerging leader of the Center-Left coalition that would win the plebiscite was none other than Patricio Aylwin Azócar, a figure with a controversial background. The president of the Christian Democrats in the final crisis months of 1973, he was perceived in 1973 by most of the Left and Christian Democrats as a hard-line Frei loyalist—in other words, as a leader who blocked a political solution to the crisis in the eyes of the Left.[27]

In the 1980s Violeta and Ricardo, along with other families in the población whose background had linked them to Allende's Unidad Popular, had begun a political discussion group that rotated from home to home. By this time in Chilean life, the nature of fear was changing subtly—from the generalized fear of the 1970s, linked to massive disappearances and killings, which made it difficult to acknowledge let alone converse with friends who were dissidents, to more specific fears, focused on particular moments such as street demonstrations, days of organized national protest, or civil disobedience actions that met with repression.[28] Grassroots discussion groups of this sort—of course, political elites were also holding such discussions—began to spring up in various shantytowns and neighborhoods.[29] As the plebiscite approached, Violeta noted, "we began to bring leaders who— where we debated the great national problems and that was very interesting. . . . It allowed us to be very much in the debate. . . . We gave ourselves a space for reflection." Some of the persons invited were persons "of great credibility" who would end up participating in Patricio Aylwin's government of democratic transition (1990–94).

In Violeta's mind, grassroots discussions such as these helped nurture the reemergence of Chile's civic culture—"all of that civic culture that somehow the country [still] had." They fostered, not without difficulty, an important foundation of political appreciation, encounter, and debate, and a series of grassroots volunteer groups to believe in and work with the plebiscite campaign. The process was not easy—not simply between Center and Left, but within the Left.

> The debate that often took place was quite, quite strong . . . very ardent, you see, even positions very conflicting—in favor of democracy, of an opening, an understanding, a consensus, and that of others who were for a hard line very far on the Left, when in reality the possibilities were not there. But somehow that allowed one to see and tell us, "Look, you could be wrong, I am talking about this, and you are interpreting me in this other way." There was a very rich debate.

In addition, some persons found it difficult, given their political memories, to accept Aylwin as the leader and presidential candidate of the Concertación (as the Center-Left coalition was known) and did not come around fully until they saw him in office. " During his government he demonstrated to many people that his position was different. We discovered that he did things with great honesty. . . . He was positive."

Processes of awakening, both personal and political, occurred within the Center as well. In the case of Violeta's extended family, they eased rapprochement. In effect, the sense of having "guessed wrong" in 1973 about the consequences of military rule convinced many Christian Democrats to put on the back burner those memories of the Frei-Allende period that caused animosity between Center and Left. Instead, they focused on memories of persecution that heightened the value placed on mutual tolerance and preserving democracy for its own sake. Persons in the Center, too, had built up versions of remembrance as persecution and awakening. The complex personal dimensions of this journey came through in a day of eating and discussion hosted by Tita, the Christian Democrat sister (mentioned earlier) who plays a vital role in the life of the extended family, and her husband, Víctor. The table was filled with siblings and cousins—the articulate 1980s youth generation of the family. When the discussions turned to politics and memory themes (a turn no doubt encouraged by my presence), we skipped lightly over the Frei-Allende period, as if in a tacit pact to respect the parental generation and to avoid the potential for division.[30] When discussions of the Pinochet period came, the language was direct and harsh and met with approval from the parental generation—notwithstanding that the Christian Democrats in the family had initially celebrated the arrival of the military period with champagne.

What was most significant of all, however, was something left unsaid. One of the cousins, the elder son of Tita and Víctor, was rumored within the family to have passed through a period of such frustration and radicalization in the 1980s that he cooperated with the Frente Patriótico Manuel Rodríguez, a group committed to resistance by armed struggle.[31] Whenever he spoke, even when he resorted to strong political language, his father—the Christian Democrat who had worked for Frei and bitterly opposed Allende—looked at him with eyes of amazing tenderness, protectiveness, and admiration. He was, in Chilean parlance, "un papá chocho." (No true English equivalent exists, but the idea is that the parent is gaga with pride and love, eager to dote on the child.) In the silence of a look that said so much, I learned that fear of the persecution that might be visited upon a family's children had struck here, too. One consequence was that the parental generation found itself pulled away from the hard-and-fast positions of its own political youth period, more drawn toward the necessity of accepting the reality of political discrepancy and placing first things first. The preservation of life, the creation of a society of democratic safeguards and tolerance, the repudiation of the tyranny that could push a child toward angry disaster—these mattered more than all else.

Experiences such as these facilitated familial as well as political rapprochement between the Center and the Left. One need not exaggerate the point nor sentimentalize it as a great family reunion. One of the Left sisters in the family, Violeta's soul mate, had to rebuild her life in exile and lacks the resources for frequent visits. Another sister is relatively withdrawn; the estrangement is a legacy of the times of political bitterness. Ricardo's family had been less than solidary about his plight in 1973; in Violeta's mind they ascribed his detention to her political beliefs, almost as if the detention and torture were somehow justified. To my knowledge, that rift has not been overcome. Notwithstanding these caveats, however, some of Violeta's siblings in the political Center can understand and respect remembrance as persecution and awakening—and not simply because they cared about Ricardo and Violeta in 1973. They and their children had experienced their own versions of persecution and awakening.

Violeta does not consider herself to be a person especially committed to the formal rituals of Catholic faith. Nonetheless, a profound sense of Christian values provided an anchor during her journey. Violeta's version of Christianity made for powerful moments between us, in part because she knew that I am a Jewish child of Holocaust survivors. More than a bridge, my background added a certain intensity—at times an interchange of family lore, at times an almost tender spiritual connection—to some of our encounters. Conversation with Violeta moved me, she knew, in part because she exposed me to a brand of life-giving Christianity that had seemed so marginalized in the Europe of the 1940s. Perhaps for this reason Violeta invited me to an outdoor gathering in Villa Francia to honor and celebrate a local priest, Father Roberto Bolton, who had just retired (in September 1996) after fifty years of service.

On a pleasant spring Sunday in mid-October, at least 1,000 people streamed in to the Plaza del Faro in Villa Francia. Behind the outdoor stage that had been built, an enormous mural with bright festive colors had been painted.

Jesus Christ dominated the center. At the right of Jesus was a portrait of Father Bolton with his Bible. At Jesus's left stood women such as Señora Herminda, with the characteristic poster pictures and slogan ("where are they?") carried by protesting relatives of the disappeared. Above them stood other scenes of protest, including a depiction of the antitorture civil disobedience group that Father Bolton had supported and in which Violeta participated for a time. Above Jesus and Father Bolton appeared the theme of the celebration: "Everything is a gift from God." [*Todo es regalo de Dios.*]

The meeting brought out the profound connections that had developed between a socially conscientious Catholicism, and experiences of persecution and awakening in hard times. This was a version of popular Catholicism that drew together the idea of "testimony" as a tradition of faith that bears witness to God's plan and glory, and the idea of "testimony" as a recounting of experience that bears witness to the truths of Chilean life that had been denied or avoided under the military regime.[32]

The vehicle was Father Bolton, as a stream of priests and women and youth from the poblaciones bore witness to their personal experiences with him and thereby activated memories of hardship, struggle, and faith. As often happens at retirement commemorations, the memories were often laced by humor—in this case enhanced by relationships more informal and democratic than the traditional deference owed a priest. One youth commented on Father Bolton's exceptionally limited dancing skills. How much could one really expect from such a person? One woman remarked on the awkwardness of Father Bolton's early moments in Villa Francia. She initially thought he was just another *cura pituco* (slang for "snobby bourgeois priest"). But there were also more serious moments that bore witness to the importance of a loving and committed Church during Chile's saga of persecution and awakening through solidarity. The wife of a disappeared person recalled how important it was when Father Bolton taught her to state without shame or fear of stigma her name and that of her disappeared husband. Father Bolton and the priests reaffirmed faith in a God who loves the poor and the oppressed, and promoted remembrance of Villa Francia's young victims of political violence during the 1980s—especially the youngster Rafael Vergara, killed in 1985—as "gifts from God."[33]

This brand of Catholicism—the commemoration included spirited religious singing and a concluding mass—was a world apart from the Catholicism that inspired Doña Elena to work in the poblaciones. In a country where Catholicism was so important, contrasting memories could also mean contrasting types of Catholicism.

The crowd in Villa Francia had been too large for me to see Violeta. In some ways this act—or more precisely, performance—of living memory was artificial. It was too one-dimensional if taken to signify life and memory in Villa Francia in the 1990s. Some of those who had come to celebrate Father Bolton no longer lived in or near Villa Francia. The cars and clothes, as well as Violeta's personal knowledge, made the point clear. When I later met and interviewed Father Bolton in his small shack in the población, he was blunt about the way a portion of the local community distanced itself from him and wanted to close the memory box of persecution. Some people specifically wanted to take down the pictures of Villa Francia's dead and disappeared, including Rafael Vergara, from an informal local chapel.[34] As Ricardo and Violeta knew all too well, moreover, the political life of the poblaciones in the Center-West of Santiago was far more heterogeneous, even in the Frei-Allende years, than the stereotype of "heroic" or combative Left communities.

Nonetheless, the reality of Violeta's remembrance—and experience—of persecution and awakening had been brought back to life. When I saw Violeta a few days later, she made the point. On the day for Father Bolton in Villa Francia, one relived "something of the atmosphere of solidarity."

The Lore of Goodness and Remorse

Memory lore—the remembered facts, stories, rumors, and meanings that people personally experienced or heard from others, and that they considered significant or curious enough to pass on to others—constitutes a kind of raw material for the building of "emblematic memories." The ways of organizing remembrance and forgetting we have explored thus far—memory as salvation, memory as rupture, memory as persecution and awakening—are emblematic memories in a double sense. On the one hand, they are emblematic because they purport to capture an essential truth about the collective experience of society. Emblematic memory tells not just what happened to my family, friends, or comrades; it tells what happened to Chile and Chileans. My story can serve as emblem of a larger story.

On the other hand, such memory frameworks are also emblematic because many people believe them. People find in them an anchor that organizes and enhances the meaning of personal experiences and knowledge that would otherwise float or circulate more loosely, as individual experiences rather disconnected from collective experience. People find their anchor credible in part because of validation by similar memory echoes in a public cultural domain—whether in the mass media, demonstrations, small group meetings, public commemorations or speeches, books or truth reports, or music or cultural festivals. The process confirms that many others are finding a similar organizing anchor for collective memory. We shall have occasion later (chapter 4) to probe more fully the theoretical or conceptual aspects of emblematic memory, and its relation to a loose memory that floats as "lore."

For now, what is important to note is the reciprocal yet selective interplay between memory lore and emblematic memories. On the one hand, as memory lore circulates, it can provide authenticity to emblematic memory. Some lore attaches readily to emblematic memory and thereby builds a foundation of credibility. As we have seen, Doña Elena could draw on considerable lore, based not only on media reports but also on personal and familial knowledge, to buttress her understanding of memory as salvation. On the other hand, not all lore fits easily within the narrative frame of major emblematic memories that have achieved a successful projection into the public cultural domain. Within the memory box of Pinochet's Chile, some lore circulates more loosely—as experiences that matter deeply yet go astray from the emblematic. Such experiences are expressive of something fundamental and powerful yet cannot necessarily serve as the anecdotal handmaiden of a framework organizing emblematic remembrance. Indeed, public expression of some such lore—beyond underground circulation as rumor, or a sharing reserved for circles of political or personal confidence—may itself become problematic.

Stories of goodness and remorse constitute such a lore, especially for those who align themselves with memory as rupture and as persecution and awakening. They capture powerfully why remembrance matters. At the same time, they sometimes unsettle the social categories of more established emblematic memories. They can introduce complications and approach taboo areas. We glimpsed the importance of goodness stories in Señora Herminda's remembrance of her disappeared children, Gerardo and Ernestito, and we observed an effort to impose guilt and remorse when Violeta's in-laws implied that as a vocal leftist, she was somehow responsible for her husband Ricardo's torture.

Even these examples suggest some of the complicating aspects of the lore of goodness and remorse. To emphasize the goodness of the victim of repression is fundamental for relatives and other persons who care about the victim—it is part of the process by which relatives affirm the victim as a human being rather than a statistic, as a person with appealing qualities tragically destroyed rather than a legal category called "victim." Affirming goodness turns the family members' loss into a larger social loss and belies the dehumanizing and criminalizing rhetoric that had been deployed to render brutal repression more acceptable. But to turn goodness into an emblematic category of remembrance, at more than a familial or a subcultural level of trust within a social circle, political party, or neighborhood community, also carries risks. From the standpoint of defending human rights, one must avoid suggesting by implication that torture, disappearance, and execution would somehow be acceptable if the victim were less than saintly. One must preserve the legal-cultural distinction between preserving the good name of a victim—the assumption of innocence unless proved otherwise by law and due process—and asserting that all victims are necessarily "good" in a moral, personal, or political sense. Upon close inspection, even the most admirable victims turn out to have been human and complicated, that is, flawed by errors, less than saintly. Given the political passions and rivalries of social actors during the Frei-Allende period, moreover, goodness stories—if carried into the national cultural arena as a struggle to define the emblematic—would invite debilitating, diversionary, and cruel debate about the "goodness" of the varied political paths chosen by many of the victims of repression.

Stories of remorse and self-doubt by those who were related to the victim open up an even more dangerous and potentially self-defeating terrain. The military rulers had in effect argued that "innocent" Chileans had nothing to fear. By this logic only those who were "guilty" of bringing Chile to a state of disaster in 1973, or of holding on to political ideas that could return Chile to disaster, had something to fear for themselves or their loved ones. Under the circumstances, discussion of a sense of remorse and partial responsibility is very difficult beyond a familial or subgroup level marked either by great mutual confidence or great necessity for intimate truth telling. The danger that remorse—guiltlike thoughts about personal errors and responsibilities—might be confused with a deeper "guilt" that transfers moral and legal responsibility for massive human rights violations away from the perpetrators is too great.

Yet for all these difficulties, the lore of goodness and remorse has proved powerful. Goodness stories matter in part because they cleanse the name of an unfairly stigmatized victim; the dehumanized targets of repression are restored to the circle of human goodness, potential, and presumption of innocence. Goodness stories, especially those from within the period of rule by dictatorship, also prove powerful for a larger reason. As we shall see, they affirm the *possibility* of humanity even in the midst of the madness and evil that destroy humanity. Stories of remorse and self-doubt are more guarded and scarce—rather invisible in the national version of the public domain. But as we shall see, they can circulate in more subtle and oblique ways in communities, neighborhoods, or social networks. When they arise, they bring home—more than statistics of death and disappearance—the depth of human tragedy. One sees in those who survived the unfinished legacy of the times of madness. Remorse stories are powerful, too, because of their massive irony: they tend to refer to the sentiments of those who suffered loss and persecution under military rule. Few architects and perpetrators of military violence express a sense of remorse or responsibility. For them memory as remorse constitutes a kind of maximum taboo.

Stories of goodness and remorse capture some of the deepest remembered meanings of the political violence of the military period, even as they bear a relationship both complicating and complementary to the emblematic memories held by the storytellers. Especially in small towns and agrarian provinces, where anonymity fades and people and their stories brush up against one another, the lore of goodness and remorse finds a reasonably prominent place inside the memory box. This situation became evident to me when I visited Chile's mythical "Lakes Region" in 1997.

The Lakes Region, known administratively as the Tenth Region, lies far in the south of Chile. Its core framed by the region's port cities of Valdivia and Puerto Montt in the northwest and south, and by the Andean mountain range in the east, the Lakes Region is a coldish territory of scenic lakes and snowcapped volcanoes, rugged forests and national parks, campgrounds and villages. The spectacular natural beauty makes the Lakes Region a prime attraction for summer tourists and adventurous winter vacationers. In addition, the region enjoys a certain historical mystique as Europe's outpost near "the end of the world." In colonial times, Valdivia—founded in 1552, abandoned in 1599, refounded in 1645–1646—emerged as the beachhead of Spanish power and culture "behind enemy lines" in the geography of frontiers and Spanish-Indian struggle. To the north of Valdivia and the Lakes Region, in today's Ninth and Eighth Regions (roughly, the area south of the Bío-Bío River, whose regional capitals are Temuco and Concepción, respectively), lay the actively contested frontier territory, where Mapuche peoples controlled land and resisted Spanish conquest for centuries. The Chilean republic would not fully conquer and incorporate the southern frontier until the 1880s. Valdivia and the Lakes Region also came to represent European culture "behind the frontier" in another sense. It concentrated the famed German settler colonization of southern Chile—that is, Chile's version of the effort by Latin American republics to bring "progress" by restocking society with European immigrants—in the late nineteenth century and the early twentieth. The economy of the Tenth Region, like the two regions to the immediate north, has retained to this day a considerable rural aspect. Cereal and potato agriculture, beef cattle raising and dairy farms, fishing and salmon farms, fruit and jam production, timber cutting and forestry: these livelihoods, along with wilderness tourism, play significant roles in the South.[1]

The rural aspects of life in the South made it, like the fertile valley provinces of central Chile, a prime area for agrarian reform organizing during the Frei-Allende period—and for vengeance under military rule. The vengeance targeted not only leftist political party militants, but also peasants and other rural folk considered agrarian reform leaders or otherwise bothersome. Of the nearly 3,200 dead or disappeared officially documented by Chile's two truth commissions (the original 1990–91 National Truth and Reconciliation Commission, and the National Corporation of Reparation and Reconciliation, established to follow up on remaining cases), the Metropolitan Region—a territory that includes both Metropolitan Santiago and some adjacent rural provinces—accounted for slightly more than 60 percent of the victims. Beyond the Metropolitan Region, only four regions accounted for at least 5 percent (160 cases) each. Not surprisingly, one of these regions was the Fifth Region, a territory to the immediate west and north of the Metropolitan Region, home both to Valparaíso and to fertile central valley provinces that had witnessed considerable agrarian reform mobilization. The other three districts were the Eighth, Ninth, and Tenth regions, which together accounted for 680 confirmed cases (21.3 percent of the national total).[2]

Significantly, in a number of agrarian provinces, the repression included salient participation by members of civil society. Landowners and other civilians supplied trucks and worked with carabineros (police) to identify and locate troublemakers—that is, to take vengeance. More than in urban Santiago, the legacy of land invasions, official transfers of property, and political conflictiveness had generated clusters of angry people ready and willing to work with the military forces and the carabineros to punish or execute individuals they considered subversives and troublemakers.[3]

In short, the economic, social, and ethnic characteristics of the South—and of agrarian provinces more generally—had generated intense political mobilization during the Frei-Allende period. It was in the South that the MIR, nourished by radical university students and youth in Concepción, developed some of its most significant agrarian grassroots work. It was in the South that idealists of varied political affiliations found some of their most graphic examples of poverty, backwardness, and social injustice sustained by the power of a landed oligarchy. It was in the South and in the countryside that there developed in civil society a personally aggrieved and activist social base for repression. It was in rural Parral (Seventh Region, the most southern of the "central" regions) that the German immigrant community known as Colonia Dignidad, founded in 1961, built up landed property, arms, and political alliances that created something of a "state within a state." After 1973, Colonia Dignidad became an eerie echo of Nazi times transported to another time—a German site of torture, disappearance, and collaboration with the DINA.[4]

Given the mobilization of civil society before and after September 1973, the agrarian South is filled with people who hold strongly to their emblematic memory frameworks and whose lore both corroborates and complicates emblematic memory. The lore includes stories of goodness and remorse.

Ramiro I., and his wife, Claudia de I., live in Osorno Province in the Lakes Region.[5] Ramiro, the son of a worker who made wheels for wooden wagons, received his higher education in Valdivia and became a young rural schoolteacher in the 1960s. Given the extreme rural poverty and social needs of the region, Ramiro and Claudia came to see teaching as a service that combined social work and pedagogical work, and they undertook many of the duties jointly. With a degree of shock tinged, perhaps, by middle-class paternalism, they learned that they would have to delouse the children periodically, work with families to promote health and hygiene as well as education, and come to terms with the social realities of the rural poor. They remember the jolt of direct encounters with extreme exploitation—what Claudia remembers, in somewhat stereotyped terms, as "the exploitation of the Indian by the German." The parents of many children held tiny land plots and had to work for a pittance on larger estates and dairy farms.

One of the moments that brought home the meaning of exploitation to Ramiro was a conversation with a child's father. "We were talking about the problem of his son," he recalled, "and his bread falls out—he used a poncho and the bread falls to the ground. And I tell him, 'Look, your tea-time snack [la once] fell down'—something like that I told him, because it was afternoon." Then came the eye opener. "Then he tells me, 'No,' he tells me, 'but this is the pay for my work today, it's my pay.'" Incredulous that a loaf of bread could constitute a day's wage, Ramiro asked for details. For whom had the father worked that day? how could this be? The peasant explained he had worked for a landowner who needed him "to break in an animal, a horse, a young colt I'm breaking in." Ramiro could not believe his ears. "'Come on now, but that cannot be,' I told him. 'Yes,' he told me, 'yes they did pay me for going around doing that work all day long with bread.' "

The idea of bread as the wage for the dangerous work of breaking in a young horse left Ramiro even more incredulous.

Ramiro and Claudia learned to take such experiences as an opportunity to put social ideals into practical action. Ramiro developed a local reputation as a dynamic schoolteacher and participated actively in the teacher trade union. During Allende's time, Ramiro received an assignment to head up a new school in a rural district, not too far from Puerto Octay, whose families worked on nearby estates and agrarian reform properties. The project proved successful. The community's families welcomed having a nearby school that eased the travel burden. Ramiro recruited dynamic and socially committed teachers, and the United Nations provided funds for educational projects. Ramiro and Claudia showed a certain willingness, as local members of the community, to work with anyone who would help community families. Although their political sympathies ran to the Left, and Ramiro had been invited to join the Socialist Party, the couple distrusted some of the local Socialists and decided they could raise up the school more effectively by avoiding political party affiliations. In addition, they valued cooperation with some landowners, who loaned trucks for transporting teachers and helped set up learning-and-apprenticeship programs, such as dairy farming workshops.

Ramiro and Claudia developed a collaborative relationship with the Peasant Trade Union "Libertador" of Puerto Octay (Sindicato Campesino El Libertador de Puerto Octay) and with the rural laborers who served as its leaders—Lucio Angulo, the president, and René Burdiles, the secretary. The collaboration began as a practical way to solve a typewriter problem. Here is the way Claudia remembered it.

> We got ourselves involved and helping the people. So, the school needed a typewriter. It did not have one, but the trade union of agricultural workers did have a typewriter, which they did not use because they did not know, did not know how to draft the papers [documents]. So we made a swap [*cambalache*], let's say. They allowed us to use the typewriter [for the school], and we helped them draft their papers. That was my work. I was the secretary, . . . we worked together.

Over time the collaboration with the Libertador trade union deepened. Claudia became a volunteer secretary who prepared documents; Ramiro became a volunteer accountant who checked to see that rural laborers were not cheated on wages and that agrarian reform beneficiaries were not cheated on product sales or account settlements with estate owners. The couple sometimes gave advice on union work plans and projects. Ramiro and Claudia remained unaffiliated with political parties, but this did not seem a handicap. As members of MAPU Obrero-Campesino, the relatively moderate wing of the MAPU aligned with Allende and the Communist Party's hopes for a negotiated resolution of the political crisis of 1973, the Libertador union's leaders, Angulo and Burdiles, were not rigid about who qualified to collaborate with their union.

The collaboration turned into a disaster after 11 September 1973.

Ramiro and Claudia set their remembrance of the 1973 collapse and of the subsequent political violence within the framework I have called memory as persecution and awakening. In their version of this emblematic memory, the emphasis is almost exclusively on persecution. Their experience of rural repression was so profoundly isolating that notions of growth or awakening, linked to a process of overcoming the culture and politics of dictatorship, have little place.

As Ramiro and Claudia understand it, "the rich"—the landowners and their allies—did what they could to deepen Chile's emerging political crisis, in part by economic sabotage including hoarding. In their understanding, the *ricos* also waited for the time when they could take vengeance. On 11 September the opportunity arrived. René Burdiles, Libertador's secretary, went that morning to the school to advise Ramiro and Claudia that a coup was truly in progress. (The couple lived in an apartment inside one of the wings of the school building.) Later, a young MAPU activist who worked in a rural education institute—the son of a landowner family, he had gone astray from his elders' class interests and politics—showed up because he needed protection. The authorities were searching for him, and he and his wife had agreed to hide in different places. With the help of other teachers, Ramiro and Claudia hid him for three days. The young man survived and eventually resettled in the Temuco area, in the Eighth Region.

Matters turned worse on 15 September. Carabineros arrested Lucio Angulo that morning in his home while he was home with his children and in-laws. His wife, Clara Pinto, was at the Puerto Octay hospital giving birth to their fifth child. The carabineros beat Angulo and took him to their station in Osorno, the Tercera Comisaría de Rahue. More than seventeen years later, the National Truth and Reconciliation Commission identified the Rahue station as a site of torture and permanent disappearance. Angulo would never reappear. The same day, the same carabinero group came for Ramiro. They took him out to the road, then decided to place him under house arrest rather than take him away. Still the same day, carabineros looked for René Burdiles. Only twenty-one years old and unmarried, Burdiles lived with his parents but was absent when the carabineros conducted the house inspection. They left notice that Burdiles should present himself. The next day, René Burdiles turned himself in voluntarily to the carabineros in Puerto Octay. Transferred to the Tercera Comisaría de Rahue, he was also disappeared permanently.[6]

After 15 September, Ramiro and Claudia would learn to live with the sensation of vigilance. For about a week and a half, they were required to keep the curtains open at night. Occasionally, lights shone in to interrupt sleep with a reminder that they were under watch. Ramiro was allowed to teach for the rest of the Chilean school year (which ends with the arrival of Christmas and summertime in December), but school documents and children's notebooks were inspected for political or other infractions. Travel away from their school apartment could not take place without specific permission. Fortunately, the rural folk in the area helped by bringing the couple vegetables, milk, wood, and sometimes meat. In February, however, Ramiro was caught cutting wood to get ready for the coming winter. "Finally, I got you!" a carabinero told him. Before the new school year began in March, Ramiro was transferred to another rural school.

The transfer marked the beginning of a much more isolated social existence, as a schoolteacher who lived as a kind of guest of owners of landed estates. Over time, Ramiro became a half teacher, half peasant. He and Claudia supplemented their fitful teaching income by growing their own food, raising animals, using the estate's pastures—and occasionally robbing pigs from the patrón. Ramiro and Claudia began to lead an extreme version of the self-enclosure that occurs in cultures of dictatorship. "I immersed myself inside my bubble," observed Ramiro, and for a time he began to drink heavily. Radio access to a local Christian Democrat station and a shortwave connection to Radio Moscow provided some sense of the outside world. But not until the late 1980s would the couple find their way to a rural school and a social and political environment that were less isolating, and not until the transition to democracy would they lose the sensation of living under vigilance.

Ramiro and Claudia can easily incorporate their experience, and those of others, within the emblematic memories with which we are now familiar. Their personal story readily finds a place in collective memory as a narrative of persecution, and it can also corroborate the narrative of rupture associated with those who died or disappeared under the dictatorship. As we shall see, however, their experience also includes a lore of goodness and remorse that complicates remembrance—especially in a public domain.

A question cuts to the emotional core of the family: Why did Ramiro survive? When the carabineros came for him on 15 September 1973, what made them decide to impose house arrest rather than take him away to the Tercera Comisaría de Rahue? The first time Ramiro told me the story of his encounter with the carabineros on the fifteenth, his two sons approached to provide support, and the eldest son wrapped him in a bear hug. The accident of survival, and the goodness story with which it is associated, are foundational for the family.

The carabineros came not in a police truck but in a private truck driven by a conservative local priest. They had brought Lucio Angulo with them to identify people who worked closely with his trade union. Angulo's appearance shocked Ramiro and Claudia. But it was not the marks of the beating he had suffered that stood out in their minds.

> CLAUDIA: . . . in the pickup truck in the back, there were rocks, stones [*bolones de piedras*], not little stones, large ones, and there they had him—
> RAMIRO:—with four blocks of cement in each corner of the pickup truck behind the cabin . . . sprouting chains, chains, and so . . . [Ramiro pauses and gathers his composure] Lucio was on his knees on that pile of rocks . . . with shackles tied to the chains, shackles here on each hand, on each ankle on his legs and on his neck, tied with chains, like a real animal, a real animal.

Then came the effort to provoke the flash of recognition that would identify Ramiro as a comrade or collaborator. Ramiro and Claudia struggled to remember exactly how to describe the scene. Their effort is worth recounting at length.

> RAMIRO: . . . they took me [out to the truck] so that the man could identify me and say "yes." I don't know what they might have asked him, if I were a leader or a comrade [*compañero*] of his? I don't know what kind of questions. . . . The point is that with a look [of recognition] it would have been

enough for him to identify me—to give signs—but I don't know how the cops [*pacos*] did not realize it, because when they took me outside, he signaled me [*me hizo gestos*], yes, he made me realize that I should *not* identify him.

AUTHOR: Was it with his head?

RAMIRO: It was with the head . . . [Ramiro knows this is not right, he corrects himself] rather with the eyes. . . .

CLAUDIA: Purely by the eyes. It was not even with any movement of the head.

RAMIRO: Yes, that's right, it was just his look, that made me understand: absolutely no [recognition]. And then they poked him [with a stick or baton], and from then I understood it, since when they poke him to look at me and to look at me—and he never looked at my face. He never looked at my face; he didn't even say my name. So, that attitude, that attitude of Lucio . . . [Ramiro pauses, then speaks softly] saved me.

Lucio Angulo's solidarity was a singularly important and life-giving act. But it was not the only significant act of goodness Ramiro and Claudia remember. As we saw earlier, peasants and other rural folk provided Ramiro and Claudia help with food during the period of house arrest. They also offered companionship, food, and labor assistance when it came time to leave. Here and there, amidst remembrance framed as a narrative of persecution, there arises a lore of goodness, often understood as solidarity with those in need.

Sometimes, however, the lore of solidarity does not line up neatly with the way the overall narrative defines "good" versus "bad" social actors. The youngest son of Ramiro and Claudia, only two years old in 1973, suffered from asthma and had to be transported to the hospital at Puerto Octay for medical relief several times in the last months of 1973. Ramiro's house arrest rendered it difficult to arrange transport and handle emergencies. In the couple's emblematic narrative of persecution, the privileged rich folk of an agrarian region are—along with some irresponsible political leaders on all parts of the political spectrum—the "bad guys" who deepened a political crisis, and took personal and class advantage of a supposed national salvation. Ramiro and Claudia know of specific cases consistent with this depiction. Within the terms of their political values and personal knowledge, the narrative framework is accurate.

But not completely. In the case of their asthmatic son, it was a young landowner—one of the co-owners on a nearby estate, Don Ramón had cooperated with Ramiro and Claudia on educational and training projects—who continued to see human beings on the other side of the fault line defining the social enemy. After Ramiro's house arrest, Don Ramón visited to check on the couple from time to time. When their son's asthma required treatment, he would use a vehicle from the estate to take the child to Puerto Octay. In one emergency he even arranged for an ambulance. Eventually, Don Ramón's acts of goodness had to stop. One day he rode over on a motorcycle—he was no longer trusted to drive a truck—to explain that his freedom had disintegrated. "Look, they have forbidden us from doing anything for you."

Arguably, the lore of goodness can be as powerful when it reverses standard roles as when it confirms them. Indeed, some of the most searing lore in the memory box of Pinochet's Chile refers to persons recruited into the secret police who sought to preserve their own humanity and that of prisoners through small acts of caring—by acting as a communication conduit between prisoners and their families, by supplying victims a bit of food or a cigarette, by speaking to prisoners as human beings rather than demons. Such persons were rare; their acts imposed risks, both psychological and physical.

The best-known case is that of Carlos Alberto Carrasco Matus, a former leftist and an army conscript recruited into the DINA. Carrasco was the person known as "Mauro" in prisoner lore—as a guard who sometimes conveyed messages between prisoners and families or supplied extra food, and who related to prisoners with a certain sweetness of disposition. Testimony in the files of the National Truth and Reconciliation Commission shows that in real life, Mauro was a complicated individual with a more complicated trajectory. Early in his time with the DINA, he had been pressured into identifying people to be detained and tortured and sometimes into witnessing and participating in torture. Mauro experienced a tremendous personal crisis and sought out an old school friend and political comrade to unburden himself. He feared that if he escaped to an embassy for asylum, the DINA would take vengeance against his relatives.

When Mauro was reassigned as a guard to Cuatro Alamos (a kind of holding jail, not an on-site torture center), he could finally act on his better instincts. But his personal crisis did not end. On 14 March 1975, Mauro—that is, Carlos Carrasco—was pushed into an operation to arrest the very friend to whom he had unburdened his soul! They had a panicky encounter and both ended up prisoners at the DINA's Villa Grimaldi torture compound. There DINA agents beat Carrasco with chains and killed him.

Carlos Carrasco's friend endured a period of political imprisonment and was eventually released and exiled to Stockholm. In his testimony to the Truth and Reconciliation Commission in 1990, he evinced no malice toward Carrasco, whom he considered a DINA prisoner coerced into becoming a different being and horrified by the process. The Carrasco he had once befriended had been "an idealistic youth and filled with love." When Carlos Carrasco was assigned to guard duty at Cuatro Alamos, perhaps he thought he could recapture his truer self through acts of goodness. Like a human interest story in a newspaper, such acts were compelling and revealing curiosities—precisely because they were so out of place in the world run by secret police. They inexorably entered the lore of prisoners. A woman who had been a political prisoner at Cuatro Alamos testified that Mauro seemed somewhat exotic, memorable because he was "sweet and soft."[7]

The lore of remorse, more scarce than that of goodness, can also prove unsettling. For the permanent disappearances of Lucio Angulo and René Burdiles, the National Truth and Reconciliation Commission assigned a clear responsibility. Agents of the state—carabineros linked to the Tercera Comisaría de Rahue in Osorno—detained and disappeared them. Yet for the case of René Burdiles, there is a lore of remorse and self-doubt whose irony brings home the depth of family tragedy. Earlier, we noted that when carabineros arrived at his parents' home on 15 September to inspect and ransack the house and arrest their son, René Burdiles was absent. When he returned home later that day, his parents told him about the incident and about the carabineros' instruction—backed by the threat of a return visit—that he turn himself in. René's mother, Señora María Verónica, accompanied her son to the carabinero post in Puerto Octay the next morning. Upon their arrival, a lieutenant exclaimed sarcastically, "Oh, here comes another Communist! Just come on in." He then told Señora María Verónica to leave. The family never saw René again. Despite their repeated efforts to find René and track state handling of him, the parents ran up against repeated denials of responsibility and knowledge.[8]

Local word had it—rightly or wrongly—that it was René's mother, Señora María Verónica, who had convinced her son to turn himself in voluntarily the next morning. The lore also had it that the remorse destroyed her. According to Claudia, "the Mom died of sheer hurting [*pura pena*], the poor woman, people say." People knew that for several years until her death, she went everywhere she could imagine to find her missing son and that she was weighed down, in Ramiro's words, by "the great remorse she began to live later, once she learned her son could be dead." The local authorities found a way to convey informally that her search would be fruitless. Claudia remembers that Señora María Verónica told her one day that "the Bishop had told her, 'Señora, your son, no, do not spend your last resources because you will not get anything.'"

In many locales across Chile, people targeted for arrest in September 1973 had to decide whether to flee or turn themselves in. Many went into hiding and exile, of course, but the number of dead or disappeared people who turned themselves in voluntarily in provincial settings is also striking. How many anxious conversations with relatives or friends took place before reaching such decisions? Even as agents of the state denied responsibility, how many persons involved in such conversations found themselves haunted by remorse—did they give poor advice? Did they fail to dissuade someone from a disastrous decision? Did they underestimate the severity of the repression? In the agrarian settings and provincial towns where carabineros were a familiar part of the lower middle-class landscape and local kinship networks, how many persons guessed wrong about the Chile they thought they knew?[9]

That terrible mistakes could be made, even after considerable evidence to the contrary, was apparent in the case of José Guillermo Barrera Barrera of Curacaví, a small town some forty kilometers west of Santiago, near the border with the Fifth Region. Barrera, a trucker active in a trade union that supported Allende (and in this way unlike most trucker unions), got into trouble with a carabinero lieutenant on 12 September 1973 because he refused to close the town's pool hall. On 16 September he was taken by carabineros, with six other prisoners, up the high hill known as Cuesta Barriga. The carabineros lined up the prisoners against an old abandoned home and shot a riff of machine gun fire to kill them. Barrera and another prisoner, Enrique Venegas, although wounded in the legs, were miraculously saved from death. The hefty body of Nicolás Gárate had fallen on top of them. The carabineros did not notice Barrera and Venegas when they checked to see that the prisoners were dead. They focused on Gárate, still agonizing, and finished off his execution with a pistol shot to the head. Once the carabineros left, Barrera and Venegas managed to leave and get help from rural folk until reunited with their respective families.

José Barrera, after receiving treatment from a doctor in Santiago, moved to the home of his in-laws in a northern province. After several months, José wanted to return home and leave clandestine life behind. The family, especially José's brother Víctor, did the work to assure his safe conduct. The contacts extended all the way from General Augusto Pinochet's secretary, Rebeca Valdebenito, to the commanding carabinero officer in the town of Talagante, who called his counterpart in Curacaví to confirm that no criminal charges were pending against José Barrera. After all the precautionary steps and official assurances of safety were in place, José Barrera returned home to Curacaví the evening of 13 March 1974. Despite the family's best efforts and judgment, they had all come to the wrong conclusion. At dawn army officers, guided by local carabineros, stormed the house and disappeared José Barrera.[10]

Remorse is a sensitive and ironic topic—and not only because most perpetrators of the political violence have so assiduously avoided it. The subject, unless handled with care, can slide subtly toward a perverse displacement of responsibilities from the perpetrators of violence to the families persecuted by it. Perhaps for these reasons, I found remorse lore more scarce than goodness lore when I lived inside the memory box of Pinochet's Chile in 1996–97. In personal interviews, people could remember and speak more easily and openly about what they termed the "errors" of the past, both personal and collective, than about sensations of remorse. Remorse lore is understandably more scarce and more guarded than goodness lore.

Nonetheless, the sentiment and lore of remorse have been powerful. An oral history study of textile worker families in Tomé (near Concepción) in the mid-1980s found that memories of pride in the work and the quality of the cloth produced were central to the workers. The context was retrospective and perhaps nostalgic, because of the crisis of the Chilean textile industry that led to a closing of the plant. But the testimonies also evinced "the sentiment of guilt, as workers, about the coup of 1973. Unanimous among all those who had been active at that time, this sentiment, almost collective, is attributed to lack of responsibility, to labor disorder, to excess demands, to 'not putting one's shoulder to it' . . . that practically led to 'making the bed' of the Popular Unity government, and that at the same time underlines the sentiment of an enormous loss."[11]

A decade later, in my own interview experience, I occasionally heard echoes of such thoughts—more readily among people from shantytown or working-class backgrounds than from leaders and political figures. Without excusing or justifying the coup of 1973 nor the political violence that ensued, and without diminishing the sense that the times of Frei-Allende were times of "joy," some people's remembrance included an idea that the pueblo and many of its political leaders had not really measured up to the awesome responsibility of carrying out an effective revolution.

Consider, for example, Marisa T. She recalls life in the poblaciones, during the times of Frei-Allende, as a period when one could aspire to a better future and experience tangible social advances, in part through direct actions that pressured the government. She found more adequate housing, mobilized successfully for a community health clinic, experienced a certain dignity in buying a new pair of pants for one of her children. (Before, her options were limited to buying used clothing or to relying on hand-me-down gifts from women like Doña Elena who visited from privileged neighborhoods.) In Frei's time she discovered a more welcoming form of Christianity—a Bible in which "I felt invited." In Allende's time she experienced "the ability to dream of a society in which we human beings were important, where we had participation." Marisa T. values these memories in their own right, but they do not imply that she is a broken or nostalgic person, condemned to a life and subjectivity organized around the lost past. On the contrary, she is an articulate grassroots leader who works on projects of collective and personal improvement for women in her población, supports human rights work—and steers clear of the kind of remorse that blames victims for their own persecution. But Marisa T. is also a person who passed through a sobering reflection about mistakes, deficiencies, and responsibilities. Even in Allende's time, "one felt that many also wanted that [socialism] would arise without great effort, without great commitment either." Some people proved dedicated and giving, but others settled for an attitude of receiving—"how great we have it, we're going to receive it, but without much in the way of commitment."

Upon reflection, Marisa T. concluded that Allende's project had not been viable, in part because too many people in civil society were not willing and able to assume responsibility for it. "Today," she observed, "I understand that what Allende was proposing, I think, was a utopia. I think that it was never going be real what he was proposing, because it was also a pueblo that was not prepared [for it]."[12]

As with Señora María Verónica, people do not confine a sense of regret or responsibility to remembrance of the crisis that unfolded before September 1973. Nor do they limit the focus to a regret that points outward, at the defects of others. The most cutting and poignant self-doubts refer to life-and-death decisions that had to be made under the dictatorship. When family members of the dead or disappeared appeared before the staff of the National Truth and Reconciliation Commission in 1990 to provide their testimonies, the sharing of goodness lore proved very important. Relatives, in addition to petitioning for investigation and confirmation of the truth of their loss by agents of a state finally willing to listen, often put forth their vision of the goodness and the appealing qualities of the loved ones they had lost. Occasionally, however, relatives also found themselves drawn to confess to one another rather complicated emotions, including self-doubt.

One striking session, for example, involved a mother who had found herself compelled to choose between searching for her missing husband and raising her young children. She decided to send the children away to be brought up by their grandparents. The endless search for the husband-father had proved fruitless and the mother's contact with the children sporadic. When the time came to provide testimonies on the case of the husband-father, the mother's sense of remorse flooded forth. She turned to her children and asked forgiveness for abandoning them. In this instance the scene concluded with tears and hugs. In other instances when the underside of family adaptation to tragedy came to the fore, the denouement could be more complicated and ambiguous. Situations such as these enable us to understand why, for personal as well as political reasons, remorse is both a theme that is touchy and guarded, and—when it surfaces and circulates—a lore that is moving and powerful.[13]

The political aspect that complicates remorse is its relationship to historical responsibility. Precisely *because* the military state had consistently denied responsibility, relatives of the dead, disappeared, and the otherwise persecuted contended with a perverse transfer of responsibility from the state to the victim-relatives. The problem was *their* problem, not the state's problem. The net effect was that even when relatives of the persecuted knew better, and even when they received assistance and expressions of support by the Vicaría or other solidarity groups, the sentiment that they bore responsibility for their loved ones hovered and intruded on consciousness.

A verbal slip in my interview with Mónica V. provides a revealing example. I asked her when she came to accept, in her own mind, that her disappeared husband was dead. Mónica evinced the difficulties of reaching and accepting that conclusion.

MÓNICA: No, I have given [him] up as dead and I have gone back to revive him and I have gone back to give him up as dead and I have gone back to revive him, eh. . . . [A long pause ensues.] As much rationally as not rationally, this process of killing him and going back to—No, not killing him, but giving him up for dead and, and—that is almost like killing him, because if you do not know.

AUTHOR, ACKNOWLEDGING THE VERBAL SLIP: I understand, yes, that is why you said it that way.

MÓNICA V.: Of course. Eh, so it has been a—so it has been until now, and I don't want to, [voice turns very emotional] I don't *want* to [accept it]. So, you see, I have been between him dying and not dying, . . . I move between "well yes," "well no." Today, rationally and scientifically [laughing as she mocks her rationalist side including research on her husband's case], with all the elements of a researcher, I say, "they killed him." . . . But there are other parts of me [that say], what do I know?—[maybe] Colonia Dignidad?—what do I know?[14]

Another example comes from Tonya R., a woman whose husband, a student leader, was sent to internal exile in a tiny town in the Calama region, in the mountains of the desert North of Chile, in 1985. The cycle of repression and protest that had broken out in 1983 had become very intense, and Tonya R. was very affected by the case of three intellectuals who had been killed, their throats slashed, in March 1985. Tonya R. managed after considerable difficulties and runarounds—the authorities kept moving her husband—to track down her husband's location. "I set myself up there . . . with him, and I said 'From here I am not going' . . . because I knew that if I was there they would not make him disappear; this is what I felt." She stayed in the isolated town with their young daughter for over a month, until her husband was released.[15]

From such an outsized sense of responsibility, transferred to its bearers by the state, it is but a short step to sheer rage at the authorities. But it is only an extra step or two to self-doubt. Did I do enough to protect or find my loved one? Did I unwittingly lay a trap or fall into one? Have I allowed myself to become too weary and discouraged? In remaining loyal to one loved one, have I neglected or harmed another one? Questions such as these yield the occasional incident or story that pins the sensation of remorse on unexpected actors. The lore of remorse strays off the established tracks that guide emblematic memories, but sometimes, like a train wreck, it draws attention and fascination. Señora María Verónica's several layers of grief about the disappearance of a son who turned himself in at her suggestion was one such case. At bottom, it was the sheer cruelty of the state's inversion of responsibility that gave the lore of remorse such irony and power.

Lucio Angulo's last act of goodness was an act of solidarity under the most extreme stress—an expression of the practical constancy with one's professed values, even under duress, known as *consecuencia* in Spanish. I understood the power of goodness lore, within remembrance of times of destruction, because I have experienced it in my own family. Shlomo Rosenzweig, my Polish grandfather, perished at Auschwitz. During the selection process that divided people into a death line and a line of potential workers who might live a while, young children could suffer confusion and fright—especially when lost or separated from a parent or a sibling sent to a different line. As Shlomo marched toward selection and death, and as my father Sam watched in shock, Shlomo's last act was to think of others. He had seen a frightened young child, lifted him up into his arms, and provided the needed hugs and companionship. He also had the presence of mind to block my father, young enough to have a chance for the line of the living, from jeopardizing himself by lifting and comforting the child.[16]

The overall frameworks that give emblematic meaning to memory of the Holocaust—to the extent that we can find meanings—necessarily focus on the capacity for human and political perversion, the specificities of German and European history that culminated in moral and political disaster, and the resultant transformation of millions of multidimensional human beings into "victims." The victims, including my grandfather Shlomo, were no doubt as flawed and as varied in "goodness" as any group of human beings. One can find faults in them if one looks closely enough, and survivor testimonies show that at least some were driven to a kind of moral disintegration, at least some of the time, by the pressure of survival in times of radical evil.[17] But notwithstanding the emblematic memories that focus on perversion and victimization, and notwithstanding the human flaws and complications of the victims, the lore of goodness moves us and finds a place in our memory chest. We find ourselves compelled to treasure it and—eventually—to share it.

In his own mind, Ramiro cannot fully explain why he survived. But he knows that Lucio Angulo's last act of goodness gave him a chance to survive. He also knows that Angulo's solidarity and presence of mind at the last moment expressed qualities that made him an appealing human being in the first place. In addition, the memory of Angulo's gift of life, and of the solidarity they received from other rural folk when they lived under house detention, turned into a foundational moral example for Ramiro and Claudia. It reminds them to bring a social ethic, even when discouraged, to their understanding of rural teaching. In the political climate of the late 1990s, this social ethic involved modest individual gestures of caring that might stretch some children's imagination or ward off discouragement—a field trip to introduce children to the awesome power of the ocean, a pair of tennis shoes to dissipate the shame of a bright shoeless girl (her mother earned pitiful wages harvesting fruit for export), a visit to a family to fortify hope and mentoring by participating in the culture of hospitality and small reciprocities common among the poor.[18]

There is no heroic narrative, no happy Hollywood ending to take the edge off the horror of Lucio Angulo's disappearance. There is no neat redemption whereby the lore of evil is somehow neutralized or cancelled out by the lore of goodness. A pair of tennis shoes, a gesture of encouragement to persons whose chances to beat the odds are improbable—these cannot measure up to nor mediate the extremes of radical evil. But perhaps it is this very imbalance, when a society makes its disastrous turn to radical evil, that gives the lore of goodness such power. As we said our good-byes and spoke politely about the book I would write, Ramiro took a moment to look at me squarely and deliver a reminder: "It is important to remember Lucio Angulo."

Chapter 3

꧁꧂

Indifferent Memory:
Closing the Box on the Past

Army Colonel Juan F. taught me something new about memory as a closed box. By the time of our interview, I had been exposed to its pervasiveness. I had seen it in the body language of an agronomist at a party. When conversation turned to my research on memories of the 1973 crisis and the political violence that ensued, he crossed his arms before him, then drew them apart quickly as if to make a giant X. Perhaps surprised by his own gesture, he explained that many lies had been stated about Chile. The conversation moved on to a more feasible theme. I sensed the closed box in the indifference of a taxi driver. An admirer of Pinochet and the benefits his rule had bestowed on Chile, he used colorful language to concede that the general's work had some rough edges. What Pinochet had produced was "a masterpiece by a cowboy" [*una obra maestra de un huaso*]. When I observed that many people thought the human rights problem was something that had ruined the military government's work and harmed the country, he replied with indifference: "Me it did not affect." (He used the Spanish form that accents the me: *A mí no me afectó.*) There was nothing more to say.

I had also heard from the conservative historian Gonzalo Vial about the way memory as a closed box translates into good manners. Politically aligned with the Center-Right, yet quite forthcoming about the problem of massive human rights violations, Vial had traveled the path of those conservatives who had grown alienated from the ongoing violence and conflictiveness associated with military rule in the 1980s. For most of the 1970s, he had backed the military regime and sought to assist its work. During 1970–73 he opposed the Allende government and was also a cofounder of the influential opposition magazine *Qué Pasa*. In 1973 he helped write the official "White Book" released by the new military junta to justify the coup. He also served briefly as education minister for the military regime after its amnesty decree in 1978, when he thought—mistakenly, in his own view—that the times of barbarity had passed. By the 1980s his political and moral journey was taking him toward an enlightened Right position: conservative social and economic values need not imply refusal to confront the reality of a continuing human rights problem. In 1990, he agreed to serve on the National Truth and Reconciliation Commission that systematically documented memory as rupture and persecution. Vial joined the Commission out of a sense of civic duty and wrote the first draft of the narrative that provided historical background and context for the events documented in the Commission's report.

After our formal interview, Vial—who writes a newspaper column as well as historical scholarship—wanted to make sure that I understood he was not representative of his political and social crowd. Talking and writing newspaper columns about human rights violations made him a bit of a maverick. You need to know, he observed, that "in my circles" talk of such themes is considered "bad taste."[1]

Again and again, I had been exposed to memory as a closed box in 1996 and 1997. I had come to learn, too, that the polemics of contrast between "memory" and "forgetting" (olvido, oblivion) can be misleading if taken to imply that amnesia had taken hold of Chilean culture.[2] Memory as a closed box was more subtle: a certain "will to forget," a social agreement that some themes and some remembrances were so explosive—conflictive and intractable—that little could be gained from a public opening and airing of the contents inside. One could visit the memory box, if one wished, but discreetly and privately, either alone or in the company of trusted friends or relatives from the same memory camp. In the public domain, an indifference that pushed the memory box to the margins and kept it shut would allow Chile to progress and look to the future.

I had become aware, as well, of the complexity of this "will to forget." For some it had become a mere habit of mind and good taste. For others it remained a more conscious desire, based ironically on remembrance, to shunt aside something formative that always led to trouble. For still others, it had become more like an oscillation between unthinking habit and conscious burial of the dangerous—like a societal effort to store and forget the accumulating radioactive waste of nuclear energy plants, only to keep rediscovering that one has to pay attention.

Two additional factors compounded the complexity of a certain will to forget, in ways that are at first sight counterintuitive. First, whatever their views of "memory" versus "forgetting" in the public domain, as a private and personal matter some victims of persecution sought to close the box on the past. To rebuild lives, or to avoid stigma or paralyzing pain, they were not likely to become social actors pushing to reopen the memory box or contribute testimony to a memory struggle in the public domain. Second, the will to forget was not limited to any one part of the political spectrum. Although the Center-Right was more consistently aligned with this stance toward memory issues, by the mid-1990s the ruling Center-Left coalition also found the politics of memory divisive and difficult, and some of its leaders suggested the time for dwelling on memory issues had passed. They might express sympathy with victims as a moral matter or support the right of victims to pursue legal actions, yet they might also beat a retreat from memory as a political and cultural matter. Chile's politicocultural divisiveness and impasse on memory questions had proven too hard and intractable; the political and cultural future lay elsewhere.[3]

By the time I spoke with Colonel Juan in May 1997, then, I had been exposed to the pervasiveness and complexity of memory as a closed box. But it was Colonel Juan who exposed me to a paradox: the passion of indifference.

Now retired from active duty and the manager of a small company, Colonel Juan began the interview with ground rules and words that signified caution.[4] The key rule: I would have to take notes rather than record the conversation on tape. History, he observed, is written by the winners, and he understood who had won in the 1990s. Civilians, even the so-called experts on the military whose works sometimes inspired a bit of laughter, often had an inaccurate impression of military life and people. Did you know—he seemed to enjoy putting the irony to a civilian—that the mentality of the Army of Chile makes it the most socialist institution in the country? The system decides all and gives all; the soldiers are treated equally; the soldier lives to serve the system. It was important that civilians understand that most soldiers are simple people with simple interests, not crazy or sick beings. "We are not monsters," he observed later when complaining about the stereotypes civilians pinned on soldiers.

As Colonel Juan recounted his experiences, and the meanings they gave to the 1973 crisis and the problem of political violence, he alternated between memory as salvation and memory as a closed box. His military experience was lengthy and varied—study at the Military Academy (Escuela Militar) in Santiago during the Allende period, duty as a young officer in the provinces in the 1970s, and promotion and service in army security functions in Santiago in the 1980s. In general he thought the military period was one of sacrifice to serve and save the nation. He remembered patrols to protect public buildings from street violence after the truckers' strike of October 1972 and the growing unease felt in the army in 1973—it was hard to understand why Allende placed no limit on the chaos. Certainly the spread of arms in the civilian population had created a problem. He had been called away from the provinces for two weeks of duty in Santiago in late September. He remembered that when the army dredged the San Carlos Canal that runs through Santiago, it discovered that many people had discreetly thrown away their arms.

What made the military's rule so important, however, was not simply putting an end to armed subversion and chaos—a task that did not prove so difficult. The biggest accomplishment was the military's will to get "to the bottom" (al fondo) of the problems suffered by Chilean society. By going to the root—by taking on the need to thoroughly reorganize the economy and society—the military government had thought about the well-being of future generations. It had turned an inefficient statist economy and social welfare system into an efficient market-driven economy. It had turned an excessively politicized society into one where technical expertise and accomplishment prevailed. In sum, the military had cured a sick country and in the 1990s gave back to the civilians a healthy society, now on a solid foundation. The one major negative mark was in the area of "social communications." Here the military government had not been very effective or efficient.

Of course, he noted, curing the nation and building a solid future exacted a social cost. Human losses were lamentable, but building for the future required it. Colonel Juan used a business metaphor to explain this reasoning. When a company has been run into bankruptcy, if the managers want to prepare the way for a healthy future, they have to accept the human cost of dismissing workers. The National Truth and Reconciliation Commission had been an escape valve for the small minority of people who had suffered and in that sense served a useful function. But its documentation of human rights violations should have encompassed the period prior to 11 September 1973, and it should have focused on the connection of cause and effect. It should have recognized the severity of the disease that required military intervention and should have asked why, by 1973, the society had come to produce so many "mentally sick people" (enfermos mentales).

As he warmed to the subject of social costs, Colonel Juan focused on the idea of patriotic sacrifice. In addition to the necessary cost borne by the civilian society, he observed, it was important to understand that there had been a sacrifice paid by the military forces. Their "best men"—the people with the best brains, the most talent—had entered into government service, a situation that weakened the professional military capacity of the armed forces.

But what about the problem of political violence? How did he remember this issue, and how did it relate to his own experiences? On this point Colonel Juan noted that he was "indifferent" and so was the vast majority of the Chilean population. The point was that not much happened and that what did happen affected very few people—within the military and within civilian society. The great mass of people was indifferent to the theme of human rights. His own experiences had been rather tranquil. To be sure, in the province where he served for several months after the eleventh, a search of a factory had turned up a closet of hidden arms. But even this event had not been very dramatic. In general, allanamientos to search for arms or to detain suspects for questioning were rather routine, orderly affairs—one knocked on the door and went about one's business. By the time he was temporarily called away for two weeks of service in Santiago on 17 September, even the capital city had settled down. It was true that army soldiers had not been trained to carry out police functions. One had to learn "as one goes" (*en camino*). In some instances the lack of preparation led to "excesses" by the undertrained young soldiers. But for Colonel Juan, like most members of the military, the work was not very dramatic.

In short, the political violence theme was unimportant and it affected very few people. It was true that when he was transferred to the south of the country there had been two or three, maybe four, active small cells of the MIR. But the violence that took place concerned only the MIR and the DINA. The people on both sides were youngsters who almost pursued their war as a "game," complete with occasional gestures of respect or appreciation for the adversary. For everyone else—in the military as well as civilian society—this war was rather irrelevant. The issue of human rights and violence, he repeated, was one that left him "indifferent," and in this regard he was like most soldiers and most civilians.[5]

Colonel Juan had closed the memory box on the violence that had been integral to policide—to curing the nation of its "mentally sick people." During our discussion, the only sign of more mixed emotions that I noticed was a clearing of the throat when he explained that not much had happened and that memories of political violence were unimportant. In general, Colonel Juan had been calm, articulate, and effective as he stripped away the drama that swirls around the theme of political violence and declared that few people cared about it.

But when the time came for me to leave, Colonel Juan changed. Like a person who obsessively returns to make sure the door is locked when leaving the house, he could not let go. He had to make sure that I *truly* understood that no one cared about such memories. He insisted on the point—again and again he repeated his own indifference, the indifference of Chileans, the emptiness and marginality of the theme. He did so not abusively or wildly, but with the passion of someone who needs to know for sure that the point has been made and that it has been convincing. Our conversation had become a monologue, and the monologue had become circular, and it went on and on. For over half an hour, it continued. Most of it took place not seated in the chairs we had used for the interview, but in the doorway of his interior office. (By then it was night, and the secretary in the outer office had left.) I stood in the doorway listening, a bit stunned and bewildered, as we kept pretending I was leaving and as he continued to make sure I understood the point.

As we failed to say goodbye, I found myself surprised by the turn of events, even though I had some idea of the mixed emotions that might produce the sudden surge of energy. I knew that Colonel Juan was closing the box on somewhat more complicated memories of political violence. A mutual acquaintance had befriended Colonel Juan when they were classmates in a course on military-civilian relations, open to both civilian and military students, in the 1990s. In an evening of camaraderie and reduced social barriers, Colonel Juan opened the memory box. When he was a junior officer who led small teams of soldiers in the allanamientos of homes common in the months that followed the 11 September takeover, he had sought to do so in a polite and peaceable manner. Normally he succeeded. But some soldiers evinced a violent "Rambo" mentality when they conducted break-ins, a situation that produced occasional ugly episodes for a young officer striving to maintain calm and good order.

In our conversation, Colonel Juan had kept the lid firmly shut on such memories. The closest he came to acknowledging them was in his comment that while nothing dramatic had happened in his own experience, it was true that army soldiers had not been trained to perform the police

functions they undertook to serve the country. For some this underprepara-
tion was a problem.

Months later, I discovered some additional contents in Colonel Juan's
memory box. From September 1973 through January 1974 (with the exception of a two-week stint in Santiago in the second half of September), he had
been stationed at Quillota, a provincial town some fifty kilometers northeast
of Valparaíso, in the fertile agricultural valley of Aconcagua known today for
its thriving fruit industry.[6] Subsequently, Colonel Juan was transferred to a
region far to the south.

In some respects the history of the entire Fifth Region, divided between
navy control in the port city of Valparaíso and army control in interior
provinces such as Quillota, conforms to Colonel Juan's placid memory of
military rule. In the section of its report dedicated to the Fifth Region in the
months after 11 September, the National Truth and Reconciliation Commission observed a complete absence of armed resistance. Its findings are
worth quoting at length.[7]

> It is relevant background for adequate understanding of the events that
> occurred in the Fifth Region . . . that the Armed Forces had taken control
> without the rise of armed clashes nor acts of violence by supporters of the
> deposed regime.
>
> Thus, neither in Valparaíso, capital of the Region, nor in the port of San
> Antonio, nor in the interior zone (Quillota, La Calera, Petorca, San Felipe,
> and Los Andes) were there acts of violence against military troops or police
> units; nor tomas [i.e., occupation and seizure of factories or properties] or
> any other form of resistance to the military *pronunciamiento*. . . . In none of
> those locales did there result any deaths, as a result of assaults by private
> individuals, of functionaries of the Armed Forces.

Notwithstanding the ease of the army's takeover in Quillota and the peace-
ableness that ensued, in January 1974 military forces in the province organized a roundup and massacre of selected leftists and peasants.[8] The official
story was that on 18 January, armed extremists attacked a military patrol
while it was transporting eight prisoners from one military site to another
(from the Escuela de Caballería to the Regimiento de Ingenieros de Quillota).
The official story also held that six were killed trying to escape, but two
managed to flee. All were well-known political leaders or activists in the
province during the Allende period. In other ways they were heterogeneous.
Politically, three were Communists, two were Socialists, one a MIRista; two

had no known political party militance but had been labor leaders in the textile factory and agrarian reform community where they worked, respectively. Occupational and professional trajectories were also diverse. Two of the eight, including the former mayor of Quillota, Socialist Pablo Gac Espinoza, worked in the former municipal government. Two had been former functionaries of the local agrarian reform. Three were textile factory workers and one a rural laborer. Six had been political prisoners since September 1973.

Ironically, and in contrast to the official escape story, three of the six prisoners held since September—agrarian reform functionary Víctor Enrique Fuenzalida Fuenzalida, municipal worker and local Socialist Party secretary Manuel Hernán Hurtado Martínez, and textile worker and factory production committee secretary Julio Arturo Loo Prado—had presented themselves voluntarily to the authorities in the orderly change of regime that took place in Quillota Province. Former mayor Pablo Gac Espinoza, one of the alleged escapees, also complied with the new regime in an orderly manner. Indeed, he had turned down an offer of asylum by the Romanian Embassy. Arrested in the third week of September, he was released on the condition that he remain in Quillota and sign in with the police (carabineros) once a week. From time to time, civilians showed up to take him to an interrogation session with military or police authorities, and he complied. When he was taken away for the last time, on 17 January 1974, the young man in civilian clothes who got out of the jeep indicated that Gac needed to go for an interview session at the local army unit (Regimiento de Ingenieros No. 2 de Quillota). The hour was early—about 2:45 A.M.—and Gac asked for some time to change his clothes. The man from the jeep agreed, and said he would leave and return. Gac took a bath, shaved, and dressed. He gave no indication to his wife that he thought this session would be different from other interrogations. He sought to calm her by saying that the civilian seemed to be a "good kid" (*buen muchacho*).[9]

When the jeep returned it contained other detainees, and Gac may have surmised that this trip would be different. He asked his wife to look for him at the army regiment if he did not return the next day.

The National Truth and Reconciliation Commission concluded that the alleged attack on the patrol was a fiction. A political massacre of unarmed and well-controlled prisoners in a military convoy had taken place. The six who had been shot in the confusion of an alleged ambush-and-escape attempt had simply been executed. The two who allegedly escaped, former mayor Gac and prominent agrarian reform lawyer and functionary Rubén Guillermo Cabezas Pares, had actually been disappeared and executed by agents of the state. The Commission observed that the prisoners had been unarmed and transported under tight military guard, and that some had presented themselves voluntarily and even contacted lawyers to help construct a legal defense. It also noted that the alleged attack occurred during curfew hours in a strategic spot under continuous military watch; that none of the alleged assailants were killed or captured, nor were any soldiers killed, even though six prisoners had been killed; and that it strained credibility to believe that former mayor Gac and agrarian lawyer Cabezas, the two prisoners who were the most well-known and prestigious (and therefore recognizable) public figures in the area, and who had been utterly cooperative when detained the day before the alleged attack, could have been the only survivors to flee successfully into anonymity.[10]

The files of the Vicaría de la Solidaridad contain additional information that renders the event even more chilling. The massacre encompassed an even larger group of prisoners, many of them peasants and former agrarian reform functionaries in the rural towns of Quillota Province. In the second week of January, the military forces issued citations calling on selected peasants and former functionaries to present themselves to the army regiment at Quillota. The roundup began as early as 11 January, when Levy Segundo Arraño Sancho complied by presenting himself voluntarily. Arraño, who had been politically aligned with the MAPU–Obrero Campesino (the "moderate" faction after the MAPU's 1973 split), was a rural laborer and former president of the agrarian reform community of San Isidro. A conscript soldier anonymously provided useful inside information. He had observed the convoy. Its size—a jeep and three military trucks—exceeded that required for a small group of eight prisoners. The last truck alone carried eight soldiers to watch over its prisoner group. He had information indicating that the total number of prisoners was actually thirty-three, that a large number of them were peasants, and that the entire group was executed.[11]

The implication of the information in the Vicaría files is that explicit acknowledgment of the individuals who had been executed or disappeared —albeit in the guise of a fabricated story—only applied in those cases for which some sort of acknowledgment could not be avoided. For eight individuals, the six known political prisoners since September and two extremely prominent local dignitaries, the alleged attack on the military patrol was a necessary fiction. For the other twenty-five or so victims of the massacre, most of them peasants, sheer denial would suffice. Secrecy and anonymity would rule; even a cover story was unnecessary.

The only exception to the anonymity rule for this group was Arraño, but as a former president of an agrarian reform community, he was prominent. The army acknowledged it had detained Arraño but stated that it had released him into liberty on 17 January. Based on the evidence (which included confidential information to the family reported by a second conscript), the Truth and Reconciliation Commission and the Vicaría both concluded that agents of the state had detained and disappeared Arraño.[12]

There was precedent for the massacre of political prisoners in provincial settings where calm order and an almost gentlemanly change of regime had seemed to prevail. In October 1973 General Sergio Arellano Stark, under authorization to intervene by General Pinochet as Army Commander and President of the Junta, led a helicopter expedition to army regiments in various provinces. The operation came to be called the Caravan of Death. The investigative journalist Patricia Verdugo, in a best-selling study originally published in 1989, established definitively that in lightning visits to several provinces, the Arellano group overrode the normal chain of army command and jurisdiction and ordered the execution of seventy-two political prisoners. In these provinces, too, a calm and almost gentlemanly repression had prevailed, and one by-product was the publicly known imprisonment of former local dignitaries and functionaries of the Unidad Popular. In these provinces, too, the roundups and executions of prisoners were explained by cover stories—meticulously analyzed and exposed as fabrications by Verdugo and the National Truth and Reconciliation Commission—that linked the deaths to alleged escape attempts.[13]

One purpose of the "Caravan of Death" massacres was precisely to impose a "hardening" of repression that would impress upon army officers and soldiers, as well as the local population, the idea that calm outward appearances were deceptive. A state of war truly existed. It required harsh repressive measures rather than a regime of gentlemanly repression. It also required the subordination of normal army hierarchy and command to special intelligence teams, in this case a team of officers and secret police who reported directly to General Pinochet in Santiago. The officers who accompanied Arellano were all part of the DINA group that had emerged (in advance of formal constitution of the DINA in 1974) already in September.

In the case of the Quillota massacre in January, the relevant intelligence group whose agents intervened in the local army scene to coordinate the roundup and massacre appears to have been not the DINA but the army's SIM (Servicio Inteligencia Militar, or Military Intelligence Service).[14]

Sudden massacres of prisoner groups under the theoretical control of regular army units were traumatic events. Not only did they upset regular institutional hierarchies and procedures. They also broke the euphemisms and the social conventions that facilitated adaptation to the new order. For regular-army soldiers, mental distance—or compartmentalization—was relatively easy when "subversives" were detained and spirited away in other places by other actors, that is, by specialized secret police bands such as the DINA. It was even possible to draw mental distance from the killing of defenseless civilians when prisoners were initially detained by a regular military or police unit, but subsequently given over to the specialists of the war against subversion. Once the specialists took over treatment and disposal of the prisoners in their own detention centers, torture houses, and military camps, those who arrested the prisoners were mentally released from their connection and responsibility.

Even within torture networks, people could try to achieve mental distance based on the division of labor. An interview with Carlos G., a former carabinero recruited into the "Community of Intelligence" network in Valparaíso, made this point chillingly clear. Carlos G. admitted he participated in some detentions. He at first identified with his role as a kind of young "James Bond." But he did *not* see himself as a torturer. He worked mainly as a secretary to an officer. Hearing the screams of prisoners tortured upstairs in the Naval War Academy disturbed him. It was only when Carlos G. personally took a prisoner upstairs to the "hell" that awaited him that he was forced to confront his own role. As he turned over the prisoner upstairs, an older navy man of inferior rank warned and mocked him, "Kid [*Cabrito*], go hide yourself because when things go the other way, they are going to recognize your face."[15]

The euphemisms and devices that enabled regular-army soldiers to compartmentalize responsibility and establish mental distance broke down if they were suddenly thrown—without recruitment and socialization into specialized "dirty war" work—as witnesses or participants into a drama of roundup and execution of prisoners. This was above all the case if the drama unfolded on their own "tranquil" turf in the provinces and if it involved a massacre without legitimizing ceremony. Execution at the margins of formal procedure was different from execution as the solemn carrying out of a sentence at the end of a military trial.

The shock waves set off by such events in provincial army settings imposed important responsibilities on officers and on specialized personnel such as military chaplains and army doctors. Colonel Eugenio Rivera was the army commander at Calama when Arellano's group arrived in October 1973 and sparked a massacre of twenty-six prisoners. When we spoke, Rivera's tense body language, his insistence that Arellano and the Santiago group had undermined normal military codes of honor and jurisdiction, his remembrance of meetings with his officers and sergeants to repair troop morale, his appreciation of the counseling offered by a military chaplain as he struggled to figure out how to orient his troops—all bore witness to the magnitude of such an event from the point of view of officer responsibility. Rivera tried to "protect the morale" of his soldiers by reestablishing their mental distance. He assured them that he need not investigate irregularities of troops forced to carry out orders issued by the Arellano group. "Señores," he told them, "here there is no problem with any of you, because the total responsibility is with General Arellano." In Rivera's case, the chain of events set off by the Calama massacre would eventually transform him into a critic of military rule. The massacre marked a new military world. This new military world violated normal jurisdictions, loyalties, and camaraderie (*compañerismo*). It dishonored officers without cause and corrupted the process of promotion. There had been "total tranquility" in Calama in the weeks following 11 September, but competence and professionalism were not the point. "Loyalty . . . broke down with the coup d'état; with it was lost all the fundamental concepts of our profession."[16]

In the case of Father Alejandro P., a military chaplain at one of the Caravan of Death massacre sites in October, the shock did not cause a questioning of the military's legitimacy as savior of the nation. In his view, Communism was atheistic and sought to impose materialism and aggressiveness on the culture; the Chilean people were Catholic and had to reject the alien ideology, hatred, and lack of faith espoused by Communists. Nonetheless, the massacre did provoke a crisis of sorts, and the stress ended up ruining his health and blood pressure. Father Alejandro's duty, as he understood it, was to attend to and somehow understand the needs, both religious and human, of everyone "in the military tent" (*bajo el techo militar*). That clientele was diverse: the political prisoners and their relatives, the soldiers and their families, the civilians who worked with the military, the officers who needed advice or information when matters were not right. In a province that had experienced a massacre of political prisoners, the work included receiving confessions by confused and frightened soldiers in search of an orientation, and responding with words that would enable them to understand what had happened and to go on with their duties as soldiers. The work also included measures that drew boundaries on the communication of knowledge. Father Alejandro personally reviewed and approved the letters soldiers sent to their families.[17]

The archives of the National Truth and Reconciliation Commission include rare documentary footprints of the tension and the orientation from above that ensued when regular-army soldiers were drawn directly into the killing or disposing of prisoners. Among the documents received by the Commission was testimony by a former conscript soldier (who required anonymity to provide the information) who served in Logistical Battalion Number 6 of Pisagua, in the northern desert region of Iquique and Pisagua.[18] The soldier had been among a group of twenty-five conscripts, most of them from the southern regions of Chile, led on a special night mission by two lieutenants and a "black beret" captain from Rancagua. The mission began in Iquique at about 2:10 A.M. on 23 February 1974. After the group arrived by jeep and truck to a site near Pisagua, it divided into two. One left with the captain toward the mountains, while the conscript's group began to dig a deep ditch. "We began to dig to a great depth . . . in my case [the hole] reached the neck, it covered my compañeros farther away. We ran into some bags. [Earlier] the Captain gave us the order that when we finished, we should lift the bags up and move them."

The lieutenant who commanded the conscript's group organized the carrying of the bags to another site, where the group began to dig a second pit, "deeper, like some 2 meters to 2 meters 20 centimeters. I had to support myself and jump to get out of there. Later we covered everything."

When the group returned to the regiment, they ate, talked about the strange and disturbing mission, and sought to draw some mental distance (by seeing themselves as "drugged"). Finally, they received counseling by an army doctor or psychologist.

> We all talked among ourselves and thought about what happened. We had the impression of being drugged, since we worked very fast and hardly felt the cold.
>   The work was very quick, my impression is that the earth was not fresh. We did not know what we were moving, until we spoke with the psycholo-

gist—like three days after the facts, approximately—who asked what we thought we were moving, just bags, we thought. . . . Then he said that what we had done was for the good of the country, that it was a soldier's duty, and that we should talk with him three times a week. . . . [So] that is how it was for two weeks. So I realized that they were human bodies.

When regular-army soldiers found themselves drawn into the active killing of prisoners or disposition of the bodies, they required guidance from above on how to remember, interpret, and draw boundaries on the experience.[19]

The scale of the roundup and massacre in Quillota, the fact that at least two conscripts were so deeply disturbed they risked providing confidential information contradicting the official story, the evidence that massacres orchestrated from above in "tranquil" army provinces required special attention to morale by military officers and counseling specialists—all these factors make it difficult to believe that Colonel Juan was unaware of the Quillota massacre or that he initially experienced it as a minor event. As an officer in an orderly provincial outpost, he had a responsibility that outstripped any personal reaction to the event, which may well have been troubled. He had to consider the morale issues—that is, to foster a process of remembrance among his subordinates that converted a dramatic shock into something less dramatic and more orderly. Did this "something less dramatic" take the form of a narrative about disciplined service in the line of duty? Did it take the form of a narrative that assigned responsibility to the intervening intelligence unit? To judge from glimpses in other cases of troop shock and confusion, disciplined duty to country and mental compartmentalization directing responsibility elsewhere served as narratives that restored morale and order.

Colonel Juan closed the memory box on the drama and legacy of policide —except, perhaps, in the most private or discreet circumstances. He closed it with a passion that at first bewildered me, as I stood in the doorway trying to leave his office. Over time, I came to understand better. He closed it not only on the memory of the occasional "Rambo" who conducted house raids too violently. He closed it, as well, on the massacre that destroyed the facade of calm, gentlemanly repression. Colonel Juan taught me that it is the explosive contents of the memory box that produce the paradox of passionate indifference.

The Accident: Temptations of Silence

Persons such as Doña Elena, Señora Herminda, Violeta, and Colonel Juan all coexisted in Chile in the mid-to-late 1990s. In their different ways, they all recognized that the overthrow of Allende by a military government in 1973 constituted a fundamental turning point in Chilean life. They all recognized, as well, that military rule had generated a contentious memory question. But these points in common do not necessarily make it possible to build a cultural conversation about the past that goes beyond argument over starting points; nor do they suffice to establish a minimal ethical baseline for the future.

Military rule bequeathed a dilemma to Chile's transitional democracy in the 1990s. How can one build a peaceful and ethical coexistence when society is populated by such different—and searing—remembrances? Beyond the goal of coexistence, after a formative period of rule by force, how does one build an ethically defensible and socially sustainable normative order? What role does justice play in reckonings with the past and its truths? For reasons we shall explore later in this book and trilogy, by 1996–97 Chile had arrived at a profound impasse on such questions. The accident described below captures the difficulties posed by the memory impasse, and the resulting temptations of cultural silence. For some, silence seemed to offer a way to sidestep the impasse, even to make believe that it did not exist.

One day in 1996, Mónica V. prepared herself for a job interview at the Chilean Ministry of Health in Santiago.[1] Six years earlier, Chile had returned to democracy after its extended period of military rule under General Augusto Pinochet (1973–90). In 1974 Mónica V. had been imprisoned and tortured by the DINA and her husband had been permanently disappeared. When Chile made its transition to democracy, Mónica V., like other survivors of the DINA's torture centers, had cooperated with the National Truth and Reconciliation Commission and also with a Chilean court case. As a witness-survivor, she could help establish the specific identities of prisoners and the specific dates, locations, and events related to their detentions. With the return to democracy in the 1990s, Mónica divided her energies between two lives—ordinary everyday life, dedicated to raising and educating her daughter, finding stable work and income, and attending to relationships with friends; and deep life, dedicated to a working through of the violent trauma she and others had experienced under military rule. The working through of deep life occurred on the one hand as an intimate process, via friends, a psychological therapist, and personal introspection, and on the other hand as a more public social process, via involvement with organizations, court proceedings, and symposia related to truth and memory issues.

The job interview belonged to ordinary everyday life. As Mónica V., accompanied by a close friend, approached the Ministry for her interview, a man strolled past her on the sidewalk. Shortly after he passed, her mind nagged her. Did she know that man? She turned to look again, only to see that something had tugged at his mind too. He had turned to stare at *her*. Then came the flash of recognition. The man had been one of the DINA agents who came to her house saying that they would take Mónica V. to see her detained husband. Indeed, the man had driven the vehicle and spoken with her in the early phase of her detention, before the blindfold came out. Perhaps strengthened by the presence of her friend, Mónica V. remembers, she strolled right up to the staring man and asked, "Are you an ex-DINA agent?" The man's eyes glazed over, and he walked away briskly.

Inside the memory box of Pinochet's Chile, it is difficult to talk across the memory camps. Within each camp, of course, there are differences of social and personal experience, political approach, and generational claim that arise and pose challenges to conversation. But from time to time, one can also incorporate such differences and problems into the cultural conversation and build a larger memory camp. Señora Herminda, Violeta and her sisters, Father Bolton, and Ramiro and Claudia can find common ground in remembrances of rupture, persecution, and awakening. Likewise, Doña Elena and Gabriela can join Father Alejandro and Colonel Juan in the cultural conversation that remembers the disaster before September 1973 that required salvation, and the necessity of looking away from the dirty and polemical aspects of the rescue. But finding common ground for a conversation between these memory camps is much more elusive. The eyes glaze over. An interlocutor shuts the box, hurries away—and remembers not to look back.

Chapter 4

※

From Loose Memory to
Emblematic Memory: Knots on the Social Body

Everyone has memories, but are everyone's memories socially significant for a history of memory? Memory is a potentially boundless theme. The contentiousness, selectivity, and ambivalences that surround the remembrance and forgetting of Chile's recent past only add to the methodological and conceptual difficulties.[1]

For these reasons, it is worthwhile to consider conceptual tools that enable one to check the potential boundlessness of the theme, and to trace more precisely the ways personally and collectively charged memories about a great trauma and turning point may project—or fail to project—into public space or imagination. In my research, I found two such tools methodologically useful because they help one focus on the making of personal and collective memory as a process, and because they avoid a rigidity that pushes aside the "messiness" of remembrance when focused on themes that are at once socially conflictive and psychologically searing, at once collective and personal. At bottom, such tools helped me to understand better the individuals portrayed in this book—how they came to frame and interpret the charged recent past the way they did, how individual narratives of remembrance connected to or diverged from social patterns, how politicocultural struggles yielded an impasse that blocked talk across memory camps by 1996–97.

These useful conceptual tools are the idea of "emblematic memory," within a process of unfolding interaction and counterpoint with the lore of "loose memory"; and the idea of "memory knots" on the social body that demand attention, calling forth publicity and contentiousness that interrupt the more unthinking flow of habitual, everyday life. Let us consider each in turn.[2]

FOUR EMBLEMATIC MEMORIES

Memory is the meaning we attach to experience, not simply recall of the events and emotions of that experience. This aspect of remembrance, especially crucial for study of collective memory, clarifies the distinction between the content (as in specific narrated events) of memory, and the organizing framework that imparts meaning. Emblematic memory refers not to a single remembrance of a specific content, not to a concrete or substantive "thing," but to a framework that organizes meaning, selectivity, and countermemory.

Consider, for example, the memory that views 11 September 1973 as the salvation of a Chile in ruins, a country whose people had passed through an enormous destructive trauma *before* the military took power. For some, the specific personal stories and memories that find meaning within this framework focus on the scarcity of goods and the long lines to purchase rationed food that redefined daily life in a large city like Santiago. For others, the specific contents of remembrance focus on incidents of violence or physical threat experienced on a landed estate affected by the agrarian reform mobilization. For still others, personal lore takes a backseat as content and emblem of national experience; they emphasize a content and symbol projected strongly by mass media and officials—for example, "Plan Z," an alleged conspiracy by the Left to assassinate military officers and prominent opposition leaders and thereby install a dictatorship in September 1973. They may also adapt and personalize the media symbol—for example, how I remember reacting to the Plan Z revelation, how I "knew" it was the awful truth. For some, the framework of salvation proves rather flat and simple: Pinochet saved the country, then turned it over in good shape to civilians in 1990. For others, the same framework has acquired a more complex layering of qualifications and historical judgments. Indeed, the layering effect might even partly contradict the original framework. An example: At first, the military junta and Pinochet saved the country, but Pinochet stayed in power too many years and finally ended up a dictator corrupted by his fondness for power and weighed down by discontent and deteriorating credibility.[3]

As a framework for collective remembrance rather than its specific content, emblematic memory imparts broad interpretive meaning and criteria of selection to personal memory, based on experiences directly lived by an individual, or on lore told by relatives, friends, comrades, or other acquaintances. The specific contents and stories that energize and provide raw material for emblematic memory, and the specific layering with caveats or qualifications, vary from one person to another. Specific emphases and layering effects also vary from one historical moment to another. In the absence of a bridge between personal memory and the emblematic memory of larger social groups, however, individual remembrances remain somewhat "loose." Disarticulated from group meaning or frameworks, personal lore or experiences cannot acquire value as symbol or emblem of a great collective experience. At best they circulate as personal anecdotes or curiosities on the margins of the social imaginary, in tiny, fragmented personal circles.

Emblematic memory circulates in some sort of public or semipublic domain —mass media reports or spectacles; government ceremonies, speeches, or media events; street demonstrations, commemorations, or protests; church or other nongovernmental institutional networks and bulletins; universities and oppositional forums including semiclandestine gatherings and underground publications; music, books, television programs, or movies that garner a mass audience. Emblematic memory functions like a moderately interactive show taking place under a big open-air tent. The performance spectacle goes on incorporating and imparting meaning to the varied specific remembrances people bring into the tent, articulating them into a wider meaning. This wider meaning defines which kinds of otherwise loose memories matter and are welcome to move forward and in effect join the show and, conversely, which kinds of memories are best forgotten or pushed back out toward the fringes. At the same time, emblematic memory imparts meaning to—encourages personal identification with—select events or lore drawn from media and public domain happenings.[4]

Up to a point, emblematic memory also creates a framework for organizing countermemory and debate. For example, memory as salvation finds a logical countermemory in the idea of treason. In discussions with ex-military people who ran into trouble under the new regime—officers dismissed from service (*exonerados*) after the 1973 coup because their political loyalties were suspect, a sailor imprisoned and tortured for alleged sedition during the run-up to the coup in August and September, an officer whose command was undermined when the October 1973 Caravan of Death arrived to execute prisoners for whom he had held responsibility—the idea that the junta rulers were traitors rather than saviors was never far from the surface, and sometimes it came forth explicitly. The junta commanders, in this view, had betrayed Chile's Constitution and thereby destroyed Chile and subjected its people. In the process, they also destroyed the military forces' professionalism, doctrine of obedience to civilian control, and camaraderie.[5] Of course, the specific stories and contents of countermemory varied. Civilian critics of the military regime, for example, remembered how quickly goods and food reappeared after 11 September 1973. In this form of countermemory, the sudden reappearance of plentiful goods seemed to prove that the rich had hoarded goods to create a crisis of rule that would bring down the government and justify military intervention. The scarcity crisis was an artifice and the "salvation" premised on it a falsehood—a political cover for the betrayal of democracy.[6]

Emblematic memory, in short, is both a framework of meaning and a way of organizing cultural argument about meaning. To frame memory as salvation is also to frame memory as a debate about salvation versus treason. A similar dance of memory versus countermemory applies to other emblematic forms of remembrance.

Yet it is worth underscoring that emblematic memory shapes the cultural framework of countermemory and debate only up to a point. The most dynamic forms of cultural and political debate about memory often take place as a contest over the primacy or "truth" of rival emblematic memories, in a competitive process to establish which frameworks will displace others and approach a hegemonic cultural influence. The emblematic memories considered to have captured the most essential collective truth gain a certain primacy of place in the society's memory box. In this sense, the voices and carriers of an emblematic memory do not succeed in imprisoning most of the pertinent debate within the terms set by their own points of departure. Memory as salvation from a treasonous betrayal of Chile before 1973 runs up against a countermemory that inverts the saviors into traitors. But its most profound challenge comes from altogether different frameworks— memory as rupture, and memory as persecution and awakening.[7]

During the quarter century since 1973, Chileans have constructed four principal emblematic memories to recall and give meaning to the 1973 crisis and military takeover, and to the subsequent wave of massive political violence organized by the state. We have already encountered these emblematic memories through the personal remembrances and experiences presented in the preceding chapters. For conceptual purposes, we need to rely here on a more formal and analytical language, on abstractions and composites derived from recurring points rather than the specific details or idiosyncrasies of any one individual's memory or experience.

Memory as salvation recalls the times of Allende's Unidad Popular coalition as a traumatic nightmare that brought society to the brink of an ultimate disaster, and it views the military takeover of 1973 as a new beginning that rescued the national community. Its key elements follow: The fundamental trauma of Chile occurred before, not after, 11 September. The economy had been taken down a path of arbitrary seizures and decisions that mired Chile in legal and economic chaos and, by late 1973, a catastrophe of falling production and ineffectual distribution. Uncontrolled violence and hatred had also spiraled out of control, taking Chile to the edge of a civil war that would include systematic massacres of real and potential opponents by the organized ultra-Left. In this context or framework, what one must remember is how truly cataclysmic and frightening a path the country had traveled between 1970 and 1973—or perhaps more accurately, in the entire Frei-Allende period of 1964 to 1973. In addition, one must remember that after September 1973 the country found a solution to its profound problems: it successfully reordered its economic life and political life, and recovered its capacity for peaceful coexistence (*convivencia*).

But what about violence by the military state, easily the most controversial aspect of military rule? Either the violence did not happen; or, human rights violations happened but as occasional excesses by individual military or police agents, who were sometimes provoked into such reactions, rather than as a systematic policy by the state; or, the violence happened but as a necessary social cost—lamentable, but necessary—to save the country.

As we saw in the case of Doña Elena (chapter 1), those who find meaning in memory as salvation build a bridge between these general ideas and the events they lived directly or heard about personally, through relatives or close friends. As one might surmise from the cases of Señora Herminda, Violeta, and Colonel Juan (chapters 2–3), a parallel process occurs with the other principal emblematic memories.

A second emblematic remembrance stands in diametric antagonism to the first. *Memory as an unresolved rupture* haunts those for whom military rule signifies a personally experienced violence by the state, especially the loss of relatives or companions, as lacerating and vivid as if it had happened today. The trauma of sorrow, fear, uncertainty, and rage destroyed the continuity of life and relationships. It defines the person's deepest self and memories. The central idea: The military government brought the country to a hell of death and torture, both physical and mental, without historical precedent or moral justification, and that hell continues. The dictatorship did not simply destroy lives. By denying the truth of torture, disappearance, and execution for years, by holding back key aspects of this truth—especially the specific detailed fate of individual victims—once total denial was no longer an option, and by engineering an amnesty that impeded full truth seeking linked to justice, General Pinochet and the other military rulers blocked the possibility of inner peace or transcendence for the families of victims. They imposed, as a consequence, an ongoing moral bankruptcy on the nation.

This profound and unhealed wound almost transforms its victims into double-persons. On the one hand, there is the normal everyday person: she (or he) competently organizes her life, tends to her family and remembers her errands, does her work and greets her acquaintances, carries on as best she can with the normal conversations and rituals of daily life. On the other hand, there is also the deep person: a human being whose most fundamental self is grounded in a living hell, a memory that reactivates the experience of unbearable wounding. This is a pain so crushing that it strips away much of the meaning of "normal" everyday life and its superficial appearances.[8]

Like remembrance as salvation, memory as an unresolved rupture provides a framework of meaning that defines what is important to remember and what can be consigned to the back burner of historical consciousness. The systematic cruelty of the repression after 1973, the absence of a true state of war despite decrees to the contrary by the junta, the international legal and moral doctrines that render unjustifiable the torture, disappearance, or execution of prisoners at the margins of legal proceedings even in a state of war, the humanity of the victim and the victim's family: these are fundamental to remember. Debate about the political choices made by the victim before 1973, or about the reasons Chile had reached a point of crisis by 1973, are either besides the point or perversely diversionary.

Memory as persecution and awakening marks those who recall the military period as a time when society and the self endured a long winter of repression and self-discovery. The violent persecution of dissidents, the collapse of democratic rights, the staying power of the dictatorship, these tested one's deepest values and social commitments, and thereby provoked—earlier for some than for others—a process of awakening. The self and society discovered not only a deepening nonconformity, or struggle for a way out, but also the self-knowledge, values, and consecuencia (moral constancy) linked to coping with fear, persecution, and in some instances rage.[9] One lived a kind of in-between life—caught between hurt and hope, persecution and revindication, stigma and solidarity.

Memory as persecution and awakening bears some resemblance to memory as rupture, but more as a cousin than a twin sister. It includes within its circle more than those who experienced the loss of a loved one directly. Its social and political base became quite large and diverse. In the 1990s, its political heterogeneity ran roughly parallel to that of the Center-Left coalition, known as the Concertación, that guided Chile's democratic transition. We tasted something of this flexibility and heterogeneity in the remembrances of Violeta and Ramiro. Violeta's moral and Christian activism during the dictatorship, and the fact that she lived in Santiago, which experienced tremendous political mobilizations and struggles in the 1980s, enabled her to recall persecution and awakening with roughly equivalent emphasis. In many ways, her personal and collective remembrance is framed as the constant unfolding tension between these two aspects of life under a dictatorship. Ramiro's internal exile and prolonged rural isolation, on the other hand, led to a kind of extreme self-enclosure. In his remembrance, the sheer weight of persecution overwhelms and suffocates any sense of social awakening, even though his inner self holds fast to Left ideals, and even though he values the solidarity he and Claudia received at crucial moments.[10]

If one returns to the metaphor of a performance spectacle under an open-air tent, memory as persecution and awakening functions as the show that invites more and more people to find their way into the tent to join their personal knowledge and experience to a wider, more emblematic meaning. Some place the accent most completely on persecution; others link their experiences to a dialectic of persecution and social awakening. Some see the awakening as having culminated in a positive way in the 1990s—in a stable and practical democratic transition, respectful of truth and citizen rights, and building realistic bases for a more equitable society in the future. Others see the awakening as a potential that came into existence but was subsequently frustrated. In this view, a wave of social movements for democracy, human rights, indigenous rights, women's rights, and economic and labor equity took hold in the 1980s, but the promise of this awakening was undermined or betrayed in the 1990s by a democratic transition too weak to reckon with the rules of the game negotiated and enforced by General

Pinochet and the outgoing military regime. Some align themselves closely, almost vicariously, with the spirit of remembrance as unresolved rupture and with its human symbols and voices; others evince a more ambivalent sympathy, respectful of those who suffered permanent rupture yet also inclined to see their needs or demands as an annoying "problem" for a stable democratic transition.[11]

The great strength and weakness of remembrance as persecution and awakening is precisely this flexibility and heterogeneity—across social groups and political sensibilities, across regionally specific experiences, across historical time from the 1970s through the 1990s. The flexibility facilitates the building of political and cultural coalitions, and it may even foster a kind of cultural hegemony. But it also leaves room for plenty of misunderstanding and friction among those in the same memory camp—who presumably share a basic understanding about the military past.[12]

A fourth emblematic remembrance, *memory as a closed box,* sees the 1973 collapse and subsequent violence as deeply troubling, divisive, and even dangerous affairs that are best put away and forgotten. If the misunderstood and contentious past is allowed to ventilate, it will poison the present and the future. It will destroy the possibilities of social reconciliation, mutual acceptance, and national progress. The theme of 11 September and subsequent military violence may be very important, and one may privately interpret them as one pleases, but such memories are so polemical and volatile that they bring danger to personal, familial, and collective life. Since the memory theme has no solution and stirs up conflict and danger, it is simply better to close the memory box. Keeping the box closed is the practical precondition for tranquility and reconciliation—whether among divided relatives who reconcile with one another and renew a family spirit, or divided citizens in the imagined national family, or even within a conflicted self that seeks psychological peace with (or distance from) one's own past. One's memories belong to a past that must be superseded by a sheer will to supersede.[13]

Memory as a closed box, like memory as persecution and awakening, bears a cousin resemblance with another emblematic memory, in this instance that of salvation. The similarity resides in the way that many of its proponents, when they are willing to open the memory chest discreetly, find meaning in a narrative of salvation. The practical effect of memory as a closed box is also rather friendly for hardcore adherents of remembrance as salvation. Closing the box facilitates—more by silence and omission than commission—the emergence of a benign veneer on the military past. In particular, it leaves unchallenged the junta's self-amnesty decree of 1978.

The resemblance and friendliness do not imply, however, a more complete or exact similitude. Remembrance as a closed box can welcome into its company political pragmatists or "realists" who dissent from remembrance of the military period as salvation, but who think that the need for justice and cultural airing of the persecutions and ruptures of the past, while understandable, is outweighed by practical political considerations. The strength of the military and its core base of supporters, and of investors who want social tranquility and stability at almost any cost, render the quest for justice and cultural airing too destabilizing and counterproductive. Like remembrance as persecution and awakening, memory as a closed box can articulate a more heterogeneous array of persons and perspectives than its "cousin" framework.

At bottom, memory as a closed box is remembrance as olvido ("oblivion" or "forgetting"). Far from the involuntary amnesia of someone who has suffered a bad fall, however, the forgetting is filled with memory and meaning. Based on remembrance, one defines the usefulness of forgetting. Based on remembrance, one defines what needs to be consigned to the back burner of cultural oblivion. Some loose memories or lore are useful because they remind one of the dangerousness that justifies closing the box. Other memories stir up trouble. Prudence allows them to drift to the margins of consciousness.[14]

In this framework, for example, it becomes less important to remember the actual human rights violations engineered by Manuel Contreras, as commander of Tejas Verdes and head of the DINA between 1973 and 1977, than to remember what happened to the country when Contreras and his second-in-command, Pedro Espinoza Bravo, were brought to justice in 1995. The final justice proceedings and sentencing to prison of Contreras and Espinoza sparked a national crisis that proved profoundly dangerous—it generated fears of a military intervention to stop human rights trials, it exposed the democratic government as too weak to take physical custody of Contreras for months, it strained political relations among democrats in the Center-Left coalition that undergirded the transition from dictatorship, and it fostered cynicism about the civilian political system. One remembers the crisis events of 1995 well, as a warning that oblivion about the 1970s may be necessary and justice may backfire. Chilean democracy survived that particular crisis, and Contreras ended up in prison (albeit one especially constructed for the case), but how many more such crises could the country survive? Precisely for that reason, one comes to appreciate a discreet memory that closes the box on the theme of 1973 and political violence.[15]

PROCESS I: THE MAKING OF EMBLEMATIC MEMORIES

These four emblematic memories—salvation, unresolved rupture, persecution and awakening, a closed box—have competed in the public domain and in people's minds as they remember the crisis of 1973 and its violent aftermath. Yet even as we note that emblematic memory is socially constructed and selective, and that it is a framework of meaning rather than a specific memory content or "thing," we need to avoid the trap of assuming that emblematic memory is an arbitrary invention or manipulation.[16]

Let us recall, in this context, three points introduced earlier (Afterword to chapter 2). First, memory is emblematic because it purports to capture an essential truth about the collective experience of society. It tells not only what happened to a person or to one's family, friends, or comrades, but suggests that this experience reveals something fundamental about a broader social circle—a political party and its sympathizers, a neighborhood or community, a social class or ethnic group, or ultimately, the imagined national family or community.[17] Second, a framework of remembrance is also emblematic because many people have come to share the idea that it represents truth. They not only find an anchor that organizes and enhances the meaning of personal knowledge and experiences that might otherwise float loosely. They also gain validation from events, relationships, and discourses in a public or semipublic domain—in the mass media or alternative informational bulletins; in street demonstrations, protests, and group meetings; in official celebrations, speeches, and controversies; or in truth reports, books, music, and cultural forums or performances. By finding a mirror or echo effect in a public cultural domain, one realizes that others have come to a similar understanding of collective memory, experience, and truth.[18]

Third, these conditions imply that the making of emblematic memory emerges from a process of reciprocal yet selective interplay between memory as emblem and memory as lore. The remembered facts, stories, rumors, and meanings that people personally experienced or heard from others— and that they considered significant, urgent, or curious enough to pass on to others—constitute a rich cultural lore and raw material for the building of emblematic memory. As we have seen (Afterword to chapter 2), not all lore attaches readily to an emblematic meaning framework. Some stories readily corroborate a major emblematic framework and find a larger meaning within it. Other memory stories, such as goodness lore and remorse lore, seem to capture a powerful truth but do not fit comfortably within major emblematic frameworks. Still other stories float loosely, more devoid of a wider social meaning or circulation, condemned to a kind of cultural marginality.

In short, the process of building emblematic memories, although it includes efforts at human persuasion and manipulation, is more complex and historically grounded than a simple idea of human invention. Emblematic memories are human inventions, but they are not arbitrary inventions. For this reason, we need to consider the historical criteria and processes that impart credibility and influence to emblematic remembrance as understandings of experience that encounter an authentic "echo" in the society and culture. It is this complex echo effect that enables an emblematic memory to gain cultural traction and "convince" people and social groups, thereby providing larger meanings to various loose memories.

Consider six interrelated criteria, some more obvious than others, that influence the capacity to "convince." First, *historicity.* Emblematic memories gain influence when they refer to a moment or time of great rupture, perceived as decisive and foundational for what came afterward by at least one or two generations. When the symbols and consequences of a rupture are widely experienced by adults and youth as "a defining issue or moment," the necessity to elaborate collective memory and meaning becomes more powerful, and the possibility of significant intergenerational dynamics and transmission also emerges more powerfully. As historians of Germany and Holocaust survivor families will recognize, a kind of intergenerational transmission can even occur through a taboolike silence that signifies that something terrible and decisive happened but that elders wish to keep the memory box shut.[19]

In the Chilean case, the sense of a society that had come to a decisive crossroads was universal by August and September 1973. In addition, the powerful symbolism of the events of 11 September underscored this sensibility. The bombing of the presidential palace of La Moneda on 11 September dramatically symbolized the historicity of the military forces' intervention. The traditional physical center of Chilean political life and democracy had destroyed Chile and would now itself be wrecked; Chile would have to build anew. President Allende's dramatic and eloquent last radio address also lent a powerful historicity to the eleventh. As many Chileans turned to the radio to follow the morning's events, he not only said good-bye to the living; he spoke to posterity.[20]

Second, *authenticity*. Memories that purport to capture an emblematic truth are more convincing when they allude to concrete "real" experiences, or to "hard" facts linked to such experiences. For example, memory as rupture was somewhat difficult to dismiss as pure invention by political centrists when it alluded to the sightings of dead bodies in the Mapocho River that many had seen and that had generated lore and rumor in Santiago, or when it alluded to moving testimonies of "real" experience collected and ratified by the Santiago Catholic Church. The authenticity of memory as rupture and persecution became even more difficult to dismiss —even in some conservative political sectors—when the Catholic Church, the mass media, and a judicial investigation confirmed that the remains of assassinated humans, discovered in 1978 in the lime ovens of Lonquén, matched up precisely with "disappeared" peasants sought for years by relatives, the Pro-Peace Committee, and the Vicariate of Solidarity. Allusions to real experience, ratified by personal knowledge, reliable testimony, or "hard" facts, were especially important to lend authenticity to dissident forms of memory.[21]

Third, *capaciousness and flexibility*. As mentioned earlier, emblematic memory functions somewhat like a performance spectacle under a large open-air tent that invites diverse people to join the proceedings and find in them a wider meaning for their specific memories. The more capacious and flexible the meaning framework, the more effectively one can build, from a multitude of diverse specific experiences brought into the tent, a collective imaginary that also seems a shared "real" experience. We have already seen, in memory as persecution and awakening, an example of a framework that eventually proved flexible enough to accommodate considerable heterogeneity. On the other hand, if one narrows the meaning framework rigidly, or ties it too tightly to memory as a specific "content" or thing, one runs up against risks. Too few people may feel themselves invited into the tent as potential co-owners of remembrance. In addition, the proponents of rival emblematic memories might expose findings that convert a crucial memory content or "thing" into a lie. For example, early versions of memory as salvation simply denied the facts of secret killings, abductions, and permanent disappearances. Presumably, the new government was too benevolent in instinct and motivation to act in such ways. When sheer denial became an obvious lie, the proponents of memory as salvation would search for more flexible approaches—whether a version of salvation that included ideas of sporadic human rights excesses and necessary social costs, or an alternative framework of remembrance that argued that the time had come to close the memory box and leave the past to the past.[22]

Fourth, *projection into public or semipublic spaces*. To the extent that remembrance is confined to a very small and enclosed ambience—something shared within a tiny circle of close relatives and friends, something that circulates at best as unconfirmed underground rumor—it proves extremely difficult to build bridges between loose personal memory and emblematic memory. The only bridge that is both safe and conducive to a validating echo effect is the bridge to the official memory propagated by the new regime. For potential dissidents, the culture of fear implies fragmentation, a self-imposed censorship that creates a certain clandestinity of deep experience (even among groups who are not engaged in clandestine political or social organizing). To become culturally influential, dissident emblematic memories must somehow break out and achieve elaboration and circulation in more or less public spaces—for example, in communications media of ample circulation, or forums of cultural and intellectual elaboration such as university life and events, or in semipublic informational networks such as reading clubs, Christian lay communities, and solidarity bulletins, or in public civic acts such as street actions or demonstrations that provoke publicity and reaction. Without such projection, potentially emblematic frameworks of remembrance remain culturally cornered and isolated; the loose memories that might sustain them remain fragmented, at best a kind of floating alternative lore.[23]

Fifth, *embodiment in a convincing social referent*. A social referent, at once concrete and symbolic, not only provides a living embodiment of emblematic remembrance. To the extent that the social referent provokes cultural respect and even sympathy, she or he invites people to identify with the human symbol, or at least to grant a certain authenticity and legitimacy to the remembrance embodied by the symbol.[24]

The emergence of convincing social referents is crucial for the building of effective emblematic memory. As Chileans in the 1970s built early versions of the four emblematic memories discussed here, they embodied the "truth" of remembrance in key human referents. Indeed, the persons presented in the preceding chapters were not only "real people." They also bear a close connection to the key symbolic referents that emerged in the 1970s.[25]

In the case of memory as salvation, the dignified and respectable Chilean woman, a person of the middle-class sectors or somewhat higher who demanded a solution to the problems of scarcity, chaos, and fear of violence, served as a galvanizing symbol of all that had gone wrong before salvation on the eleventh. Doña Elena, a woman with a strong sense of dignity, manners, and order, but who felt her world torn apart before the military intervened to set Chile right, is a living example of this symbolism. For the proponents of remembrance as salvation, military intervention on the eleventh was a "pronouncement" (pronunciamiento) rather than a "coup" (golpe) precisely because Chilean society, especially respectable women in the name of society, had demanded an energetic and effective solution to the imminent catastrophe. The women had demonstrated against Allende and banged their empty pots to signify the urgency of their problems finding food and their fear that the disorder would expose their relatives to violence. The military's pronunciamiento responded to the call of the women, and it turned Chile to a path whereby respectable Chilean women and their families could recover their world of order, dignity, and progress.[26]

For memory as unresolved rupture, women also embodied the suffering of society. In this case, however, the social referent was women such as Señora Herminda—mothers and wives who suffered the worst pain imaginable, that of losing a relative by action of a state that not only kidnapped or killed loved ones, but cruelly refused to respond to the love and sorrow of the women with honest and reliable information.

Women in search of their disappeared loved ones became an extremely powerful social referent, projected into the public domain by the women's own actions as well as sympathetic publicity through church-based solidarity. The symbolism was so powerful that it provoked not only sympathy and solidarity but also a ferocious hostility. Those who did not wish to hear or believe the women, or who wished to undermine their credibility, would have to stigmatize them. On the spectrum of stigmatization, the most hateful pole might brand the women as "fanatics," or their loved ones as "subversives" who engaged in wild military actions and deserved whatever befell them, or the "presumed" disappeared as irresponsible people who abandoned families for lovers or a new life. A softer, more paternalist form of stigma recognized that to lose a relative of course brought great personal grief, but suggested that such grief could understandably lead the women into distorted expectations of the state and obsessions with the past.[27]

Given the heterogeneous co-ownership of remembrance as persecution and awakening, and its flexibility as a meaning framework, its historical evolution after 1973 was complex and its key symbolic referents shifted and multiplied over time. In the 1980s, when street protest erupted and public political spaces became crowded and turbulent, several key referents emerged: shantytown youth caught between the rage induced by violent persecution of their communities by an apparently unending dictatorship, and their yearning for democracy and a future; women *pobladoras* who suffered economic misery and political repression in their shantytowns but also awakened, through human rights work and political mobilization, to discover their own strength as women and their rights as citizens; political leaders of the Center-Left who discovered, through their processing of political failure and the devastating truths of persecution, a renewed commitment to cherish democracy and human rights, and to place collaboration on behalf of a sustainable democracy above ideology.[28]

In the 1970s, however, when government and official truth held greater control of public space, people such as Violeta symbolized remembrance as persecution and awakening. Persons of profound moral conscience—especially male priests and religious leaders, but also laymen and laywomen who felt the call of faith or conscience—could not turn a blind eye to the truth of a human rights emergency. Christian faith and morality impelled one to recognize human needs and persecution, and to work with organizations such as the Pro-Peace Committee or the Vicariate of Solidarity to provide testimonial voice to "people without voice." In a Catholic society whose military rulers proclaimed fidelity to Christianity as a basic principle and where political polarization and bitterness had run deep, a social referent that questioned official truth on the basis of religious conscience was culturally and practically feasible. Religious conscience framed the question of violence and human rights as transcendent. These were themes beyond mundane political calculations, rules, and fault lines. Those who insisted on defending fundamental human rights had a right to do so because they were acting not as a political opposition, but as Chileans of conscience. Theirs was a moral insistence legitimized, organized, and partially protected by the Santiago Catholic Church.[29]

For memory as a closed box, which became especially important after the promulgation of the 1978 amnesty decree, a culturally convincing social referent did not emerge as clearly or coherently as in the other cases. The Chileans who symbolically justified a closing of the box ranged from the specific—combatants on all sides who had fallen in supposed armed confrontations, in a sad phase of history that could now be left behind—to a more general sense that Chilean citizens and families were tired of conflicts and now wanted to turn away from the hatred and excesses of the past. In this more opaque symbolic context, Colonel Juan more or less connects to the human symbolism. It was the officers and soldiers who had been called upon to serve the country at an extremely difficult juncture, presumably, who had the most pressing need to leave the past in the past.[30]

A sixth element in the capacity to convince and create echo effects is as indispensable as it is obvious: *effective carriers or spokespersons (portavoces).* Human voices, committed and organized to share remembered experiences and truths, to project them into a domain beyond personal circles of mutual confidence, to insist on them even to those who might not want to listen—these are fundamental to the making of emblematic memories. Without human actors who make, interpret, and insist on one or another form of collective remembrance—who engage in a pushy politicocultural performance of memory—none of the other elements mentioned above can truly "happen."

We shall expand on this point later in this chapter, when we discuss memory knots. Our main purpose here has been to suggest the ways that the meaning frameworks we have called emblematic memory, although a human creation and inherently selective, are not at all an arbitrary human creation. Merely to list the varied elements that influence the cultural resonance or echo effect of emblematic memory—historicity of the remembered rupture, authenticity and allusion to authenticity, capaciousness and flexibility, projection into public or semipublic space, embodiment in a culturally convincing social referent, and backing and projection by organized human spokespersons—exposes the ways that emblematic memories cannot emerge by mere chance or manipulation.

Emblematic memories are ways of organizing and thinking about experience, and in this sense they are by definition a human invention. But to carry cultural weight, they must connect to the "real" events and experiences of at least one or two generations. They must relate to the necessities and sensibilities generated by such experiences in significant social groups or in broad swaths of society at large.

PROCESS 2: MEMORY KNOTS ON THE SOCIAL BODY

The necessary echo effect between loose personal memory or lore on the one hand, and emblematic meaning on the other, brings us face to face with the making of emblematic memories as a human activity. Emblematic memory emerges from multiple human efforts, conflictual and competitive, to give meaning to a great collective rupture, trauma, or turning point—an experience perceived as decisive or transformational and therefore "historical."

These efforts constitute a learning process. Spokespersons and their potential publics *discover* how to construct bridges to emblematic memory and thereby find their collective truth. The process is more practical than theoretical, a kind of learning by trial, error, and improvisation in the face of rival meaning frameworks and, for those who organize dissident memory, in the face of state hostility and repression. In effect, the human organizers of memory learn "as they go," with varying degrees of success, how to handle matters such as authenticity, flexibility, projection into public domains, and embodiment in sympathetic human referents.[31]

The specific social groups, networks, and leaders who are sufficiently motivated to organize and insist on memory constitute troublesome "knots" on the social body. They interrupt a more unthinking and habitual life, they demand that people construct bridges between their personal imaginary and loose personal experiences on the one hand, and a more collective and emblematic imaginary on the other.[32]

The idea of a memory knot is a metaphor inspired by the human body.[33] Consider a knot in the stomach when one is nervous, a lump in the throat when one is moved, a nerve-and-muscle mass that spasms and cries out for relief. Such bodily events break the "normal" flow of everyday life and habit, the physical and mental existence that relies on reflexes (whether learned or instinctive) to lessen the need for conscious thought and memory. Suddenly, we experience a heightened consciousness, a demand that we take notice—that we think, feel, or respond.

Memory knots on the social body also interrupt the normal flow of "unthinking" reflexes and habits. They force charged issues of memory and forgetfulness into a public domain. They make claims or cause problems that heighten attention and consciousness, thereby unsettling reflexive everyday habits and euphemisms that foster numbing. One responds even if the purpose of response is merely to find "relief" and return to normalcy.

Expressed theoretically: memory knots are sites of society, place, and time so bothersome, insistent, or conflictive that they move human beings, at least temporarily, beyond the *homo habitus* postulated by anthropologist Pierre Bourdieu.[34] Expressed colloquially: memory knots are sites where the social body screams.

These sites are multidimensional. Memory knots, as I am using the term, refer to sites of humanity, sites in time, and sites of physical matter or geography. Specific human groups and leaders, specific events and dates, and specific physical sites all seem to stir up, collect, and concentrate memories, thereby "projecting" memory and polemics about memory into public space or imagination.[35]

Let us review briefly these three dimensions.[36] *Sites of humanity.* Particular human groups—whether high officials and civilian collaborators of a military government and its public relations offices, or members and supporters of relatives-of-the-disappeared networks, or leaders and activists in human rights or religious organizations, or members and staff of a civilian government's truth commission, or journalists determined to expose a hidden truth or legitimize an official one, or simply persons who feel drawn to participate in a street commemoration or a protest—developed intense motivations to organize and project particular kinds of emblematic memories into a public domain. Such actors created information, events, commemorations, publicity, and scandals that drew people together in remembrance, or at least obliged some form (whether approving or disapproving, fair or tendentious, naïve or skeptical) of media coverage.

To one degree or another, the persons we met in preceding chapters all participated in or were influenced by human memory knots that formed after 11 September 1973. Doña Elena was an intermittent participant in the making of heroic memory. She joined the giant street rallies celebrating the first 11 September anniversaries as the salvation of Chile. She relied on officialist reporting in *El Mercurio* and on Radio Agricultura to distinguish truth from rumor, and to frame the meaning of events. For a time she worked with the National Women's Secretariat, whose outreach activities and publications promoted the idea of a national salvation from ruin led by military men but assisted by a volunteer women's auxiliary. Señora Herminda and Violeta were more consistently activist makers of memory. They participated over long periods of time in dissident memory knots, particularly the organization of relatives of the disappeared and the Vicaría de la Solidaridad. They relied on alternative information outlets, such as the

Vicaría's magazine *Solidaridad* and its confidential human rights bulletins, to link personal experience and witness to collective truths. They joined brave scandal-producing actions, including a dramatic hunger strike by relatives demanding a return of the disappeared and a truthful accounting of their fate, and sudden noisy demonstrations in prominent civic spaces to expose torture and rally moral consciousness.

Compared to these three women, Colonel Juan was the least "activist" organizer of public memory. He had no direct official connection to army communications or public relations work. Nor did he enjoy a rank or responsibility high enough to forge official public memory by his own statements or actions. But as an officer, he participated in the army's internal ceremonies of commemoration and memory transmission and in its codes of silence and euphemism. As an officer, too, he had a place in the chain of responsibility to maintain morale and discipline—to frame events properly, to deflect or neutralize any doubts—among soldiers under his command. He in turn followed the lead of superiors and official communications when dismissing human rights as a minor by-product of "war" that affected few people, naturally spawned a few excesses by individual combatants, and in any event belonged to a superseded era. In sum, Colonel Juan was part audience, part transmission belt of Chilean Army memory, though it goes too far to see him as a direct actor or leader within military knots making and insisting on official memory.

Sites in time. Particular events and dates, whether spectacular scandals such as car bomb murders of former Chilean dignitaries on foreign soil, or culturally charged anniversary dates such as 11 September or May Day, concentrated the symbolic power to "convene" or project memory. Indeed, the first three September memory seasons—periods of official celebration, facilitated by speeches, parades, mass gatherings, and media retrospectives, of the 1973 "rescue" action, of the army and military role in national history, and of national independence day—were also accompanied by compelling international homicide incidents. The DINA organized the car bomb assassination of General Carlos Prats, the army commander in chief displaced in August 1973 to clear a path for the coup, and his wife, Anita Fresno, in Buenos Aires in 1974; the shooting that gravely wounded Christian Democrat leader Bernardo Leighton and his wife, Sofia Cuthbert, in Rome in 1975; and the car bomb killing of Socialist leader Orlando Letelier and his colleague Ronni Moffit in Washington, D.C., in 1976. The symbolic power of May Day derived from the fact that the labor movement had developed such a strong political and cultural presence in Chile before September 1973. Difficult to ignore or suppress, such events and anniversaries *demanded* human efforts of interpretation, control, and projection. They widened the circle of attention to remembrance.

The cultural magic of charged calendar dates, moreover, presented opportunities for organizing and publicity by motivated human groups seeking to magnify the "call" of collective remembrance. Such was the case with International Women's Day. By the 1980s the 8 March celebration became a date, like 11 September or May Day, to which people felt compelled to respond and which they freighted with memory struggle. Such was the case, too, with anniversaries of especially notorious human rights scandals, such as the DINA's botched attempt, in July 1975, to explain 119 disappearances as the result of Left fratricide and shoot-outs in Argentina.[37]

Sites of physical matter or geography. Particular physical places or artifacts could evince a power of almost sacred connection to the past, and consequently stir up and project polemics about memory and amnesia. When the remains of disappeared peasants were discovered in the abandoned lime ovens of Lonquén in 1978 (see chapter 2), the site and the cadavers pushed the problem of the disappeared onto a wider public stage. Lonquén and its cadavers became objects of memorial processions, judicial proceedings and news reports, and struggles for control. Theoretically speaking, physical places or matter exert a certain cultural magic in part because they descend directly from the great historical trauma or turn, as in a torture house, a massacre or assassination site, or suddenly discovered cadavers; and in part because the sites become infused with a sense of intimate connection to sacred history via human invention "after the fact," as in a moving museum, monument, movie, or testimonial book. It is the interplay between direct physical descent and cultural invention that counts—that sparks the imagination that makes remembrance compelling—even if the balance or "play" of variables differs from one physical site to another. A site directly descendant from the trauma must come to be recognized as such through cultural interpretation or struggle. A museum, memorial, or film created after the fact establishes a more sacred or "authentic" connection to the past if it houses artifacts such as physical instruments, bodily remains, sounds, or photos directly connected to the great trauma.

Whatever the process and its mix of physical descent and cultural creation, once a place becomes endowed with sacred connection to a traumatic and still polemical past, it can unleash ferocious ongoing memory struggles. As with charged events and anniversary dates, motivated human groups can feel a "call" to recognize or create physical sites connected to their sense of collective remembrance, or alternatively, to shun or render culturally invisible those sites that lend credibility and organizing energy to rival memories. In the case of Lonquén, for example, the military government found it necessary to arrange a politically friendly transfer of ownership that culminated in March 1980 with the dynamiting of the sacred mines. Their very existence as physical matter and place catalyzed too many people, too many processions, too many consciences—too many struggles.[38]

Strongly motivated human groups, symbolically powerful events and anniversary or commemoration dates, haunting remains and places—these "memory knots" in society, time, and space provide a useful methodological focus for historians of collective remembrance. To express the point more formally and theoretically: the human relations and activities organized either to create or to respond to memory knots enable us to trace the making and unmaking of emblematic memories—the contentious processes that project some ways of organizing memory forcefully into the public cultural domain, as essential "truths" through which people build bridges between personal knowledge or experience and the imagined national community of experience, while pushing other lore and narratives to the margins.

POLITICS AND CHRONOLOGY

The making of collective memory is an intensely political process, in ways both obvious and not obvious. After all, it is the terrifying and often divisive times of trauma, rupture, and historical turning point that generate intense efforts to shape memory. It is the struggles over memory that play a major role in winning or losing political "hearts and minds." That is, they widen or narrow the legitimacy of a new ruling regime that takes control amidst crisis and controversy, of dissenters who challenge the regime or its policies, or of a transitional regime premised on achieving apparent national reconciliation. Especially in cases of violent military dictatorship, fragile democratic transition, and concentrated economic and media ownership, moreover, the structure of power and constraint organized from above figures strongly in available paths for effective memory struggle from below.[39]

In short, memory and politics bear a reciprocal relationship. Political upheaval and attendant atrocities generate memory struggles; politics and power, in turn, shape memory's playing field. In a dictatorship determined to remake society drastically and project its version of truth, and willing to repress dissent violently, power and fear exert an obvious influence on the capacity of human actors to persuade: to mobilize people to gather, to challenge propaganda and misinformation, to project dissenting versions of emblematic memory into a public or semipublic domain. More subtly, considerations of politics and power can also channel the very language of memory struggle. In the mid-1970s, for example, the extreme violence (not only extreme in its effect on the victim, but unbounded by law or known rules) of state repression, the regime of formal and informal media control, the denunciation of politics and politicians as illegitimate, the annihilation of directorates of Left political parties and the crackdown on Christian Democrats, the coerced closure of the Pro-Peace Committee as an ecumenical network to defend human rights—all served to drive human rights–oriented memory work toward appeals on a moral rather than political basis, and toward the Santiago Catholic Church, as a vehicle for dissent and pressure. Not surprisingly, Christian responsibility and moral conscience weighed heavily in the emerging language of memory as rupture, persecution, and awakening.[40]

The political aspect of memory making is especially evident if one considers the chronology of memory struggles and their cultural influence. The four emblematic memory frameworks—salvation, rupture, persecution and awakening, the closed box—did not emerge all at once, nor did they prove equally influential at all moments in time.

A succinct chronology demonstrates the point.[41] The first decade of military rule, roughly 1973 to 1982, was a "foundational" era in memory making. As with so many other aspects of Chilean life—economic, political, educational, institutional—these years involved a thorough revamping of society enforced by raw power. Within this initial phase, moreover, the frameworks emerged more or less in succession, as part of a struggle within a society with radically redrawn lines of power. During 1973 to 1976, the new military junta unleashed intense violence against the Left, dissenters, and social undesirables or troublemakers, shut down adversarial media and purged government ministries, schools and universities, and the military branches, and defined psychological war as one of the several missions of the secret police. The potent mix of repression, self-censorship, and propaganda in the public domain launched memory as salvation. State power and terror made it very difficult for critics to make headway against the waves of information, misinformation, commemoration, and news reporting that drove home the idea of a September 1973 rescue "just in time" from a violent civil war and takeover planned by the Left, and that also drove home the idea of a good-faith rebuilding of a better society by Chile's new rulers.

The launch of memory as salvation did not go uncontested, but dissident emblematic frameworks—cruel and wounding ruptures that never end, persecutions that also prod witnessing and awakening—could not crack into the public domain very powerfully and coherently until the 1975–79 period. It was during these years that organizers of dissident memory began achieving the durability and Catholic Church backing, the practical networking and experience, and the publication outlets and media presence that projected alternative readings of reality into public and semipublic domains. Such achievements put the legitimacy of the regime and its favored memory framework under more open pressure. In these years, relatives of the disappeared organized themselves and found allies, forged their own "reading" of Chilean life and an increasingly coherent public voice, launched dramatic street actions including hunger strikes and self-chaining to buildings, and thickened international solidarity connections. Human rights lawyers and activists who had begun with the ecumenical Pro-Peace Committee, forced to close under pressure by Pinochet late in 1975, found a more resilient institutional shield and a platform for an alternative popular magazine within the Vicaría de la Solidaridad of the Santiago Catholic Church. Chilean lawyers and journalists learned to master the art of international synergy, that is, to use transnational relationships with their professional counterparts to generate human rights news and political news, legal conflicts, and controversies abroad that could not be silenced fully within Chile.

In short, the human actors who congealed into dissident memory knots learned how to work the practical rules and fault lines of domestic and international power, even as they lived under a dictatorship that formally banished "politics." They learned to push into public and semipublic domains the reality of rupture, persecution, and moral awakening by persons of conscience, and they put greater pressure on official memory-truths. Significantly, by 1978–79 such memory struggles gained increasing force not only because of cumulative learning and experience by actors organizing dissident memory, but also because splits had become more intense within the realms of high politics. Splits widened between military leaders and branches, mainly air force generals led by Gustavo Leigh versus the army and Pinochetistas; between elites who favored a return to economic policies based on state-led development with assistance and market protections for business and labor, and devotees of the "Chicago Boys" reforms, a neoliberal dismantling of state presence and protections in the economy; and between states, as border tensions nearly flared into war with Argentina, and as tension mounted with the U.S. Carter administration over human rights and the Letelier-Moffit murders.

Memory as a closed box did not emerge as a powerful, coherent framework for reading the traumatic recent past until the 1978–82 period. It was the intensifying crises of 1978–79—stoked by intense public struggles over ways to define the true meaning and purpose of the 1973 coup, and the true reality of human rights under military rule—that generated a new politics of memory from above. Led by Pinochet's close political counselor, Interior Minister Sergio Fernández, the turn began in the pressure cooker year of 1978. The point now was to define the salvation of Chile as a sadly necessary stage of history—a war against subversives—that had been successfully concluded and could be thankfully left behind. Chileans could now look forward, not behind, as the country moved from its emergency years and ad hoc solutions toward a new institutionalization and a new Constitution. Modernized institutions, including constitutional protection against democratic excesses, would build a bright future. It would do no good to Chilean unity, to former "combatants" on any side, or to the bright future at hand to reexamine the "dirty war" aspects of the past. An amnesty excusing combatants of dirty war through 10 March 1978 would provide the legal closure that formally left the past behind.

Significantly, it was also during 1978–82 that the cultural idea of "memory" itself, and the related idea of a struggle between "memory" and "forgetting," congealed as a cultural language and rallying cry. Earlier in the 1970s, the language of memory conflicts rarely invoked "memory" as a sacred or strategic idea. When counterofficial voices contested official versions of Chile's recent and current reality, language focused on the truth of the events of violence and persecution, the need for justice and answers, the imperatives of moral awakening to human rights, and the like. It was struggle against memory as a closed box that added to the code words truth, justice, and human rights an additional cultural vocabulary: *memory*. The politics of struggle over how to document, draw meaning from, and respond to recent and current experience generated new language—or imbued old words with a new cultural twist or electricity. Just as to *disappear* had turned into a sinister transitive verb—to kidnap someone forever without leaving a memory trace—so it was that *memory* changed. For counterofficial Chile, *memory* had become strategic, since it had become clear that the politics of regime rule and legitimacy was premised on its erasure. *Memory* had also become sacred, a matter of keeping trust with those whose disappearance, deaths, torture, or other persecutions would otherwise vanish, as if they were not real or human.[42]

One could carry on the point past the first decade of military rule. The chronology of memory underscores its interplay with political context and social power. Memory conflicts turned into more of a mass experience— cultural wars to determine which memory frameworks would prevail, and to add new symbols and layers of meaning to old frameworks—during 1983–88. The turn coincided with the shattering of the dictatorship's facade of political control under pressure from mass street protests in 1983–86 and the impending plebiscite on Pinochet's continuing rule in 1988. The politics of memory would also be evident in the 1990s. Documenting and coming to terms with human rights violations under military rule played an important role in the political legitimacy of the ruling Center-Left coalition that steered Chile's democratic transition in 1989–91. At the same time, the continuing power of Pinochet, the military, and the business sector in the 1990s imposed sharp constraints on Center-Left memory strategies, and it eventually bred a demoralizing sense of impasse. Majority belief in the truth of massive and unjustifiable human rights violations—memory as rupture and persecution—and in the consequent imperative of criminal justice kept running up against ambivalence. Right or wrong, many also believed that the large minority of Pinochetista supporters and sympathizers included sectors too powerful to challenge too hard. The partial unraveling of memory impasse after 1998, in turn, bore a close connection to realignments of power including Pinochet's retirement as army commander in chief in March, and his criminal arrest in London in October.

Yet if the making of emblematic memory and the organizing of "knots" on the social body are deeply influenced by politics and power, it goes too far to reduce memory to a matter of politics only. Paradoxically, what gives memory struggles about times of great human rupture and trauma such forcefulness—and potential to influence political legitimacy and alignments—is precisely the inability to reduce memory to a mere political instrument or strategy.

Memory was moral and existential, not simply political. The language of moral suasion that emerged in the human rights memory camp, for example, in part reflected narrow limits of the possible under conditions of dictatorship, and the prominent role of the Santiago Catholic Church, during the formative 1970s period. Over time, however, such language drew adherents and "awakened" people of varied political inclinations precisely because human rights memory *did* transcend politics in the usual or narrow sense. The idea that human rights ought override mere calculation of political advantage versus disadvantage, or regime sympathy versus regime opposition, became a new cultural argument in Chilean life. In a culture with a long political party tradition, where people could quickly spot and reject manipulation, the idea of human rights memory as transcendent gained traction. People found themselves moved or even shattered by confrontation with moral atrocity. Some found that the moral urgency of human rights memory drew them into collaborations that cut across older political divisions. Beyond the specific lives spared or partially repaired by human rights activity including memory work, it was this wider cultural sensitization to human rights as a fundamental value in its own right—too important to be buried by the vagaries of politics or convenience—that constituted the most important achievement of those aligned with memory as rupture, persecution, and awakening.

Just as significant, it was the existential aspect of memory that generated passion and persistence in the face of fear and adversity. What do I do if I have experienced or witnessed atrocity beyond the imaginable? Radical evil and rupture of life can bring in their wake a powerful call to bear witness. For some survivors, relatives of victims, and witnesses, memory became an obligation and a condition of existence in the world, if one were to remain true and loyal to the self, to loved ones, or to friends and comrades. It was this existential aspect that inspired people such as Señora Herminda and Violeta to make the leap into extraordinary risks—a hunger strike to demand accountability for the disappeared, a street demonstration to expose torture—under a violent dictatorship. It was this existential aspect, too, that could inspire quieter feats of resolve—the decision to somehow gather energies to keep insisting on memory, despite the exhaustion, demoralization, and aging that set in as one continues with work that provides precious few results.[43]

Memory knots on the social body organize and demand cultural attention to a charged historical trauma or turning point—an experience profoundly important to at least one or two still living generations, and in some way recognized as decisive by those who have followed them. They help us to understand the process of selective interaction between the major frameworks of meaning we have called emblematic memory, and the personal experiences and lore we have called loose memory. They also help us to understand the social conflictiveness, multiplicity of experiences, and rival claims of remembrance "ownership" embedded in such interactions.[44]

Although concepts such as emblematic remembrance and memory knots offer a check on the boundlessness of memory as an analytical theme, and a means to study the making of collective memory as a process, we also need to remain cognizant of ambiguities. The latter specify the limits of any conceptual scheme, and they remind us to tolerate a degree of necessary "messiness." Especially for the theme of charged collective remembrance, too much conceptual tidiness may be as self-defeating as too little of it.

Three ambiguities or qualifications require special comment. First, the distinction between emblematic memory and loose memory should be understood less as a dichotomy than as a spectrum or better, as a kind of bridge on which people find relatively strong or relatively attenuated connections between personal experience and social experience. On one extreme end of the bridge or spectrum, an emblematic meaning framework shapes personal remembrance so powerfully that a person's experience seems an almost classic version of a group experience. It is worth remembering, however, that emblematic remembrance can gain such cultural power precisely because it uses as "authentic raw material" the testimonial lore and stories that arise from personal experience. On the opposite extreme of the bridge, remembered personal experiences linked to a great social theme or trauma may seem too idiosyncratic to resonate substantially with major emblematic frameworks. Nonetheless, as Maurice Halbwachs demonstrated many years ago, even the most "personal" or individualized memories arise from a social process of remembrance—a familial or group circle that verbalizes and circulates an experience found to be meaningful. In this sense, even a remembrance so idiosyncratic that it connects poorly or loosely to major emblematic frameworks often bears traces of some sort of social process of remembrance and forgetting, and the cultural and political contestations that gave rise to rival emblematic meaning frameworks may well have exerted an indirect influence.[45]

People build their sense of remembered experience at different places in the bridges that connect the emblematic and the loose. Among the proponents of remembrance as salvation, for example, Doña Elena is closer to a classic expression of the key elements of the emblematic framework, while Gabriela (introduced in the Afterword to chapter 1) evinces a more attenuated or fragmentary connection. But at various points along the bridge, what one sees is not a mutually exclusive dichotomy between emblematic group meaning and loose personal experience, but differently balanced interplays between collective and personal remembrance.

Second, as we observed in the cases of goodness lore and remorse lore (Afterword to chapter 2), some kinds of remembrance are socially important yet bear a problematic relationship to emblematic meaning frameworks. Such stories circulate as a cultural lore that tells a powerful truth, but a truth that escapes an easy fit with nationally influential meaning frameworks. The lore may veer away from emblematic story lines, as when remorse stories seem to invert (perversely and tragically) who bears a subjective sense of responsibility for human rights violations, or as when goodness lore inverts the social class or political identity of those who display admirable human solidarity with the persecuted. Or, the lore may seem to fit with emblematic story lines but introduces a threatening double edge. As we have seen, goodness lore, if tied too firmly to memory as rupture, may seem to imply that only the "good" victim (at the extreme, the innocent depoliticized victim) deserves protection from torture and other human rights violations. It may also invite diversionary and cruel debate about the relative goodness of the political choices made by the victim. In short, even as we find the making of emblematic memory methodologically useful to chart the main contours of struggle and meaning related to remembrance, we *also* need to be attentive to a lore of remembrance that breaks away from emblematic moldings and struggles yet circulates and becomes socially meaningful as truth in its own right.

Third, emblematic meaning frameworks develop not only at the level of the national imaginary but also at the level of specific regions, locales, and social groups. This plurality of memory processes complicates and relativizes the interplay of emblematic memory and looser memory lore. Beyond the obvious fact that the specific human groups who constitute "memory knots" seeking to influence the national imaginary are themselves "subnational" networks (even national officials who claim to speak in the voice of the national community and its experience are specifically grounded in regions, institutions, or subcultures that cannot encompass the entire "nation"), there also arises a more subtle issue. A meaning framework that becomes emblematic of remembered experience within a specific locale or subnational grouping may not match up identically with the framework adapted to a struggle to influence the national imaginary. Under such circumstances, a certain relativity qualifies the line of analysis developed thus far. For example, at the level of the national imaginary in the 1990s, we have noted that goodness stories present dangers if attached too firmly—as essential defining elements—to memory as unresolved rupture. One result is that goodness stories circulate somewhat more loosely and flexibly, as a powerful lore. Yet it is also true that at a subnational level—in a barrio commemoration of disappeared youths in La Legua, in a political party such as the Communist Party that suffered persecution, in a human rights organization such as the Agrupación de Familiares de Detenidos-Desaparecidos —the "goodness" that Señora Herminda remembered in her missing children Gerardo and Ernestito can become an essential cornerstone of group memory as unresolved rupture. It defines the full meaning and injustice of the loss; it inspires the group to carry its battles into a contest for the national imaginary.[46]

In short, even as we chart the making and unmaking of collective memory, including emblematic remembrance, at the national level, we must also bear in mind that such processes are driven by actors rooted in specific subcultures, networks, and locales. One result is that actors relativize meaning frameworks, adapting them to the social arena in which they wish to promote an emblematic remembrance. They may even move (ambivalently, in some instances) between one meaning framework and a friendly cousin framework depending on the social arena and circumstances. For example, Colonel Juan and other former army officers can, in the context of a private military commemoration of 11 September within the Military Academy (Escuela Militar), reaffirm their group needs and identities by *celebrating* memory as a national salvation undertaken by patriotic and self-sacrificing soldiers. Here, they are free to energize themselves by remembering or reactivating what others cannot or will not understand. When remembrance issues are discussed in a national arena whose civilian leaders accept the truth of a definitive documenting of human rights violations under military rule, however, Colonel Juan and his colleagues can adapt by promoting memory as a closed box. What is important in this arena is neither to celebrate nor to condemn, but to remember that the country can move ahead only if it cultivates a certain indifference to its volatile past.

These qualifications—the constant interplay rather than dichotomy between the loose and the emblematic, the lore that matters yet escapes enclosure within major meaning frameworks, the adaptations and relativity that define the simultaneous making of remembrance in national and subnational imaginaries—caution against too rigid a reliance on the concepts presented in this chapter. Theorization is a tool, not a formula. Culturally charged memory themes induce messiness and ambiguity precisely because so many persons and groups claim a certain ownership in and valid perspective on the experience. The human processing of a controversial and defining experience cannot be contained within neat conceptual categories or borders.

Nonetheless, the making and unmaking of emblematic memories that selectively draw on loose memory, the knots of bothersome people, times, and places that concentrate collective remembrance and the struggle to shape its meaning—these are useful conceptual tools. They are useful in part because they help us to discern the making of silence. The same process that brings certain meanings, remembrances, and voices to the fore also buries others. For as we are about to see, some human carriers and experiences get pushed to the bottom of the memory box. There, the floor opens and they fall away—into the tomb of oblivion.

Memory Tomb of the Unknown Soldier

The cassette tape of our interview records its peculiar circumstances. There we were, parked on the shoulder of a highway outside of Santiago. The rhythmic whoosh of the cars passing by, the occasional roar of a large truck, the cheery chirping of birds on a bright spring day, Cristián U.'s voice and tears—all found their way onto the tape.[1]

We had ended up on the highway because Cristián almost cancelled the interview. When we were about to begin our talk early that October morning, Cristián had stated that he could not go forward with our meeting. The fear had suddenly overwhelmed him. General Pinochet was still commander in chief of the army, he explained, and the military intelligence services still operated. If I talk about my life as a soldier, maybe something could happen to me or my family, he said. We don't live in a full democracy yet.

We continued to talk. I assured Cristián that we would use a pseudonym for him, and he helped choose it. We agreed to leave Santiago and talk on the side of a highway where no one could overhear fragments of the conversation. As an extra precaution, we would keep his real name off the cassette tape. The truth was that once he had opened the door to talking about his memories, he could not let go. He felt compelled to talk even as he felt afraid to talk.

Born in 1956, Cristián grew up in a working-class family. His father worked as a diesel engine mechanic for a state bus company (Empresa de Transportes Colectivos del Estado), at first in the southern city of Concepción, then in Santiago after the 1962 World Cup. His mother raised the children —Cristián was the third of five—and did embroidery work to bring in additional money. Cristián remembers the early family years as a life of learning to make do on a very limited income, but without suffering hunger and without suffering moral or educational neglect by his parents. It was a life of "a rather dignified poverty," and the medical and pension services of the state company also helped when his father turned out to suffer from diabetes. In addition, Cristián remembers his late father, "of a socialist tendency," with pride. Although poorly educated, Cristián's father had made himself into a good mechanic by watching and doing. In addition, he had a strength of character—"he was very much of the pueblo, a man of struggle and in addition very honest"—that impressed his coworkers, who elected him a union delegate.

As the children moved into adolescence, they began to chart their occupational futures and to contribute to the family income pool. Cristián's older brother completed technical school (the equivalent of an eighth- or a ninth-grade education, supplemented by special skill training), found work at RCA as an electrician, and gave a share of the wages to their mother. His older sister found a job in a shoe factory and also channeled wages into the family fund. These transitions coincided with the emerging political crisis of Chile. Cristián, like his brother, went to technical school. He finished in 1972 and began to work his practicum period as a mechanic in the bus company. But this trajectory was cut short when Cristián was called up in March 1973 to perform his obligatory military service.

Life as a conscript soldier in metropolitan Santiago changed everything. Even before September, Cristián's regiment had been mobilized from time to time, but mainly as theater—a show of force to restore the veneer of order to parts of Santiago that had experienced street troubles. Cristián and the other youngsters in his unit had grown up in times of political turmoil and ascribed a certain normalcy to it. Even when they were called out to restore a sense of order, they did not fully understand how serious a turn Chile was taking in 1973. "We were kids, eighteen, nineteen years old, you know; for us it even became a bit of fun to go out on the streets. . . . We didn't see the gravity of the events at the time. . . . Think of it, at seventeen, eighteen years of age a person isn't very mature, right?"

After 11 September 1973, Cristián and his comrades would grow up quickly. In the weeks that followed, Cristián's regiment, based in the shanty-town zones that sprawl south of Santiago, participated in the sweeps and allanamientos that fell upon the "rather conflictive poblaciones." As we have seen for the case of La Legua (chapter 2), some such sweeps aimed to intimidate the general population of a neighborhood by roughly inspecting all the homes for subversive materials and alleged hidden arms, and by rounding up all the young males for arrest. Some allanamientos, however, also focused on specific individuals to be found and arrested.

When I asked Cristián to tell what happened at a break-in that he had said he would never forget, his composure broke. After his apology ("forgive me for breaking"), and my offer of Kleenex tissue with an observation that everyone has the right to cry, Cristián tried to explain why he had turned so emotional. "I don't know, I, I remember this and it so saddens me because I—Well, I'm a father now [his voice begins to break again] and I wouldn't want such a thing done to my children [now he is crying]. Never!"

In late September or early October, Cristián and a small group of soldiers commanded by a lieutenant with the assistance of a sergeant received orders to arrest a local labor leader and conduct a break-in of his home in a shantytown neighborhood of southern Santiago. "We arrived at that house with orders to tear up everything, the mattresses, furniture, ceilings . . . in order to find weapons, uh, subversive material." As was customary on such operations, the small arresting band (six soldiers in this case) was backed by a larger force of soldiers and vehicles to seal off the area and intimidate neighbors. The labor leader was not at home, but his wife and three children were ordered to lie on the floor face down while the search and ransacking proceeded. The sight and sounds of armed men bursting in to search for their father and take apart the inside of their home frightened the children. The youngest child, perhaps four or five years old, began to cry.

The events Cristián could never forget then ensued quickly. The lieutenant shouted at the child to hush, but to no avail. The child continued to wail. As the shouting and wailing proceeded, the lieutenant grew furious: "I don't know, he entered into a furious state, since the kid wouldn't obey him." Finally, the lieutenant took his rifle butt and smashed the child's jaw. His mother leaped off the floor.

> She throws herself against the lieutenant, "Damned murderer, damned bastard," she shouted, and he hits her with the rifle, the woman falls to the ground. . . . [Cristián pauses, gathers himself.] And he gives an order to a conscript to kill the woman. Then the soldier [Cristián begins to sob]—the conscript doesn't, doesn't obey, he takes his weapon, the rifle, and he throws it at the feet of the lieutenant. He says he's not a murderer, and the lieutenant pulls out his revolver and says, "If you don't kill her, you'll be the one I kill." The moments are so terrible, think of it. . . . So the lieutenant steps forward and shoots the conscript [Cristián is crying more fully], he killed our compañero!
> AUTHOR: The lieutenant killed the conscript?
> CRISTIÁN, HIS VOICE LOUD AND CRYING: The conscript—right in front of us!

The sergeant in the group took control. He hit the lieutenant hard enough in the back to knock him to the floor, then ordered the other three conscripts to disarm him. In a rage, the officer "screamed like a crazy, 'I'll kill all of you, I'm going to kill you all.' " Eventually, some other officers came in to restore order. The lieutenant, who had obviously lost control over his subalterns, was transferred, and Cristián would never see him again. (He later heard rumors that the officer died in a presumed shoot-out with leftists.) The conscript who had refused to shoot the mother—known as "Larita" by his soldier comrades, who had attached a diminutive to his formal last name, Lara—had died quickly from a pistol shot to the head.[2]

Cristián was a survivor. As we spoke, it became evident that Larita symbolized for him the ethical stance that Cristián should have taken, as well as the extreme danger of thinking ethically. As a survivor, Cristián drew the lesson. Questioning an order placed one under suspicion of treason, and the consequences could be severe: "either you obey or you die."

As we spoke, it also became evident that Larita drew into focus Cristián's sense that he had not lived up to the values of the socialist father he loved and admired. During one family visitation time when Cristián was still on duty, his father, saddened by the persecution he saw in Chile, reminded Cristián not to take human life "because my father—he's a very healthy man [in his values]—he asked me not to go kill anyone."

But the realities of life and fear, for a conscript soldier subjected to vertical command and a war mentality, pointed away from his father's values. One wondered or occasionally heard a rumor about what happened to an officer or a conscript considered too hesitant, unreliable, or insubordinate. One worried about how the new lieutenants brought in on an emerging rotation system might react to their subalterns. One feared falling prey to a leftist sniper, if one thought too much on night patrol during curfew. "Many soldiers, lots of folks in the troops who didn't intend to hurt anyone, did it to protect their own skin." Cristián found it difficult to evade the sense that fear and the desire to survive had plunged him into an impossible world.

Even after his release from military service in 1975, the memories would not go away. He suffered nightmares in which he would see the killing of Larita again, and a vivid splattering of Larita's brains. He sensed that even during the day, somewhere in his mind, he was thinking about "what I saw, what I did, what I didn't do, what I could have done and didn't do it, so [these are] things that start to eat away at you bit by bit. Bit by bit it becomes a thing

that's there. You can't get rid of it, you want to forget about it but you can't."
Like other Chileans, Cristián coped with the economic depression of the
mid-1970s by working for a time as a farm laborer in Argentina. He hoped
that the physical distance would also help him get over the past, but he
proved wrong.

Once, before his father died in 1982, Cristián talked openly about his
experiences and they cried together. To his mother, he had been more dis-
honest. "I shared [things] with him, to my mother no, to my mom I never
told her anything. With her I'd just make her think that everything was easy,
that there wasn't any evil, that what was being talked about and what was
being speculated about were a lot of lies. I think my mother died in peace
because of it."

Cristián's fears were not exaggerated. In 1973, about half the soldiers in the
Chilean Army, which numbered about 32,000 troops, were conscripts.[3] As
Colonel Juan (chapter 3) noted when discussing the occasional problem that
beset soldiers during the allanamientos of late September and October
1973, the army had trained its personnel for war, not police work. An additional issue he left unmentioned, however, also complicated the repressive
work of September and October. Draftees tended to come from the humble
social backgrounds that had provided Allende and the Unidad Popular a
political base. Indeed, the armed forces drew in people of all political ten-
dencies in a Chile where politics had become a contest of passionate convictions. Under these circumstances, the military takeover required not
only action to control, isolate, or discipline Constitutionalist officers, and
not only action, such as the October Caravan of Death, to harden the repression and to subordinate apparently "tranquil" provinces and officers to
Santiago.

The takeover also required that even the lowliest soldier—even if he har-
bored leftist sympathies, had leftist relatives, or simply felt repelled by the
repression—understand that duty and vertical command took priority above
all else. Especially in the navy, the stage had been set for such intimidation
by the polemics of August and early September about seditious sailors and
their torture, and about leftist infiltration of the armed forces.[4] Nonetheless,
the idea of Chile as a democracy, unique in Latin America for its tolerance of
political discrepancy and its respect for individual rights, died hard. In some
civilian and military quarters the idea of democracy mutated, after 11 September, into an idea that a soft repression—temporary and civilized, funda-

mentally tolerant of most of those who had taken the wrong political side—might mark the change of regimes. As we saw in Quillota and elsewhere, one consequence, especially in the provinces, was that many persons affiliated with the defeated regime, including local political authorities, turned themselves in voluntarily to the new military authorities. They did not expect, as long as they behaved reasonably under the new regime, that their political defeat or errors would translate into torture, execution, or disappearance. What would happen if soldiers of diverse social and political backgrounds also assumed that a culture of experience with political discrepancy implied that they enjoyed certain rights and protections?

Michel Selim Nash Sáez, an army conscript soldier on duty in the northern province of Iquique in September, perhaps thought along these lines. Only nineteen years old, Nash had been a member of the Young Communists and did not want to participate in the repression. On 11 September his unit was ordered to conduct some allanamientos, but in the words of his mother, "he wasn't a person cut out for such brutality. So, this wasn't for him." Nash talked over his dilemma with a soldier friend and decided that he would present his misgivings to his superiors with a request to be excused from duty. As his mother later heard it, "he explained that he couldn't continue on there, that this wasn't his way of thinking." The officers appeared to understand and granted the request. The permission, consistent with the mutating idea of a traditionally pluralistic and democratic Chile, turned out to be a lie. Arrested upon leaving the base, Nash would be transported to the concentration camp for political prisoners in Pisagua and was permanently disappeared.[5]

Incidents such as these probably occurred infrequently, especially at the conscript level of military life. Precisely because they fed an undercurrent of frightening rumors and lore about what "happened" to soldiers judged hesitant or disloyal, such incidents did not need to happen often. Survivors drew the appropriate lessons from the fears with which they lived. They did what they were told.

Although the allanamiento that led to the killing of Larita haunted Cristián —symbolically, it brought home an intolerable ethic of survival and set him against his father—I sensed in our conversation that something more had been eating away at Cristián.

Most of Cristián's duties in the weeks following 11 September involved not participation in allanamientos that had a specific objective, but night patrol duty during curfews—a more vague and uncertain activity. Cristián remembered the night patrols as tense and frightening. One induced fear in the poblaciones by firing shots in the air to simulate shoot-outs or sniper fire. At the same time, one feared that a real sniper might exist out there in the night, somewhere. One worried, too, that an aggressive officer or a hot-headed soldier might turn dangerous or accusatory.

Finally, there was the problem of understanding one's own strange state of mind as one went out on patrol. As we saw earlier (chapter 3), the idea that conscript soldiers had been drugged into an unnatural aggressiveness entered the lore they told about themselves.

> I don't know it for sure, but there's something to it, I think. Afterwards, later I heard a lot of versions, there was lots of speculating, and I think there was something to it, because they gave us the rancho [slang for the meals given to soldiers]. And they threw something into the food, . . . because a person would go out . . . like eager to destroy, to be brutal, to shoot. We were begging for a shootout, you get it?

Maybe because the beans were of such poor quality, maybe because something had indeed been added—"I'd be lying if I tell you [I know for certain] they put something in it"—they just did not taste right. "They gave us some beans with an acid taste and made us eat it." The result was speculation among the soldiers about what might have been added to the food.[6]

Whatever the explanation of aggressiveness and however varied the individual motivations—Cristián brought up arrogant power-lust, and extreme fear, in addition to possible drugging—the formal procedures to be followed on night patrol did not seem realistic. Upon encountering a civilian during curfew hours, first one was supposed to shout an order that the person halt, then one was supposed to fire in the air. If these measures failed, one could then fire at the person. Given the tension, however, "things went backwards." The state of fear and aggressiveness, compounded by the varying personalities of those on patrol, could create confusion about how to react.

Cristián had circled somewhat warily around the theme of night patrols. For this theme, he seemed to prefer to talk about soldier experiences in general, not personally about the details of his own experience. But the conversation drew us anyway to an obligatory question. While on night patrol, I asked, did you yourself run across a situation in which "you encountered a person during curfew and didn't know what to do?" Here is how Cristián struggled for words.[7]

I, [a short pause] . . . I don't know,—I give thanks to God, and I tell you truly, geez [*puchas*], I don't know, I tell you—Look, I believe there is a God, there's a Supreme Being, and I ask of this God *many* [with some emotion] things. . . . I shot at other people [his voice begins to drop], I fired. I shot when—at moments when my life was in danger, you're cornered in one place and see that over there they're firing at you. . . . I shot, I wounded people also. Killed? I don't know [a pause] . . . and maybe I did, I don't know, [he starts to cry] I don't want to know either. But [crying more] that's the, that, that's the remorse and suffering I carry inside, I'll carry it until I die maybe. You understand? So—[Now he is crying fully and cannot continue talking.]

Cristián and I had touched bottom. Additional details were beside the point. Which mattered more? To know precisely whom he shot, under precisely what circumstances, by precisely which forgotten or twisted details he mediated memory and remorse? Or to know that a lowly conscript soldier, drafted into the dirty work of a terrifying repression, could also experience a devastating rupture without healing? Somewhere in his most interior self, Cristián had come to the ruinous conclusion that he wanted to live too much.

In the memory box of Pinochet's Chile, as of 1996–97, there existed no place for Cristián's voice or remorse. The voices of military memory were controlled from the top. Too many socially determining factors suffocated the possibility of conscript memory as one legitimate cultural expression of military memory—the vertical command ethos of a military still led by Pinochet, the fears of former soldiers about the consequences of breaking silence or speaking in a critical voice, the cultural and media elitism that marginalized dissident expression from the lower layers of society, the all too understandable temptations of memory as a closed box. Former conscripts had not and could not congeal into a meaningful "memory knot" in their own right. The only voices of dissident military memory that carried cultural weight were those of a handful of prominent former officers.

In addition, in the struggles through which Chileans built their collective memory box, conscript soldiers had not become a key symbolic referent for any of the contending memory camps. For reasons that are entirely legitimate, from the perspective of human suffering as well as cultural effectiveness, the afflicted female relative of a disappeared or executed victim became the key social referent of memory as unresolved rupture.

Under the circumstances, Cristián's type of remembrance—a potential alignment with memory as rupture from within a military background—could not "erupt" into the public domain as socially meaningful expression.[8] Loose rather than emblematic, Cristián's memories float in his mind and perhaps among a few confidants. They cannot connect to the social making of memory. His memories and turmoil are a personal problem. From cultural and political points of view, they remain entombed with the experiences of other unknown soldiers.

Yet Cristián's identity and memory split into the superficial and deep layers recognizable to those afflicted by memory as a devastating, still active rupture. In normal everyday life and memory, Cristián carries on like most people. He seems a reasonably competent worker in his brother's shop, an enjoyable conversationalist in networks of male sociability, a reasonably attentive father and husband. Deep inside, however, the lacerating wound refuses to heal. Cristián's brother understands intuitively. Once in a while, at a family affair or party where the point is to have fun, Cristián cannot put deep memory aside. He moves to a corner, where he begins to break down and cry. His older brother comes over, gives him an affectionate pat on the head, and simply says, "Easy, brother, easy."

Conclusion

❀

Memories and Silences of the Heart

On the eve of 1998, the memory question—how to remember the military takeover of 1973, the furious violence against perceived enemies and critics under military rule—remained divisive and potent. It could not be otherwise. Memory had proved central to struggles for political and cultural legitimacy during a quarter century. Memory's power to move people—its role as experienced truth, the meaning of shattering times—transcended simple manipulation and instrumentalism, even as it invited efforts to manipulate. Its connection to life-and-death struggles to save people and remain true to them inspired renewed energy and persistence when the spirits of human rights activists and victim-survivors flagged. In the opposed memory camp, the idea of military rescue "just in time" from bloodbath in a world gone mad could also inspire fierce loyalty. For all sides, too, memory struggles placed into play key rules of the game in the 1990s: the legal precepts governing truth, justice, and accountability; the politicocultural value to be placed on human rights as sine qua non of a civilized and democratic society; the social legitimacy of the new democracy and its undemocratic aspect, oversized zones of military power and political-minority power; and the relative influence of social actors and their voices. The still-present aspects of memory, in the formative years of transition from military rule, meant that struggles over the military past were also struggles to chart the present and future. At stake: the quality and stability of an emerging democracy.

Above all, the memory question overflowed boundaries that might otherwise compartmentalize life and its social actors. Memory connected the political, the moral, and the existential. It sometimes challenged standard political party loyalties and alliances. It entangled the personal and the public. Politics in the 1990s had yielded a certain memory impasse—tense standoffs between majority desire and minority power on truth-and-justice issues, frustrations when seeking cultural conversation across memory camps, returns to a sensation of deadlock or "moving impasse" after breaking a standoff on a particular issue. The Truth and Reconciliation Commission could definitively establish the factual truth of systematic state repression in its 1991 report, but how its documentary foundation might play out in court or affect the military's 1978 self-amnesty law was another matter, another standoff to accept, erode, or somehow break. The civilian government could, after months of hide-and-seek, finally enforce a court order to jail former secret police head Manuel Contreras in 1995, but whether this power would prove precedent or exception was another matter, yet to be resolved.[1]

Yet if politics yielded impasse or return to impasse between distinct memory camps, *experience* rendered the impasse "intimate." The issues in play were more searing and personal and meaningful than routine political struggle or manipulation. For more than one generation, the crisis of 1973 and the transforming world of military rule had made memory a matter of heart as well as mind. The point held for various sides. As Doña Elena had put it, 11 September 1973 had been "the happiest day of my life."

The principal purpose of this book has been to provide human portraits of this world of intimate memory impasse. On the basis of such life stories and their historical contexts, I have also sought to render more real and accessible—and to build a foundation for—a theoretical and analytical understanding of memory struggles as a historical process. In the Chilean case, the process of memory making and struggle unfolded both during and after the times of atrocity. In the culminating theoretical essay (chapter 4), I have sought a language appropriate for the Chilean case, yet informed by and useful for studies of other cases.

Beyond these main purposes and the narratives and arguments to develop them in specific chapters, if one steps back to reconsider the whole, three broad conclusions come into view.

First, the making of memory in Chile was a deeply symbolic process. Precisely for this reason, the line between social memory and personal memory could readily blur. More than recollection with an interpretive slant, memory of shattering and historic times emerged from selective interplays between personal lore and experience on the one hand, frameworks of collective meaning and experience on the other. Such frameworks turned remembrance toward the "emblematic." My story—the story I experienced or heard from my relatives and friends—is the story of Chile. It is an emblem of something larger you see and hear echoed in the public domain. Likewise, the memory camp to which I am drawn puts forth a memory-*truth*, not an arbitrary invention nor a remembrance of the insignificant. Its preferred narratives and emblems—mobilized in the public domain via speeches and mass media reports, court cases and cultural forums, commemorations and demonstrations, live testimony and cultural expression in books, movies, music, art, and photography—are authentic. They capture a meaning and reality that run deep. They evoke and stand for experiences I know to be true.

To be sure, degrees of interplay and fit between personal memory and social memory varied. Doña Elena's remembrance of salvation was more coherent and more deeply entangled with collective memory making than Gabriela's. Some memories remained more "loose" from social anchoring and meaning than others. The case of Cristián, the conscript whose inner devastation could not find social expression, was an extreme example. For social actors building collective memory, moreover, a certain capaciousness —the flexibility to include many individual stories and variations—was essential to achieving cultural influence and authenticity. The memory tent of persecution and awakening could include a Violeta, who emphasized both repression and moral awakening as essential aspects of her life journey and the journey of Chile; and a Ramiro, who accented the isolating and suffocating effects of rural persecution. Emblematic memory was more effective as a framework of meaning, not as prescribed content of facts to remember. Notwithstanding these qualifications, symbolism infused the memory-building process and could merge the public and the intimate, the emblematic and the idiosyncratic.

The symbolic aspect came through in the four persons whose life stories introduced the main memory frameworks influential in Chile on the eve of 1998: salvation, rupture, persecution and awakening, a closed box. Each person turned out to connect to a key social referent, a culturally convincing symbol that embodied emblematic remembrance and invited identification, empathy, or at least respect from broad sectors of society. Doña Elena was not only her own person with her own idiosyncrasies; she also matched up well with the dignified and respectable Chilean woman who demanded salvation from the scarcity, chaos, and fear of violence afflicting Chilean families in 1973. As a mother of disappeared sons, Señora Herminda was a living symbol of the limitless rupture—the mothers and wives who had to bear unprecedented and unending cruelty to life and family—that opened wounds throughout Chile after 11 September 1973. Violeta exemplified the drama of solidarity in the 1970s. Chileans of deep moral conscience found themselves pulled into witnessing a ferocious persecution, and awakening to the call of Christian duty to affirm life and help those in need. Colonel Juan symbolized one of the kinds of people who could lay cultural claim to a closing of the memory box: the soldier who was not a monster but an ordinary person, who had served his country well in desperate times, and who now needed to be allowed to move on. Did connection to such culturally powerful symbols—socially valid identities—condition the ways these individuals came to understand themselves and their memories? I think so, but one cannot provide a definitive answer.

What *can* be verified is appeal to the emblematic. Each person saw inside her or his own experience a parallel or a connection—a kind of distilling in microcosm—to Chile's true and larger reality. This link to the emblematic was not unusual in my interviews in the mid-to-late 1990s, even among the many people who considered themselves "unimportant," nor was it unusual in the documentary trail of memory struggles prior to the mid-1990s. It also cut across memory camps. Consider the heroic and indifferent narratives that put a benign veneer on military rule and minimized the significance of human rights. Doña Elena's family lore confirmed the truth of a heroic memory narrative. Good people and good families across Chile had indeed been brought to economic ruin and insecurity during the Frei-Allende era. They had indeed tasted violence and intimidation, did indeed need rescue from guerrilla armies plotting civil war and Communist dictatorship. They were indeed saved by a military that built a successful country out of ruins. Colonel Juan repeatedly made the point that his indifference to the human rights question—dirty war affected such a tiny group of people on both sides—was the indifference of almost all Chileans. Soldiers were normal people like everyone else. Almost everyone in Chile was unmoved by the human rights question. Almost everyone saw no good reason to keep returning to and quarreling about tough times of war that exacted a modest social cost.

Consider, too, the dissident memory narratives people built to challenge the official story of military rule. Señora Herminda's photos of her disappeared sons, Gerardo and Ernestito, are not only badges of suffering to wear on her sweater at a meeting or a demonstration. The disturbing question on each photo seals the fusion of the personal and the symbolic. Each picture, like those worn by other relatives of the disappeared, is of one missing person, one family's tragedy. The question that accompanies the photo turns the person and the family into an example of something bigger: widespread disappearance as an instrument of state terror. "Where Are They?" is the question, not "Where Is He?" Violeta draws out the connection in a different way. She understands her narrative of persecution and awakening—a life in solidarity work—as a journey of encounter. Through solidarity, I came to meet the true Chile, the true pueblo, my truest self and values.

A second conclusion is that the making of emblematic memories involved not merely differences of perspective and experience, but struggles for legitimacy and primacy. Such struggles were at once cultural and political: arguments to shape values, understandings of reality, and influential social voices; and simultaneously, efforts to shape or restrict the exercise of state power. The making of memory emerged not as a natural or smoothly unfolding process, but in fits and starts, in a rhythm shaped by events that demanded notice, by seasons and places freighted with symbolism, and above all, by motivated social actors. Memory knots—bothersome people, times, and places—interrupted the flow and reflexes of unthinking life, insisted that the social body take notice. They turned struggles about the past into struggles to shape the present.

We can see traces of the struggle aspect of memory making in various ways: in chronology, narrative, and body language. The overlapping chronologies of emblematic memory frameworks bore witness to intense contesting of the still-present past. Raw power and violence allowed for strong projection of memory as salvation into the public domain in 1973–76, as part of a campaign to build a free hand to remake Chile for the long run rather than accede to a soft interim of military rule. Organizers of dissident memory frameworks—ruptures with no end in sight, persecutions that also spark witnessing and awakening—had to learn how to survive and build influence amidst dictatorship. They only began cracking into the public domain coherently and forcefully during 1975–79. By 1978–79, as dissenters gained experience and put greater pressure on official memory-truths, and as their challenges coincided with splits and tensions at the level of high politics (internal junta tensions and international tensions), a new politics of memory began emerging from above. The salvation of Chile had been a necessary and sad stage, successfully concluded. To build a bright and unified future required a closing of the memory box and the conflicts it sparked. Closing the memory box yielded key legal corollaries: an amnesty for the "combatants" in 1978, a new Constitution in 1980.

In sum, the basic chronology of memory creation and influence cannot be understood apart from struggles over legitimacy and power. Not surprisingly, during 1978–82, when memory as a closed box emerged as a new official narrative arguing for a conscious forgetting of ugly times, the idea of "memory" itself—as a sacred struggle against "forgetting"—gained traction as cultural language and rallying cry.[2]

Beyond chronology, one can see traces of memory struggle in individual life stories. At one level, the connection emerges in the spoken narratives. Some such traces are subtle. For example, Doña Elena can openly acknowledge—over the objection of her husband, let us remember—a certain propaganda war by her own side, to tear down the other side's myths and define the true nature of military rule and salvation. But more subtle traces also appear if one compares her narrative of the mid-to-late 1990s, which conceded the reality of human rights violations but framed them as modest social cost, with the flat denials that marked her earlier discourse. The retreat emerged under the pressure of an ongoing memory fight. The balance of the conflict shifted as a result of the cultural and political impact of findings by the Truth and Reconciliation Commission in 1990–91.

Señora Herminda's spoken narrative also reflects memory struggle in ways obvious and not so obvious. The experience of always having had to fight against misinformation and official stories to discover the truth about her disappeared children infuses her narrative of remembrance. More subtly, a certain *consistency* appears in the whole of her life story, notwithstanding the profound rupture she suffered and suffers. Life in a working-class shantytown built up from scratch in the 1950s, and alignment with the subculture of Communist politics, had taught her the value of struggling for one's rights—not alone, but collectively. Without a social struggle and a combining of forces, one could expect little justice. Her experience with military dictatorship is of a piece with this larger life lesson, even though the injustice committed was far more cruel and shattering than anything she could have imagined in the 1950s or 1960s.

At another level, the connection between life stories and memory as a process of desperate struggle came through in body language, not simply in words. Recall the restlessness of Violeta when our interview turned toward Lonquén, the abandoned lime ovens where remains of the disappeared were for the first time discovered in December 1978. Lonquén not only became a major emblem of the dissident memory camp; it constituted a breakthrough within a devastating and conflictual experience. Lonquén provided the first hard forensic proof—after years of dismissal and questioning of credibility by state authorities and officialist media—that relatives of the disappeared had told the truth about permanent and denied abduction of their loved ones. It also forced direct confrontation with the reality that disappearance probably meant that a relative suffered bodily cruelty and death. Violeta's body language—the sudden squeezing of the hands, the pulling at the nails—conveyed the enormity of the memory struggle more quickly than her words.

Consider, too, the time when words and body language diverged. Colonel Juan's calm narrative of indifference was at first belied only mildly if at all. He needed to clear his throat when he explained that not much had happened, that people overdramatized military rule, that political violence was rather unimportant. The more blatant body language suggesting something more complex and conflicted came later, when he could not let me out his office door—and kept standing there with me to make sure, passionately and again and again, that I truly understood that practically everyone in Chile was indifferent to the human rights theme, that it was a marginal issue.

It was the body language, a surprise that turned into a puzzle, that inspired me to keep investigating and wondering and eventually led me to the Quillota massacre. Memory as a closed box and a reassuring tranquility bore traces of a struggle to tame the explosive.

The interpretive approach to the memory question taken here argues for a process of competing selective remembrances. In times of a great and shattering turn, as a sense of unprecedented crisis and violence takes hold and spreads trauma and shock, people come to struggle about ways to define meaning and draw legitimacy from the experience. Social actors seek to define what is true and what matters about the experience, and thereby resolve the problems they consider urgent. During the times of atrocity as well as the subsequent transition, they pit one memory framework against another, testimony against testimony. The necessary selectivity of such memory making renders a memory-against-forgetting dichotomy too narrow and restrictive for purposes of analysis. But it also suggests a key byproduct and a third major conclusion: the making of memory is also the making of silence.[3]

Two aspects of silence making as inherently tied to memory making are obvious. First, consider selectivity. Making emblematic memory requires a highlighting of that which is significant and demands attention, a marginalizing of that which is beside the point or plays into the hands of the other memory camp. Partisans of memory as salvation had every reason to focus attention on the Frei-Allende years as root cause and justification of "war" against violent subversives, and of extraordinary state powers to cleanse and transform Chilean society and politics. Activists who built counterofficial memories under military rule rightfully saw the pre-1973 focus as a diversionary tactic—a way to silence and eventually erase the reality of massive unjustifiable atrocities by the state against a portion of its own citizenry, committed despite the absence of armed insurgency. One group's necessary memory focus becomes another group's necessary silence.

A second obvious link between memory and silence occurs when we consider memory as a closed box. Its entire premise is a certain "will to forget," that is, to silence that which is remembered but too explosive or intractable to air publicly.

In a sense, the Afterwords that follow each chapter of this book have steadily built up an argument about silence, both its obvious and less obvious aspects. On the one hand, they have exposed the diversity of motives for silence, as a cultural response integrally tied to remembrance. Gabriela, the child who feared for the life of her father in times of urban land invasion, at bottom believes in memory as salvation. But she is attracted to silence. The human rights problem is intractable; discussions of military times turn quarrelsome and make her out to be a less caring person than she wants to be. In public and in most social settings, memory as a closed box has its virtues. The DINA agent confronted by Mónica on a downtown Santiago street has deeper reason to hold to a code of silence. The memory impasse may erode if one forgets that it is dangerous to get drawn into conversation across camps. Activists and victim-survivors may succeed in besmirching the reputation or even placing in criminal jeopardy people once defined as serving the country.

The Afterwords also brought into view more subtle aspects of memory tied to silence: touchy taboo areas, and the problem of social voice. As we have seen, personal lore serves as a kind of raw material for the making of emblematic memory. Yet among the memory lore that matters—that circulates and seems to capture experienced truths—are rumors and stories that sit uneasily with major memory frameworks. They go astray from standard story lines, raise issues that might lessen cultural appeal, and risk unsettling a proper understanding of responsibility and victimization. In a word, some memory lore treads on the touchy.

The paradoxical result, as we saw for goodness lore and especially remorse lore (Afterword to chapter 2), is a weave of memory and silence. On the one hand, the lore threads its way around because it is so meaningful to people. Relatives wish to remember the goodness and idealism of their loved ones; friends wish to remember the goodness and solidarity of their lost comrades. The qualities of a Lucio Angulo, reduced to an animal in chains yet somehow able to save Ramiro by resisting pressure to identify him, draw out the magnitude of what has been destroyed. People also remember the curious compelling exception: the prison guard who cared about the prisoners, the soldier who apologized for having to conduct a house raid. The exception proves the rule of cruelty yet somehow reaffirms the possibility of humanity. In the hands of an Ariel Dorfman, it can inspire a moving poetry of possibility.[4] Nor can Ramiro, Claudia, and others forget the remorse of Señora María Verónica as she searched for René Burdiles, the disappeared son who—at her behest, rumor had it—turned himself in voluntarily to carabineros at Puerto Octay. What an overpowering example of the naïveté and confusions, the descent into inferno and tragedy, that spread in the provinces of Chile after 11 September 1973!

On the other hand, the lore is dangerous and can therefore also inspire silence. Even goodness lore can become touchy if taken too far—if carried into an unfriendly public arena that might question the goodness of a victim's pre-1973 political choices, or sever the essential point that human beings have rights to life, bodily integrity, and due process independent of their "goodness." More touchy still is the question of remorse. Misinterpreted, the lore of remorse and self-questioning by those who suffered can seem to invert perversely the map of who is responsible and who is victimized. It can seem to play into the hands of perpetrators who reject making their own remorseful acknowledgment of responsibility for atrocities. Small wonder that remorse is usually a kind of underground lore that circulates among the few and remains guarded from the many. Taboo areas are both compelling and unsettling; they tend to encourage a tight weave of memory with silence.

Finally, the isolation and turmoil of Cristián, the conscript who wanted to live too much, brought us face to face with another subtle tie of memory and silence: the making of effective social voices. At bottom, human actors make and dispute emblematic memories. They organize themselves into "knots" that demand attention to their memory-truth and experience and push their way into the collective imagination. Some such actors are more politically powerful than others. Some learn to organize more effectively than others. Some enjoy more cultural respectability or social advantage and connection than others. The struggle to make influential emblematic memories—my experience, my group's memory-truth, is the truth of Chile—is also a struggle about whose social voice counts. The raising up of some social voices to a position of influence is also a silencing of other potential voices. In the Chilean world of intimate memory impasse, Cristián is a stark reminder that the process of memory struggle left little effective room for one potential voice: conscripts and low-rank troops who experienced fright, coercion, rupture—and remorse.

The world of memory impasse was actually a world in motion, not a world frozen. Over the course of a quarter century after 1973, human rights and memory struggles produced frustration after frustration, yet the sensation of frustration could also be misleading. Beyond the specific lives saved and the individuals and families who received a measure of solace or repair, the people who built a memory camp of rupture, persecution, and awakening also achieved something larger: cultural sensitization to human rights and democracy as values in their own right.[5]

By the mid-to-late 1990s, a quarter century of cultural argument had especially transformed the ways people understood and valued the term *human rights,* a minor part of cultural vocabulary in the 1960s. What could be legitimately stated in public by any political actor, including those who had supported military rule, about the use of state violence against citizens had changed dramatically since the 1970s. State violence at the margins of legitimate due process respecting fundamental human rights could not be condoned or treated as a nonissue, not even in times of stress or emergency.

Even in the times of impasse in the 1990s, when majority desire on truth-and-justice issues kept running up against de facto powers of a political minority, and an army still under command of General Pinochet, time did not really stand still. Chileans eroded or broke impasses on specific issues—the truth of systematic state violation of human rights, the criminal accountability of the former head of the secret police, among others—while returning to tense standoffs on related specific issues. This was the rolling impasse of a society in (slow) motion, not impasse once and for all. In 1998, when Pinochet retired from his post as army commander in chief and later found himself arrested in London, political and cultural circumstances changed. Motion on the memory question accelerated, a more decisive (if still partial) unraveling of impasse soon became apparent. But that is another story for another book.

Abbreviations Used in Notes
and Essay on Sources

AAVPS	Archivo Audiovisual de la Vicaría de Pastoral Social (Santiago)
ACNVR	Archivo de la Comisión Nacional de Verdad y Reconciliación (as incorporated into Archivo de la Corporación Nacional de Reparación y Reconciliación)
ACPPVG	Archivo, Corporación Parque Por La Paz Villa Grimaldi
AFDD	Agrupación de Familiares de Detenidos-Desaparecidos
AFDDCD	AFDD, Centro de Documentación
AGAS	Archivo Gráfico del Arzobispado de Santiago
AGPHH	Archivo Gráfico Personal de Helen Hughes
AGPMAL	Archivo Gráfico Personal de Miguel Angel Larrea
AICT	Archivo Intendencia Cautín (Temuco; subsequently incorporated into Archivo Regional de Araucanía, Temuco)
APAF	Archivo Personal de Alicia Frohmann
APDPC	Archivo Personal de Diego Portales Cifuentes
APER	Archivo Personal de Eugenia Rodríguez
APJCC	Archivo Personal de Juan Campos Cifuentes
APMEH	Archivo Personal de María Eugenia Hirmas
APMM	Archivo Personal de "MM"
APSS	Archivo Personal de Sol Serrano
APTV	Archivo Personal de Teresa Valdés
ASVS	Arzobispado de Santiago, Vicaría de la Solidaridad
ASXX	Archivo Siglo XX del Archivo Nacional
BF	Biblioteca de FLACSO (Facultad Latinoamericana de Ciencias Sociales–Chile)
BF, AEH	BF, Archivo Eduardo Hamuy
BN	Biblioteca Nacional
CODEPU	Comité de Defensa de los Derechos del Pueblo
CODEPUCD	CODEPU, Centro de Documentación
DETDES	ASVS, *Detenidos desaparecidos: Documento de trabajo,* 8 vols. (Santiago: ASVS, 1993)
ECO	Educación y Comunicaciones
ECOCD	ECO, Centro de Documentación
FASIC	Fundación de Ayuda Social de las Iglesias Cristianas
FAV	Fundación de Documentación y Archivo de la Vicaría de la Solidaridad, Arzobispado de Santiago
FSA	Fundación Salvador Allende, Centro de Documentación (Santiago)

FSA, ASI	FSA, Archivo Sergio Insunza
ICNVR	Comisión Nacional de Verdad y Reconciliación, *Informe de la Comisión Nacional de Verdad y Reconciliación,* 2 vols. in 3 books (Santiago: Ministerio Secretaría General de Gobierno, 1991)
ICTUSCD	Ictus, Centro de Documentación
LHORM	Ascanio Cavallo Castro, Manuel Salazar Salvo, and Oscar Sepúlveda Pacheco, *La historia oculta del régimen militar: Chile, 1973–1988* (1988; reprint, Santiago: Antártica, 1990)
LHOT	Ascanio Cavallo, *La historia oculta de la transición: Memoria de una época, 1990–1998* (Santiago: Grijalbo, 1998)
PIDEE	Fundación para la Protección de la Infancia Dañada por los Estados de Emergencia
PIDEECD	PIDEE, Centro de Documentación
PUC	Princeton University Library Pamphlet Collection, Chile ("Main" and "Supplement" collections, as microfilmed by Scholarly Resources, Inc., by agreement with Princeton University Library)
SHSWA	State Historical Society of Wisconsin Archives
TVNCD	Televisión Nacional, Centro de Documentación

Notes

Introduction to the Trilogy: Memory Box of Pinochet's Chile

1 Guillermo O'Donnell's pioneering work is a fine guide to social science scholarship on bureaucratic authoritarianism, and (to a more limited extent) subsequent literatures on transitions and democratization. See esp. *Modernization
and Bureaucratic-Authoritarianism*, 2nd ed. (1973; Berkeley: University of California Press, 1979); *Bureaucratic Authoritarianism: Argentina, 1966–1973, in
Comparative Perspective* (Berkeley: University of California Press, 1988); and the
adapted reprints and mature reflections in *Counterpoints: Selected Essays on
Authoritarianism and Democratization* (Notre Dame, Ind.: University of Notre
Dame Press, 1999). Cf. David Collier, ed., *The New Authoritarianism in Latin
America* (Princeton, N.J.: Princeton University Press, 1979); Manuel Antonio
Garretón, *El proceso político chileno* (Santiago: FLACSO, 1983); Guillermo O'Don-
nell, Phillippe Schmitter, and Laurence Whitehead, eds., *Transitions from Au-
thoritarian Rule: Prospects for Democracy*, 4 vols. (Baltimore: Johns Hopkins
University Press, 1986); and Scott Mainwaring, Guillermo O'Donnell, and J.
Samuel Valenzuela, eds., *Issues in Democratic Consolidation: The New South
American Democracies in Comparative Perspective* (Notre Dame, Ind.: University
of Notre Dame Press, 1992). It should be noted that a comparative spirit marks
this social science literature and often includes consideration of authoritarian
regimes and democratic transitions in southern Europe.

For fine work that built on this literature while extending it in new directions
—toward themes such as the culture of fear, the fate and resilience of labor, and
the dilemmas of transitional justice—see Juan E. Corradi, Patricia Weiss Fagen,
and Manuel Antonio Garretón, eds., *Fear at the Edge: State Terror and Resistance
in Latin America* (Berkeley: University of California Press, 1992); Paul W.
Drake, *Labor Movements and Dictatorships: The Southern Cone in Comparative
Perspective* (Baltimore: Johns Hopkins University Press, 1996); and A. James
McAdams, ed., *Transitional Justice and the Rule of Law in New Democracies*
(Notre Dame, Ind.: University of Notre Dame Press, 1997).

For a superb recent reflection, rooted in Holocaust history, on the larger
connections of modernity, technocracy, and state terror in the twentieth century, see Omer Bartov, *Mirrors of Destruction: War, Genocide, and Modern Identity*
(New York: Oxford University Press, 2000).

2   For a bottom-up perspective in which protest becomes the obverse social phenomenon—an explosion and realization of an underground potential amidst
    top-down control and repression—see, e.g., Cathy Lisa Schneider, *Shantytown
    Protest in Pinochet's Chile* (Philadelphia: Temple University Press, 1995). For the
    recent conceptual turn by historians of Latin America that eschews the analytical dichotomy of top down versus bottom up, in favor of focus on more interactive, mutually constituting, and mediated political dynamics, see Steve J. Stern,
    "Between Tragedy and Promise: The Politics of Writing Latin American History in the Late Twentieth Century," in *Reclaiming the Political in Latin American
    History: Essays from the North*, ed. Gilbert M. Joseph (Durham, N.C.: Duke
    University Press, 2001), 32–77, esp. 41–47. Mexican historians have been very
    prominent in this turn: e.g., Gilbert M. Joseph and Daniel Nugent, eds., *Everyday Forms of State Formation: Revolution and the Negotiation of Rule in Modern
    Mexico* (Durham, N.C.: Duke University Press, 1994); Florencia E. Mallon,
    Peasant and Nation: The Making of Postcolonial Mexico and Peru (Berkeley: University of California Press, 1995); Mary Kay Vaughan, *Cultural Politics in Revolution: Teachers, Peasants, and Schools in Mexico, 1930–1940* (Tucson: University of
    Arizona Press, 1997).

3   The death-and-disappearance figures have received the most attention and require a detailed explanation. For tabulation of individual deaths and disappearances documented by Chile's two official commissions (the Truth and
    Reconciliation Commission of 1990–91, often nicknamed the Rettig Commission after its chair, and the follow-up organism known as Corporation of Repair
    and Reconciliation), see Comisión Chilena de Derechos Humanos (hereinafter
    CCHDH), *Nunca más en Chile: Síntesis corregida y actualizada del Informe Rettig*
    (Santiago: LOM, 1999), esp. 229. The state-certified figures run as follows:
    2,905 cases documented as death or disappearance by state agents or those in
    their hire, and 139 deaths by political violence, which in most instances involved the shooting of civilians by state agents in curfew hours.

        The conservative methodology for an estimated toll of 3,500–4,500 deaths
    and disappearances is based on several factors, beyond the slowly growing pile
    of anecdotal evidence of individual cases evident through newspaper accounts,
    my field research, and knowledge acquired in human rights and lawyer circles.
    On the latter point, see, e.g., the testimony of the former chair of Chile's Truth
    and Reconciliation Commission, Raúl Rettig, in Margarita Serrano's interview-
    book, *La historia de un "bandido": Raúl Rettig* (Santiago: Los Andes, 1999),
    83, 89.

        First among the factors I have considered is an important account by Adam
    Schesch, a U.S. survivor of arrest at the National Stadium in September 1973,
    which documents probable deaths of some 400 additional persons at the National Stadium. Schesch and his then wife, Pat Garret-Schesch, were detained
    in a part of the stadium that enabled them to count meticulously squads of

prisoners taken out for execution and to hear the machine-gun fire cutting them down (in some instances, the prisoners sang just before execution), despite the use of the stadium's large ventilator fans to muffle sounds in the holding cells and lockers away from the field. Schesch returned to Chile in May 2002 to provide sworn testimony in criminal investigations by Judge Juan Guzmán. See his interview in *El Siglo*, 24-V-02; cf. the 1973 press conference and congressional testimony documents in SHSWA, Adam Schesch Papers, tape 823A, reel 3 (press conference, 2-X-73), and Manuscript 534. I am also grateful to him for numerous conversations about his experiences in Chile and at the National Stadium. Schesch's testimony raises the estimate toward 3,500, even if one does not assume that for each session of group execution, about an equal number of prisoners were taken out to the central field from the other side of the stadium. (In one instance, Schesch was able to infer such a two-sided grouping practice, by subtracting the number of people he saw removed from his side from the total number of prisoners mentioned by a soldier returning to his area.)

Second, the fear factor inhibited presentation of cases (or adequate corroboration of them), especially in countryside and provincial settings and in cases of persons not prominent in political party or other activism. The case of the roundup of leftists and peasants in Quillota in January 1974 is extremely suggestive because it offers a rare opportunity to document the rural anonymity and fear problem in quantitative terms. The documentary trail for specific individuals enabled the state's Truth and Reconciliation Commission to demonstrate definitively the deaths or disappearances of eight individuals in the Quillota roundup and massacre, but the Catholic Church's Vicariate of Solidarity files had inside information (two anonymous conscript testimonies) indicating the massacred group numbered thirty-three. In this instance, the ratio of anonymous to known deaths is chilling: about three to one! For detailed discussion and documentation, see Book One, chapter 3, of this trilogy.

Compounding the anonymity and fear problem were ethnic social barriers, and indigenous cultural interpretations of links between social relationships and events of death and misfortune, in southern areas that had substantial Mapuche populations and were subject to fierce repression. For an important in-depth study, see Roberta Bacic Herzfeld, Teresa Durán Pérez, and Pau Pérez Sales, *Muerte y desaparición forzada en la Araucanía: Una aproximación étnica* (Temuco and Santiago: Ediciones Universidad Católica de Temuco and LOM, 1998). If one sets aside the Santiago Metropolitan Region and assumes that elsewhere the fear-and-anonymity factor screened out definitive individual documentation by the democratic state of only one-third of actual deaths and disappearances, the toll in the provinces rises by about 587. This pushes the conservative estimate up to the 4,000–4,100 zone. (For a breakdown of official figures by regions, see CCHDH, *Nunca más en Chile*, 231.)

Last, assigning a more modest fear-and-anonymity factor (15–20 percent) to the Santiago Metropolitan Region, while setting aside the National Stadium figures modified by the Schesch testimony to avoid double-counting, pushes the estimate toward 4,500.

Under the circumstances, a 3,500–4,500 estimate is quite conservative. The reality may have been higher. It is noteworthy that this estimate squares well with testimony given to the Chilean Senate Human Rights Commission in 1999 by former agents of the military government, stating that actual disappearances amounted to more than 2,000 (about 800 beyond the cases documented by the state). See the disclosure by the chair, Senator Jorge Lavandero, in *La Tercera*: www.tercera.cl, 13-VII-00; see also *Clarín* (Buenos Aires), 14-VII-00. This estimate also squares well with the assumption that in at least half the 1,289 alleged cases of death or disappearance by human rights violations or political violence presented to the two commissions, and for which the commissions could *not* establish definitive proof, the cases were genuine rather than frivolous. For statistics on cases presented but not definitively proved, see Corporación Nacional de Reparación y Reconciliación, *Informe a Su Excelencia el Presidente de la República sobre las actividades desarrolladas al 15 de mayo de 1996* (Santiago: La Nación, 1996), 19 (Cuadro 1).

Finally, it should be noted that this rather conservative estimate in no way disparages the superb work of Chile's Truth and Reconciliation Commission and its follow-up Corporation of Repair and Reconciliation. Based on the 3,500–4,500 estimate, the two organisms managed under adverse circumstances to account, on a definitive and individualized basis, for some 65–85 percent of the toll—without subsequent disproof of a single case. This is a remarkable achievement. It also sufficed to demonstrate the systematic and massive quality of repression.

The other figures do not require as detailed a discussion here. For the technically complex issue of torture estimates by rigorous definition, a full documented discussion is offered in trilogy Book Three, chapter 2. For documented political arrests, the 82,000 baseline figure is based on the 42,386 arrests acknowledged by the regime as of 6 February 1976, and an additional 40,043 arrests registered by the Santiago Catholic Church's Vicariate of Solidarity once it began operating in 1976, cited in FAV, caja A. T. no. 2, Casos: "Algunas cifras sobre atentados a los derechos humanos durante el régimen militar [1990?]." The more realistic yet conservative estimate of 150,000 to 200,000 is based on discussion with José Zalaquett, 27-X-01, who is exceptionally well informed and rigorous in methodology and who has included short-term political detentions (at least a day) via crackdowns and roundups in the poblaciones, along with the more long-term cases. Zalaquett's background and expertise, and his penchant for conservative methodology, are documented in Books Two and Three of this trilogy. For exile estimates, which include both an initial wave impelled by political persecution and later waves impelled by mixed political and economic motives, see Thomas Wright and Rody Oñate, *Flight from Chile: Voices of Exile* (Albuquerque: University of New Mexico Press, 1998), esp. 8 (note); for a serious estimate as high as 400,000, see Carmen Norambuena Carrasco, "Exilio y retorno: Chile 1973–1994," in *Memoria para un nuevo siglo: Chile, miradas a la segunda mitad del siglo XX*, ed. Mario Garcés et al. (Santiago: LOM, 2000), 178 esp. n. 13.

4 The assumptions about a "soft" coup in a fundamentally law-abiding and democratic Chile, and the related issue of voluntary compliance with arrest lists and orders, are thoroughly documented in the trilogy. See Book One, chapter 3; Book Two, chapters 1–2. For the pattern of voluntary compliance, see also the case files assembled in DETDES.

5 The Brazilian case gave rise to a pioneering early study that documented political nonradicalism and conservatism among a substantial sector of shantytown dwellers, a finding that seemed counterintuitive at the time. See Janice E. Perlman, *The Myth of Marginality: Urban Poverty and Politics in Rio de Janeiro* (Berkeley: University of California Press, 1976), esp. 162–91.

6 North of Chile, Peru also succumbed to a "new" style of military government in 1968. The Peruvian military, however, followed a different path, albeit one influenced by the climate of mobilization and polarization about injustice. Led by General Juan Velasco Alvarado, it launched a "revolution" of Left-leaning reforms, including expropriation of foreign oil holdings, an agrarian reform in the highlands and coastal provinces, and worker cooperatives. Nonetheless, the result was a giant swath of military regimes in South America by the early-to-mid 1970s. Another important result was that the Nixon administration saw Peru and Chile, after Allende's election in 1970, as a large contiguous territory hostile to U.S. interests and propitious to Left politics. The forthcoming book by John Dinges (tentatively entitled *The Condor Years*), and Peter Kornbluh, *The Pinochet File: A Declassified Dossier on Atrocity and Accountability* (New York: New Press, 2003), cast fresh light on transnational aspects of the rise of "dirty war" regimes, in large part through declassified U.S. documents released in the Clinton administration and through use of the Freedom of Information Act.

The Southern Cone experience gave rise to a small industry of fine analytical and comparative writings by political scientists and sociologists, first about authoritarianism and the new style of dictatorships and subsequently about problems of democratic transition. See note 1 in this chapter.

7 See Kathryn Sikkink, "The Emergence, Evolution, and Effectiveness of the Latin American Human Rights Network," in *Constructing Democracy: Human Rights, Citizenship, and Society in Latin America*, ed. Elizabeth Jelin and Eric Hershberg (Boulder, Colo.: Westview Press, 1996), 59–84, esp. 63–64. Cf. Margaret E. Keck and Kathryn Sikkink, *Activists Beyond Borders: Advocacy Networks in International Politics* (Ithaca, N.Y.: Cornell University Press, 1998); for

more on Chile and transnational human rights agendas, *NACLA Report on the Americas* 36:3 (November–December 2002): thematic issue on "NACLA: A 35 Year Retrospective"; and Book Two, chapter 3, of this trilogy.

8   The myth of Chilean exceptionalism is well known to scholars. For a striking example of Allende's effort to invoke it, amidst grave crisis, see trilogy Book Two, Afterword to chapter 1. Cf. Marc Cooper, *Pinochet and Me: A Chilean Anti-memoir* (London: Verso, 2001), 81. The myth was most influential in middle-class urban society and in political elite circles; the forthcoming studies of Florencia Mallon and Claudio Barrientos on southern regions and (in Mallon's case) indigenous Mapuche peoples will do much to clarify the implicit regional, class, and ethnoracial parameters of such beliefs.

9   Two of the finest works that argue along these lines, and from which I have learned much, are Tomás Moulian, *Chile Actual: Anatomía de un mito* (Santiago: LOM, 1997); and Tina Rosenberg, *Children of Cain: Violence and the Violent in Latin America* (1991; reprint, New York: Penguin, 1992), 333–87. Cf. Cooper, *Pinochet and Me*. Significantly, Rosenberg also ponders the German problem. "Sophistication," she writes, "was not the solution . . . The more cultured the Chileans were, the more willing they appeared to blind themselves to what was going on around them" (380).

For recent work in Chile that evinces both the pervasiveness of the memory-versus-forgetting dichotomy and intellectual efforts to break out of its confines, see Mario Garcés et al., *Memoria para un nuevo siglo*. Cf. Nelly Richard, ed., *Políticas y estéticas de la memoria* (Santiago: Cuarto Propio, 2000). On memory as a process of competing selective remembrance within a society's wider political and cultural struggles, see, aside from chapter 4 in this book, the seminal theoretical essay by Argentine scholars Elizabeth Jelin and Susana G. Kaufman, "Layers of Memories: Twenty Years After in Argentina," in *The Politics of War Memory and Commemoration*, ed. T. G. Ashplant, Graham Dawson, and Michael Roper (New York: Routledge, 2000), 89–110; and the fuller reflection in Jelin, *Los trabajos de la memoria* (Madrid: Siglo XXI, 2002). New doctoral research on Chile with a regional focus informed by similar theoretical perspectives includes Lessie Jo Frazier, "Memory and State Violence in Chile: A Historical Ethnography of Tarapacá, 1890–1995" (PhD diss., University of Michigan, 1998); and Claudio Barrientos, "Emblems and Narratives of the Past: The Cultural Construction of Memories and Violence in Peasant Communities of Southern Chile, 1970–2000" (PhD diss., University of Wisconsin, Madison, 2003).

10 My fuller reflection on the problem of representing the impossible, a theme that haunts discussion of relationships between "history" and "memory," is presented in trilogy Book Three, Afterword to chapter 2. There I explore searing human experiences and inherent narrative dilemmas as they related to the work of Chile's National Truth and Reconciliation Commission. For the

history-versus-memory problem as conceptualized by Pierre Nora, see his multivolume memory project, *Realms of Memory: The Construction of the French Past,* ed. Lawrence C. Kritzman, trans. Arthur Goldhammer (French ed. 7 vols., 1984–92; English ed. 3 vols., New York: Columbia University Press, 1996–98), esp. "General Introduction: Between Memory and History," 1:1–23, cf. xv–xxiv. For helpful context and critique, less bound to a history-versus-memory dichotomy, see Natalie Zemon Davis and Randolph Starn, "Introduction" to *representations* 26 (spring 1989), thematic issue "Memory and Counter-memory," 1–6; and Tony Judt, "A la Recherche du Temps Perdu," *New York Review of Books* (3-XII-98), 51–58. Cf. the history-memory problem as developed in Yosef Hayim Yerushalmi, *Zakhor: Jewish History and Jewish Memory* (Seattle: University of Washington Press, 1982). See also related reflections by Amos Funkenstein, "Collective Memory and Historical Consciousness," *History and Memory* 1, no. 1 (1989): 5–26; and David Myers, "Remembering *Zakhor:* A Super-Commentary," *History and Memory* 4, no. 2 (1992): 129–46 (with reply by Funkenstein, 147–48). For a perceptive and multifaceted brief reflection on the relationship of history and memory, Jelin, *Los trabajos de la memoria,* 63–78. For a fuller discussion and guide to literature, and the related problem of representation, an excellent starting point is recent work by Dominick LaCapra, *History and Memory after Auschwitz* (Ithaca, N.Y.: Cornell University Press, 1998); and *Writing History, Writing Trauma* (Baltimore: Johns Hopkins University Press, 2001). Cf. Michael Bernard-Donals and Richard Glejzer, *Between Witness and Testimony: The Holocaust and the Limits of Representation* (Albany: State University of New York Press, 2001).

11 Benedetti's phrase ("el olvido está lleno de memoria") appears on the wall of remembrance of known political prisoners killed or disappeared at the largest torture camp of the DINA (secret police, formally Dirección de Inteligencia Nacional), Villa Grimaldi, inaugurated as a Peace Park in 1997. See also the contribution of Mireya García Ramírez, a leader-activist of the Agrupación de Familiares de Detenidos-Desaparecidos (AFDD; Association of Relatives of the Detained-Disappeared), in Garcés et al., *Memoria para un nuevo siglo,* 447–50. The notion of "obstinate memory" was coined by documentary filmmaker Patricio Guzmán, in his moving *Chile: La memoria obstinada* (1997, available on video via First Run Icarus Films).

Introduction to Book One: Remembering Pinochet's Chile

1 For a theorized analytical approach to intersections of memory and generation, a fine starting point is Harold Marcuse, *Legacies of Dachau: The Uses and Abuses of a Concentration Camp, 1933–2001* (New York: Cambridge University Press, 2001). Cf. reflections in Elizabeth Jelin, *Los trabajos de la memoria* (Madrid:

Siglo XXI, 2002), 117–33; and for a revealing Chilean case study, see Katherine Hite, *When the Romance Ended: Leaders of the Chilean Left, 1968–1998* (New York: Columbia University Press, 2000).

2 See James E. Young, *The Texture of Memory: Holocaust Memorials and Meanings* (New Haven, Conn.: Yale University Press, 1993); and Young, *At Memory's Edge: After-Images of the Holocaust in Contemporary Art and Architecture* (New Haven, Conn.: Yale University Press, 2000). It is worth noting that in his earlier book and research cycle (on Israel as well as Europe), Young also illuminated the importance of sites in time: e.g., "When a Day Remembers: A Performative History of *Yom ha-Shoah*," *History and Memory* 2, no. 2 (1990): 54–75. For the broader context of memorialization in Germany, see also Rudy Koshar, *Germany's Transient Pasts: Preservation and National Memory in the Twentieth Century* (Chapel Hill: University of North Carolina Press, 1998).

3 For Nora and helpful critiques, see Notes to General Introduction, n. 10. For suggestion that his framework may become more apt in Chile in the twenty-first century, see Book Three of this trilogy, Afterword to chapter 4.

4 My awareness of the emerging new scholarship on Latin America derives not only from my work in the field in Chile but also from the privilege of participating as a collaborating faculty member in the Social Science Research Council's training and research project, directed by Elizabeth Jelin and Eric Hershberg with Carlos Iván Degregori, on memory, political repression, and democratization in South America (Southern Cone countries and Peru) during 1998–2001. The project faculty worked with Latin American fellows in order to build a critical mass of research and of well-trained and networked young intellectuals working on memory-related issues. My own thinking on memory has been enriched and influenced by this collaboration. A series of volumes (up to twelve) by the publisher Siglo XXI will disseminate many of the results under the umbrella title "Memorias de la represión." As of 2002, three had appeared: Jelin, *Los trabajos de la memoria*; Claudia Feld, *Del estrado a la pantalla: Las imágenes del juicio a los excomandantes en Argentina* (Madrid: Siglo XXI, 2002); and Elizabeth Jelin, ed., *Las conmemoraciones: Las disputas en las fechas "infelices"* (Madrid: Siglo XXI, 2002).

Chapter 1: Heroic Memory

1 For the evolution of public opinion during the years of democratic transition, and pertinent survey and election results, see Book Three of this trilogy.

2 All quotations given for the case of Doña Elena F. are from my interview with her in Santiago on 29-VIII-96. Most of the information about her experiences and memories derives from the interview. As is obvious in the text, however, I supplemented the interview with numerous informal conversations, more in

the tradition of ethnographic participant-observation, held with Doña Elena and some of her relatives before and after the interview session.

3 Despite the controversies that attend on matters of interpretive analysis, most of the empirical information I present in this chapter as contextual background is common knowledge for Chilean specialists. For a brief and reliable guide to the general political history of Chile between the 1920s and 1973, and whose analytical outlines I have largely followed in this chapter, see Brian Loveman's superb *Chile: The Legacy of Hispanic Capitalism*, 2nd ed. (New York: Oxford University Press, 1988), esp. chaps. 8–9. To avoid confusing readers about the source of statistics, particularly since precise figures sometimes vary slightly from one source to another, unless otherwise indicated I have relied on the numbers cited in the Loveman text.

Readers who wish additional reliable analysis on Chilean history between the 1920s and early 1970s may wish to consult the following fine works, to which I am also considerably indebted. (The list that follows must be a ruthlessly selective sampling, given the vast historiography, and I intend no slight to the contributions of many fine scholars who go unmentioned here.) On the history of the Christian Democrats and the Catholic Church, see Michael Fleet, *The Rise and Fall of Chilean Christian Democracy* (Princeton, N.J.: Princeton University Press, 1985); and Brian Smith, *The Church and Politics in Chile: Challenges to Modern Catholicism* (Princeton, N.J.: Princeton University Press, 1982). For additional insights from a key leader of Christian Democratic doctrine, see Jaime Castillo Velasco, *Las fuentes de la democracia cristiana* (Santiago: Editorial del Pacífico, 1963).

For Left and working-class politics between the 1930s and early 1960s, see Paul W. Drake, *Socialism and Populism in Chile, 1932–1952* (Urbana: University of Illinois Press, 1978); Thomas Miller Klubock, *Contested Communities: Class, Gender, and Politics in Chile's El Teniente Copper Mine, 1904–1951* (Durham, N.C.: Duke University Press, 1998); Karin A. Rosemblatt, *Gendered Compromises: Political Cultures and the State in Chile, 1920–1950* (Chapel Hill: University of North Carolina Press, 2000); and the background commentary included in the early chapters of Peter Winn, *Weavers of Revolution: The Yarur Workers and Chile's Road to Socialism* (New York: Oxford University Press, 1986). For the pre-1930s context of labor and social movements, especially in central and northern Chile, see Peter De Shazo, *Urban Workers and Labor Unions in Chile, 1902–1927* (Madison: University of Wisconsin Press, 1984); Julio Pinto, *Trabajos y rebeldías en la pampa salitrera* (Santiago: Universidad de Santiago de Chile, 1998); and Elizabeth Quay Hutchison, *Labors Appropriate to Their Sex: Gender, Labor, and Politics in Urban Chile, 1900–1930* (Durham, N.C.: Duke University Press, 2002). For additional broad portraits of the "unruly" dimensions of Chilean popular culture and politics, and the related issues of institutional response and social disciplining, see Lorena Godoy et al., eds., *Disciplina y desacato: Construcción de identidad en Chile, Siglos XIX y XX* (Santiago: SUR, 1995); Gabriel Salazar, *Labradores, peones y proletarios* (Santiago: SUR, 1985); and Salazar, *Violencia política popular en las "grandes alamedas": Santiago de Chile, 1947–1987* (Santiago: SUR, 1990).

For the countryside, the background of political effervescence and repression is ably presented in Brian Loveman, *Struggle in the Countryside: Politics and Rural Labor in Chile, 1919–1973* (Bloomington: University of Indiana Press, 1976), and further illuminated in new research by Florencia E. Mallon, forthcoming publications on politics and society in the Temuco region; Heidi Tinsman, *Partners in Conflict: The Politics of Gender, Sexuality, and Labor in the Chilean Agrarian Reform, 1950–1973* (Durham, N.C.: Duke University Press, 2002); and Claudio Barrientos's "Emblems and Narratives of the Past: The Cultural Construction of Memories and Violence in Peasant Communities of Southern Chile, 1970–2000" (PhD diss., University of Wisconsin, Madison, 2003). For a superb evocation of the mix of cultural conservatism and political effervescence that developed in rural regions, see Isabel Allende's celebrated novel, *La casa de los espíritus* (Madrid: Plaza & Janes, 1982), also available in English as *The House of the Spirits*, trans. Magda Bogin (New York: Alfred Knopf, 1985). For the ways that strong family ties and social networks knit together leading political elites into a culture of conservatism, partly anchored in the rural milieu described in this chapter, and encouraging of "gentleman pacts" in politics, see the astute observations of Alicia Frohmann, "Chile: External Actors and the Transition to Democracy," in *Beyond Sovereignty: Collectively Defending Democracy in the Americas*, ed. Tom Farer (Baltimore: Johns Hopkins University Press, 1996); and the closely documented study of the coalesced web of landlords, capitalists, and family in the dominant class of Chile in the mid-1960s by Maurice Zeitlin and Richard Earl Ratcliff, *Landlords and Capitalists: The Dominant Class of Chile* (Princeton, N.J.: Princeton University Press, 1988). Cf. the reflections on politics and the middle class based on research in a similar time frame, in James Petras, *Politics and Social Forces in Chilean Development* (Berkeley: University of California Press, 1969). For additional historical background on Chile's system of landed estates and peasant servility (*inquilinaje*), the classic starting points are Mario Góngora, *Origen de los inquilinos de Chile central*, 2nd ed. (Santiago: Instituto de Capacitación e Investigación en Reforma Agraria, 1974); and Arnold Bauer, *Chilean Rural Society from the Spanish Conquest to 1930* (Cambridge: Cambridge University Press, 1975). See also Jean Borde and Mario Góngora, *Evolución de la propiedad rural en el Valle del Puangue*, 2 vols. (Santiago: Editorial Universitaria, 1956).

On the evolution of the political party system and for the making of a severe institutional crisis by the early 1970s, two excellent starting points are Tomás Moulian, *La forja de ilusiones: El sistema de partidos, 1932–1973* (Santiago: Universidad ARCIS, 1993); and Arturo Valenzuela, *The Breakdown of Democratic Re-*

gimes: Chile (Baltimore: Johns Hopkins University Press, 1978). See also the views and exchanges presented by Chilean political elites, journalists, and scholars in Matías Tagle D., ed., *La crisis de la democracia en Chile: Antecedentes y causas* (Santiago: Editorial Andrés Bello, 1992), which may be usefully supplemented by the following retrospective visions by political elites from the Right, Center, and Left respectively: Alberto Cardemil, *El camino de la utopía: Alessandri, Frei, Allende, Pensamiento y obra* (Santiago: Editorial Andrés Bello, 1997); Edgardo Boeninger, *Democracia en Chile: Lecciones para la gobernabilidad* (Santiago: Editorial Andrés Bello, 1997); and Sergio Bitar, *Chile, 1970–1973: Asumir la historia para construir el futuro* (Santiago: Pehuén, 1995). It should be noted that the book by Valenzuela, *Breakdown of Democratic Regimes,* cited earlier, was part 3 of a larger comparative political science project, published simultaneously in one cloth volume and in four separate paperback volumes and including a broad theoretical essay as well as treatment of diverse cases in Europe and Latin America, by Juan J. Linz and Alfred Stepan, eds., *The Breakdown of Democratic Regimes* (Baltimore: Johns Hopkins University Press, 1978). For context on the institutional and political history of the military in Chile before and after 1973, see Frederick M. Nunn, *The Military in Chilean History: Essays on Civil-Military Relations, 1810–1973* (Albuquerque: University of New Mexico Press, 1976); Augusto Varas, *Los militares en el poder: Régimen y gobierno militar en Chile, 1973– 1986* (Santiago: Pehuén, 1987); Varas, *Las Fuerzas Armadas en la transición y consolidación democrática en Chile* (Santiago: Centro de Estudios del Desarrollo, 1987); and Claudio Fuentes, "El discurso militar en la transición chilena," paper published in Nueva Serie FLACSO (Santiago: FLACSO, 1996).

Finally, for additional sources that refer specifically to the years of Allende's presidency, see also notes 8 and 15 in this chapter.

4   By the late 1950s, massive migration to major cities—accompanied by urban land invasions of zones surrounding the central city core, mobilization to develop an infrastructure of urban services in the new urban communities, and opportunities for populists and political parties to develop new clienteles—had become common features of life in many Latin American countries. For an illuminating example of Allende's political identification with the new urban communities (in this case the famed "La Victoria" district of metropolitan Santiago) and the important role of the Communist Party, see Orlando Millas, *Memorias, 1957–1991: Una digresión* (Santiago: CESOC, 1996), 15–27. For the long-term impact of political party mobilization and organizing on the culture and combativeness of specific shantytown communities, see Cathy Lisa Schneider, *Shantytown Protest in Pinochet's Chile* (Philadelphia: Temple University Press, 1995).

For additional insight on history and culture of *poblaciones* (neighborhoods of urban poor and working-class people, often with a background as shantytowns that began with land invasions and flimsy housing), see Edward L. Murphy, "Surviving Development: *Pobladores* and Social Identity in Santiago, Chile,

1967–1997" (master's thesis, Georgetown University, 1998); Manuel Castells, *The City and the Grassroots* (Berkeley: University of California Press, 1983); Vicente Espinosa, *Para una historia de los pobres de la ciudad* (Santiago: SUR, 1988); Rosa Quintanilla, ed., *Yo soy pobladora* (Santiago: PIRET, 1990); Jorge Chateau et al., *Espacio y poder: Los pobladores* (Santiago: FLACSO, 1987); Teresa Valdés and Marisa Weinstein, *Mujeres que sueñan: Las organizaciones de pobladoras en Chile, 1973–1989* (Santiago: FLACSO, 1993); and Francisco Sabatini, *Barrio y participación: Mujeres pobladoras de Santiago* (Santiago: SUR, 1995). It is worth noting, in this context, that by the 1980s the term *poblaciones* had become the dominant referent for neighborhoods of the urban poor and working classes; the more varied pre-1973 nomenclature, whose common terms included reference to *callampas* (mushrooms) and *campamentos* (tent towns, squatter towns) as well as *poblaciones,* had fallen into disuse.

For the ways populist political responses to the new urban migrations and mobilization were part of the wider Latin American scene—restricted neither to multiparty democracies such as Chile, nor to countries with dominant new populists such as Argentina's Perón—the case of Peru is quite instructive. See Carlos Iván Degregori, Cecilia Blondet, and Nicolás Lynch, *Conquistadores de un nuevo mundo: De invasores a ciudadanos en San Martín de Porres* (Lima: Instituto de Estudios Peruanos, 1986); also Steve Stein, *Populism in Peru: The Emergence of the Masses and the Politics of Social Control* (Madison: University of Wisconsin Press, 1980).

5 The gender gap in presidential voting for Allende was substantial in the electoral races in 1958, 1964, and 1970. The comparative percentages for Allende ran as follows: in 1958, 22.3 percent of the female vote, 32.4 percent of the male vote; in 1964, 32.1 percent of the female vote, 45.1 percent of the male vote; in 1970, 31.0 percent of the female vote, 42.0 percent of the male vote. Since female participation in the total presidential vote rose sharply in those years (to 35.1 percent in 1958, 44.1 percent in 1964, and 48.8 percent in 1970), the electoral consequences were important. Women, for example, proved crucial to Frei's resounding majority vote in 1964. Frei beat Allende by only a slender margin among men (49.6 percent to 45.1 percent) but nearly doubled Allende's vote among women (63.1 percent to 32.1 percent). For the electoral figures cited above, see Germán Urzúa Valenzuela, *Historia política de Chile y su evolución electoral (desde 1810 a 1992)* (Santiago: Editorial Jurídica de Chile, 1992), 551–53, 594, 635, 640–43. See also Institute for the Comparative Study of Political Systems, *The Chilean Presidential Election of September 4, 1964,* report published in 2 parts (Institute for the Comparative Study of Political Systems, Washington, D.C., 1965), esp. pt. 2:10–11, 14–16.

The gender gap should not be construed to mean that Allende failed to carry the female vote in working-class or other districts where he held unusually strong appeal. See, for example, the figures that show Allende carrying the female vote in Santiago's working-class neighborhoods in the 1970 elections, in Urzúa Valenzuela, *Historia política*, 641–43. Nonetheless, it is probably the case that even in the working-class and regional districts that constituted his electoral strongholds, Allende fared somewhat more poorly among women than among men and that the gap lessened his overall electoral strength. To my knowledge, we still lack a rigorous study of Allende and the female vote that controls for class, regional political culture, and rural versus urban voting.

6 The 1964 literacy rate is based on Comisión Económica para América Latina (Economic Commission for Latin America), *Boletín estadístico de América Latina . . . 1967* (New York: United Nations, 1967), 203; and Markos J. Mamalakis, *Historical Statistics of Chile*, 6 vols. (Westport, Conn.: Greenwood, 1978–89), 2:142. The estimated percentages of national population in urban locales of varying sizes and in metropolitan Santiago are adapted from the figures in Comisión Económica para América Latina y el Caribe (Economic Commission for Latin America and the Caribbean), *Anuario estadístico de América Latina y el Caribe . . . 1994* (Santiago: United Nations, 1995), 7, 9 (cf. 10, which shows that metropolitan Santiago and Valparaíso alone accounted for nearly 40 percent of the national population). The population of greater Santiago is drawn from Mamalakis, *Historical Statistics*, 2:413. As noted earlier, all figures not specifically credited to a different source are from Loveman, *Chile*, chaps. 8–9.

7 On political conflicts in the countryside, the superb starting point is Loveman, *Struggle in the Countryside;* pioneering new studies are Florencia E. Mallon, "Land, Morality and Exploitation in Southern Chile: Rural Conflict and the Discourses of Agrarian Reform in Cautín, 1928–1974," *Political Power and Social Theory* 14 (2000), 143–95; and Heidi Tinsman, *Partners in Conflict: The Politics of Gender, Sexuality, and Labor in the Chilean Agrarian Reform, 1950–1973* (Durham, N.C.: Duke University Press, 2002). On the Alliance for Progress and the agrarian reform question under Alessandri and Frei, a sympathetic account may be found in Paul E. Sigmund, *The United States and Democracy in Chile* (Baltimore: Johns Hopkins University Press, 1993), chap. 2.

8 The most controversial point of this paragraph is assessment of the practical impact that U.S. funds had on Chilean political life. The net impact on the 1964 elections is a matter of dispute, but the facts of the funding are not. A fundamental source on U.S. covert involvement in Chilean political life in the 1960s through 1973 is the U.S. Congress, through the hearings led by Senator Frank Church in 1975. The domestic political context was the uproar about government covert action and abuse of power raised by the combined effect of the Vietnam War and the Nixon administration's Watergate crisis. Less than a year after Nixon's resignation, Senator Church's committee conducted an extensive investigation of government abuse of power and rogue actions, both domestic and international. Covert action in Chile became an emblematic example of covert action more generally. For U.S. action in Chile, see especially U.S. Con-

gress, Senate Select Committee to Study Governmental Operations Staff Report, *Covert Action in Chile, 1963–1973*, 94th Cong., 1st Sess. (Washington, D.C.: Government Printing Office, 1975); and *Hearings before the Select Committee to Study Governmental Operations with Respect to Intelligence Activities . . . Ninety-fourth Congress, First Session*, 7 vols., Hearings from 16 September 1975 to 4 December 1975 (Washington, D.C.: U.S. Government Printing Office, 1976), vol. 7 (see p. 2 for Chile as an emblematic example). See also the same committee's *Alleged Assassination Plots Involving Foreign Leaders: An Interim Report . . . Together with Additional . . . Views* (New York: W. W. Norton, 1976), 5, 225–54, 262, 272, 273. For more recent releases of documents on U.S. involvement in Chilean political life, see the Chile project of the National Security Archive, at www.nsarchive.org.

To illuminate the facts that are not in dispute while bearing in mind divergent points of interpretation, it is useful to compare Sigmund, *The United States and Democracy*, with James Petras and Morris Morley, *The United States and Chile* (New York: Monthly Review Press, 1975); and with Armando Uribe, *The Black Book of American Intervention in Chile* (Boston: Beacon Press, 1975). The Sigmund book is also useful for its meticulous dissections of the claims made in accounts by key U.S. actors: Nathaniel Davis (former U.S. ambassador to Chile), *The Last Two Years of Salvador Allende* (Ithaca, N.Y.: Cornell University Press, 1985); Henry Kissinger, *White House Years* (Boston: Little, Brown, and Co., 1979); and Seymour Hersh (the *New York Times* journalist who wrote influential exposés of politics during the 1970s and early 1980s), *The Price of Power: Kissinger in the Nixon White House* (New York: Simon and Schuster, 1983). For Sigmund's overall views and analysis of the Frei-Allende years, see *The Overthrow of Allende and the Politics of Chile, 1964–1976* (Pittsburgh: University of Pittsburgh Press, 1977).

9   Here I must record my thanks to the many Chilean relatives I have gained through marriage to Florencia E. Mallon—for visits to the family fundo San Pancho; and for conversations with relatives, guests, and laborers amidst walks and horseback rides, as well as around the meal table at San Pancho and in Santiago, during 1996 and 1997. The social interactions and conversations about family lore, past and present, helped illuminate the rural milieu of the 1940s to 1960s in ways that would be difficult to discern from written documents and novels alone.

10 The potential for an archaeology of the production technologies and organization of the landed estate system prior to the agrarian reform was brought home to me during a walking tour with my cousin Gastón Gómez Bernales, of the "ruins" still visible on the family fundo San Pancho. On the inquilino-based agrarian system consolidated in the late nineteenth century and the early twentieth, see Loveman, *Struggle in the Countryside;* Góngora, *Origen de los inquilinos;* and Bauer, *Chilean Rural Society.*

11 It is worth comparing the quotations that appear below with the analysis of the political languages of morality, efficiency, and exploitation in Mallon, "Land, Morality and Exploitation"; and with the detailed study of agrarian reform and its tensions in Tinsman, *Partners in Conflict*.

12 In recent years, serious study of the Left has begun to emerge, especially on the appearance and subsequent trajectory of the "1960s generation" in Latin American politics. For Chile, the most illuminating research is by Katherine Hite, *When the Romance Ended: Leaders of the Chilean Left, 1968–1998* (New York: Columbia University Press, 2000). See also Norbert Lechner, *Los patios interiores de la democracia* (Santiago: FLACSO, 1988); Kenneth M. Roberts, *Deepening Democracy? The Modern Left and Social Movements in Chile and Peru* (Stanford, Calif.: Stanford University Press, 1998); and Steve J. Stern, ed., *Shining and Other Paths: War and Society in Peru, 1980–1995* (Durham, N.C.: Duke University Press, 1998), esp. pt. I. For Latin America more generally, the best starting point is Barry Carr and Steve Ellner, eds., *The Latin American Left: From the Fall of Allende to Perestroika* (Boulder, Colo.: Westview Press, 1993). For useful supplementation, see various specific articles and special numbers in two Left-oriented journals, NACLA (North American Congress on Latin America) *Report on the Americas* and *Latin American Perspectives*. Also see Jorge Castañeda, *Utopia Unarmed: The Latin American Left after the Cold War* (New York: Random House, 1994). For the 1960s generation as an international phenomenon beyond Latin America, see Todd Gitlin, *The Sixties: Years of Hope, Days of Rage* (New York: Bantam, 1993); and Eric Hobsbawm, *The Age of Extremes: A History of the World, 1914–1991* (New York: Pantheon, 1994), esp. 295–301, 329–34, 344–57, 443–49. For the Catholic Church and reformist stirrings, the best starting point for Chile is B. Smith, *Church and Politics;* and for a more general overview, Penny Lernoux, *Cry of the People* (1980; reprint, New York: Penguin, 1982).

13 I am especially grateful to Ramón Huidobro for a conversation on 22 July 1997, which illuminated the personal "magic" Allende brought to his style of politics and face-to-face encounter. Huidobro was a close personal friend of Allende and a relative by marriage (he is the adoptive father of the novelist Isabel Allende), and he served as Chile's ambassador to Argentina in the Allende government. I am also grateful to Allende's daughter, Isabel Allende Bussi, for several conversations in the family home in Providencia between May and July 1997 that also illuminated Salvador Allende's personal qualities. It should be noted that it was not simply Allende's relatives and loyalists who noted his skills at human rapport, persuasion, and manipulation. Critical journalists and political opponents readily acknowledged these attributes, and they became part of the larger public image of Allende. Note, in this regard, the impressions of Allende by Doña Elena, cited later in this chapter; and the reluctance of coup leaders to talk directly with Allende (see note 23 below).

14 FSA, "Exposición del Presidente de la República de Chile, Dr. Salvador Allende Gossens, en el XXVII período de sesiones de la Asamblea General de las Naciones Unidas . . . Nueva York, 4 de diciembre de 1972," typescript of original version in presidential office.

15 My reference to a "coup foretold" borrows from the title (and sensibilities) of the novella by Gabriel García Márquez, *Crónica de una muerte anunciada* (Bogotá: Editorial La Oveja Negra, 1981). Given the controversy, international symbolism, and sense of Greek tragedy that surround the topic, the literature on the Allende experiment and its disastrous denouement is enormous. Aside from the sources, memoirs cited in notes 3 and 8 in this chapter, see, for an early essay that outlines distinct perspectives on the Allende years and the coup and remains a useful guide for assessing literature, Arturo Valenzuela and J. Samuel Valenzuela, "Visions of Chile," *Latin American Research Review* 10, no. 3 (autumn 1975): 155–76. See also the early assessments by Genaro Arriagada, *De la "vía chilena" a la "vía insurreccional"* (Santiago: Editorial del Pacífico, 1974); Stefan de Vylder, *Allende's Chile: The Political Economy of the Rise and Fall of the Unidad Popular* (Cambridge: Cambridge University Press, 1976); Edward Boorstein, *Allende's Chile: An Inside View* (New York: International Publishers, 1977); Sergio Bitar, *Transición, socialismo y democracia: La experiencia chilena* (Mexico City: Siglo XXI, 1979); and the articles in *Latin American Perspectives*, 1 (summer 1974): special issue on Chile. For an excellent recent reflection, see Tomás Moulian, *Chile Actual: Anatomía de un mito* (Santiago: LOM, 1997), 151–70.

Two of the most illuminating "inside" accounts of the period are by military leaders on opposite sides of the constitutionalism question: Carlos Prats González, *Memorias: Testimonio de un soldado* (Santiago: Pehuén, 1985), for the perspective of the army Constitutionalist general who worked with Allende to stabilize the country during 1972–73 and who would be assassinated by agents of the junta in Buenos Aires in 1974; and José Toribio Merino C., *Bitácora de un almirante: Memorias* (Santiago: Editorial Andrés Bello, 1998), for the navy leader and junta member in the vanguard of organizing the coup.

An additional important inside account may appear within several years. Patricio Aylwin, the key Christian Democrat who conducted his party's negotiations with Allende and who would later serve as Chile's president and key architect of the transition from military rule, has been working on a major project of memoirs, one volume of which would review the Allende years. As of 2003, only the memoir of the military period has been published, and its treatment of the Allende period and crisis is exceedingly brief: Patricio Aylwin Azócar, *El reencuentro de los demócratas: Del golpe al triunfo del No* (Santiago: Ediciones Grupo Zeta, 1998). Interview and conversations with Don Patricio Aylwin, 20 June and 15 July 1997.

16 The Kissinger quote comes from the investigative report by journalist Seymour

M. Hersh on CIA censorship of 168 passages (among them the Kissinger quote) in a book by two former intelligence officials, in *New York Times*, 11 September 1974. For the original book (with deleted sections noted, and with comments on the legal struggle over censorship), see Victor Marchetti and John D. Marks, *The CIA and the Cult of Intelligence* (New York: Knopf, 1974), esp. xi–xxvi. The CIA originally ordered 339 deletions. A court battle reduced the number of legally approved deletions to 168, but as a practical matter, ongoing litigation prevented publication of an additional 140 items in the book. The Hersh article enables one to infer that the deleted Kissinger quote was to have appeared on p. 14.

Hersh incorporated the Kissinger remark in his wider depiction of Kissinger and U.S. relations with Chile and Allende, in his 1983 book, *Price of Power*, esp. 258–96. Kissinger did not know much about Chile, but in his geopolitical vision, Chile's influence and its borders with Peru, Bolivia, and Argentina rendered Allende a disaster for U.S. interests in turning back radicalism in South America. His vision was probably colored, as well, by anxieties about Communist social bases and politics in Western Europe, especially Italy. See Kissinger, *White House Years*, 653–83 (esp. 657), and on Italy, 100–4, 920–22. Cf. Hersh, *Price of Power*, 270; and Kissinger's later response to Euro-Communism, in *Years of Renewal* (New York: Touchstone [Simon and Schuster], 1999), 626–32. For the Nixon meeting with Helms and notes from the meeting, see U.S. Congress, Senate Select Committee to Study Governmental Operations Staff Report, *Hearings before the Select Committee*, 7:96; and *Alleged Assassination Plots*, 227.

For additional detail and context on Nixon-Kissinger and U.S. relations with Chile, see Mónica González, *La conjura: Los mil y un días del golpe* (Santiago: Ediciones B, 2000), 86–95, and note 8 in this chapter. The controversial quality comes through vividly in the competing accounts of U.S. government involvement or complicity in the execution (and related cover-up, familial research, and justice issues) of U.S. citizen Charles Horman shortly after the 1973 coup. For accounts by Horman's family and acquaintances, filmmaker Costa-Gavras (Konstatinos Gavras), and former U.S. ambassador to Chile Nathaniel Davis, respectively, see Thomas Hauser, *The Execution of Charles Horman: An American Sacrifice* (New York: Harcourt Brace Jovanovich, 1978); *Missing* (1982, directed by Costa-Gavras and starring Jack Lemmon and Sissy Spacek); and Davis, *Last Two Years of Salvador Allende*, esp. 351–53, 377–82. See also Peter Kornbluh, *The Pinochet File: A Declassified Dossier on Atrocity and Accountability* (New York: New Press, 2003), 267–322. The controversy also comes through clearly in Kissinger's replies to critics in *White House Years*, 653–83. Cf. *Years of Upheaval* (Boston: Little, Brown and Co., 1982), 374–413; and *Years of Renewal*, 310–43 (esp. 314–20, 328–30), 749–60. For Allende's bitterness that Soviet solidarity had turned more verbal than tangible as economic and political crisis deepened late in 1972 (even Davis, *Last Two Years of Salvador Allende*, 130, estimates new short-to-medium credits promised in Allende's Moscow trip in December 1972 at only $30 to $50 million), I am grateful to journalist Emilio Filippi, a strong critic of Allende who accompanied him on his Moscow trip, interview, 3-IV-97. Cf. Elizabeth Subercaseaux, *Gabriel Valdés: Señales de historia* (Santiago: Aguilar, 1998), 163.

17 Defining an inflation figure is complicated by the impact of the coup crisis itself in the September–December period. The official figures of the Chilean Central Bank estimated 1973 inflation at 508.1 percent; see Loveman, *Chile*, 329. If one discounts the impact of the coup crisis and its immediate aftermath, the calculation from August 1972 to August 1973 runs at 303.6 percent, and the September 1972–September 1973 estimate is 286.0 percent; see Valenzuela, *Breakdown of Democratic Regimes*, 55 (based on reports of the Instituto Nacional de Estadística). The 1973 negative GDP growth rate (not as worrisome as inflation and supply shortages at the time, and a figure also affected by the coup crisis itself) was −5.6 percent (Loveman, *Chile*, 329). Boorstein, *Allende's Chile*, is a fascinating account of economic policy making amidst the economic and political challenges of the period.

18 Both critics and supporters of Allende are aware of the profound implications of Allende's commitment to clear major policy matters with a committee comprising heads of the major UP parties. Patricio Aylwin Azócar, interview, 20-VI-97; Emilio Filippi, interview, 3-IV-97; Sergio Insunza, discussion of Allende's final days and the difficulties of a speedy announcement of the plebiscite option in September 1973, interview, 28-XI-96; and conversation with Gonzalo Falabella, 14-VI-97, about Allende's determination not to break apart the Unidad Popular despite the difficulties this posed as he searched for a political solution to the 1973 crisis. Filippi summed up the issue as follows: "[Allende] preferred continuing to be loyal to the UP [Unidad Popular], [but] the UP wasn't loyal to him." For the connection of such issues to plebiscite announcement timing and strategy, see also González, *La conjura*, 313–16.

The point is a sensitive one, because it is unclear that Allende could have constructed an alternate strategy with his coalition, because Allende sought to provide some counterweight to the commitment by personally insisting on his prerogatives as president and on his unwillingness to go into exile if politically undermined, and because the point places some responsibility for the political disaster of 1973 on maximalist ("ultra") leaders whose intransigence undermined negotiations with Christian Democrats in August and delayed the crucial announcement of a plebiscite originally intended for 10 September. An additional sensitive aspect is that Allende's difficulties in disciplining his own coalition related to some of his own cherished and otherwise appealing values —the value he placed on personal loyalty, and on preference for Left unity over sectarianism. For some indications of the sensitivities that surround the theme of the partial tying of Allende's hands by his own coalition, it is helpful to compare the retrospectives of the "moderate" Millas, *Memorias*, 97–106; and the "ultra" Carlos Altamirano, interviewed in Patricia Politzer, *Altamirano* (Buenos Aires: Ediciones Grupo Zeta, 1989), esp. 51–59, 127–44. See also Bitar, *Chile, 1970–1973*, 365–68; Prats, *Memorias*, 509–10; and the account of Allende's effort to reach an accord with the Christian Democrats, and the obstacles he faced from his own allies as well as hard-liners among the Christian Democrats, in the memoirs of Santiago's archbishop, Cardenal Raúl Silva Henríquez, *Memorias*, ed. Ascanio Cavallo, 3 vols. (Santiago: Copygraph, 1991), 2:249–80, esp. 255–56, 259, 260, 262, 267, 270–71, 275–76, 278–80.

19 See Winn, *Weavers of Revolution*.

20 Three of the most well-known cases of the family and generational dynamics that complicated political debate and tolerance between ultra and moderate leaders involved top MIR leaders who were relatives of high officials in the UP government. Miguel Enríquez Espinoza and Edgardo Enríquez Espinoza were sons of Education Minister Edgardo Enríquez, and Andrés Pascal Allende was the nephew of President Allende. All three would become high priority targets of the DINA. The DINA tracked down Miguel Enríquez in October 1974 and killed him in the shoot-out that ensued. Pascal Allende barely escaped assassination when the DINA traced him to a safe house in November 1975. Agents of the Argentine Army and the Chilean DINA permanently "disappeared" Edgardo Enríquez Espinoza in Buenos Aires in April 1976. See *LHORM*, 56–59, 101, 136–37; and *ICNVR*, vol. 2, 132. Historical knowledge of the MIR focuses mainly on the leadership, but new and forthcoming research by Florencia E. Mallon sheds light on grassroots activism. See Mallon, "*Barbudos*, Warriors, and *Rotos*: The MIR, Masculinity, and Power in the Chilean Agrarian Reform, 1965–1974," *Changing Men and Masculinities in Latin America*, ed. Matthew C. Gutmann (Durham, N.C.: Duke University Press, 2003), 179–215.

21 For Sáenz quotes and SOFOFA seminar, see González, *La conjura*, 119, also 137–38.

22 The previous five paragraphs on the "disloyal opposition" problem, the specter of violence, and the "disloyal government" issue (from the perspective of Allende's opponents) raise profoundly controversial issues—assignment of historical responsibility for the making of disaster, analytical distinction between violence as verbal theatrics and as genuine threat. In retrospect, the ease of the military takeover and the scale of political violence committed by the state's military and police forces after 11 September 1973 impart a naive, theatrical character to Left discourses before 11 September about armed organizing to block civil war or to win a confrontation. But despite controversy on points of analysis and interpretation, the existence of an atmosphere of violence that affected political thinking, and that gained additional impetus by the results of the March 1973

election and by the abortive coup attempt on 29 June, is not a controversial point.

For the rhetoric of potentially imminent civil war that made its way strongly into the press during the last months of the UP government, see the major national newspapers, between June and September 1973: esp. *El Mercurio, La Tercera, Ultimas Noticias,* and *La Segunda* for the major opposition press; and *Clarín, El Siglo, Puro Chile,* and *La Nación* for the major progovernment newspapers. See also the magazines *Ercilla* and *Qué Pasa* for reporting and interpretation of such discourses from the Center and Right, and *Chile Hoy* and *Punto Final* for reporting and perspective from the Left. Arguably, press reporting itself contributed to the atmosphere of violence, through lurid treatments of specific violent street confrontations, and irreconcilable contrasts in basic descriptions of the same event. See, for example, the coverage of the shooting that occurred during an opposition march near the Congress on 21 August 1973, in Chile's three most important newspapers: *El Mercurio, La Tercera,* and *Clarín,* 22 August 1973. Upon reading such divergent descriptions, one might have thought one was reading about two different countries. For meticulous chronology of the Allende era, helpful to place media reports in perspective, see Manuel Garretón et al., *Chile: Cronología del período 1970–1973,* 7 vols. (Santiago: FLACSO, 1978).

For President Allende's own discussions with his Cabinet, after the clumsy and abortive coup attempt in June, about the problem of violence and the difficulty of finding a political solution to Chile's crisis, see the notes reproduced in Bitar, *Chile, 1970–1973,* 365–67. Cf. the assessments given in Prats, *Memorias,* 312; and Merino, *Bitácora,* 178–226.

On the complexities of timing and degree of concern about violence, see also note 23.

23 For the roles of violence as specter and as action by determined groups, see, aside from note 22, González, *La conjura;* Manuel Fuentes W., *Memorias secretas de Patria y Libertad* (Santiago: Grijalbo, 1999). On the perceived atmosphere of violence, even before the truckers' strike of October 1972, see the August 1972 poll published in *Ercilla,* 13-IX-72, p. 11 (cited, as well, in Valenzuela, *Breakdown of Democratic Regimes,* 69–70). For the relative weight given to economic rather than violence problems, and for political evaluations of Allende higher than those of his government, the survey data in BF, AEH, Investigación no. 42 (Greater Santiago, December 1972–January 1973) and no. 45 (Greater Santiago, February 1973) are revealing. When a sample of 426 respondents was asked, in the first survey, to identify the principal problems of Chileans, they overwhelmingly focused on economic difficulties—specifically the lack of goods and inflation (64.3 percent and 12.0 percent respectively, for a total of 76.3 percent). Political instability, intransigent opposition that undermined governability, and physical insecurity (6.3 percent, 2.3 percent, and 1.9 percent

respectively, for a total of 10.5 percent) trailed notably. Even when allowed a second answer, the majority (64.8 percent) failed to name a second problem, and only a tiny minority (3.7 percent) named political instability, violence, and related issues as a key secondary concern. In the same survey, 60.8 percent of the respondents agreed that there existed "a climate of insecurity" but when asked to specify its most important manifestations, 31.5 percent pointed to work, 16.0 percent specified the difficulty of making future plans, 12.7 percent pointed to personal liberty, 7.0 percent mentioned personal property or wealth, and only 4.0 percent mentioned "physical integrity."

The February 1973 survey, based on 754 interviews, pointed in a similar direction but also specified the distinction people drew between the figure of President Allende and their assessment of his government. When asked their rating of Allende's government, only a third (33.4 percent) of the respondents provided a positive rating (excellent, very good, or good); an additional third (30.8 percent) provided a "so-so" ("regular") evaluation; and the remaining third (33.3 percent) provided a negative (bad or very bad) rating. When asked about President Allende himself, however, the positive approval score rose to nearly half (49.6 percent), and the so-so and poor ratings dropped accordingly (22.8 percent and 22.1 percent, respectively). When asked the degree of political support they provided to Allende, the February survey results for Greater Santiago ran close to the results of the March congressional elections and pointed to the political difficulties that lay ahead. Two-fifths (39.5 percent) indicated support ("total support" and "considerable support" at 26.0 percent and 13.5 percent, respectively). About a fifth (17.4 percent) responded with a so-so waffle (*regular apoyo*). The remaining two-fifths (39.8 percent) opposed the government ("little support" and "no support" at 7.2 percent and 32.6 percent, respectively). For additional discussions of Eduardo Hamuy's surveys before and during the Allende period, see Fleet, *Rise and Fall*, chaps. 2–4, passim; cf. their use in B. Smith, *Church and Politics*.

The connection between the timing of the coup and the announcement of a plebiscite remains a controversial point—and a complex one—because, arguably, such an announcement would not have "solved" the political crisis. See, e.g., Prats, *Memorias*, 509–10. But the reluctance of the junta leaders, on 11 September, to talk with Allende and thereby expose themselves to his muñeca, is well known. See Ignacio González Camus, *El día en que murió Allende*, 2nd expanded ed. (Santiago: CESOC, 1990), 261, 288–89. Cf. Patricia Verdugo, *Interferencia secreta: 11 de septiembre de 1973* (Santiago: Editorial Sudamericana, 1998), 111–12, 116, 120–23, 141–43, and accompanying compact disk recording with the same title.

24 Moulian, *Chile Actual*, 158–70, is the most perceptive interpretation of the self-deceptions and romance that produced, among other effects, a theater of violence and a certain assumption that expressive discourse itself—declarations of

loyalty to ultimate goals or utopias—might somehow yield the magic of political solution. One result was that even as Unidad Popular activists and leaders sought to escape the logic of political violence as an iron law of revolution and history, they also deployed discourses that stimulated fear and hatred—in other words, a social base for violence to stop the Unidad Popular. (My understanding of these issues has also been enhanced by numerous interviews and conversations.) For a fine update and critique of the political uses of the idea of pre-1973 violence in the post-1973 context, see Verónica Valdivia Ortiz de Zárate, "Terrorism and Political Violence during the Pinochet Years: Chile, 1973–1989," *Radical History Review* 85 (winter 2003), 182–90.

25 On oral history as a method of gaining insight into the meanings people attribute to their experiences, and thereby providing an important source for historians even when the "facts" recounted are empirically false or mistaken, see Alessandro Portelli, *The Death of Luigi Trastulli and Other Stories: Form and Meaning in Oral History* (Albany: State University of New York Press, 1991), esp. 1–26. Cf. Luisa Passerini, *Fascism in Popular Memory: The Cultural Experience of the Turin Working Class* (New York: Cambridge University Press, 1987); and Daniel James, *Doña María's Story: Life History, Memory, and Political Identity* (Durham, N.C.: Duke University Press, 2000).

26 The "radical evil" concept, as I am using it, draws especially on Hannah Arendt and Carlos Santiago Nino, and it refers to violations of human integrity and dignity so massive, organized, and profound that they defy the boundaries of conventional moral evaluation and response. Similar in spirit to the concept of "crimes against humanity," radical evil imposes a moral devastation so severe, so beyond the limits of normal experience, that it draws humanity into a logic of action and experience that defies even a minimal sense of moral or ethical order, or human capacity to control and comprehend. In this sense, the evil becomes radically challenging, paradoxical, and destructive.

In the twentieth-century context, the Holocaust has been the foundational event for reflections on radical evil. For Hannah Arendt's incisive formulation of radical evil as willed crimes so extreme that they defy the normal realm of the punishable and forgivable, see *The Human Condition: A Study of the Central Dilemmas Facing Modern Man* (1958; reprint, New York: Doubleday Anchor, 1959), 212–23, esp. 215–16. Cf. Arendt's controversial but profoundly important and chilling depiction of Eichmann's mental and social world, where banality becomes the paradoxical handmaiden of monstrosity, in *Eichmann in Jerusalem: A Report on the Banality of Evil*, rev. and expanded ed. (New York: Viking Press, 1964). Holocaust survivors have contributed powerful and courageous reflections on the moral devastation and questioning wrought by radical evil, including its creation of a norm-defying world with a distinct logic of human relations, suspended in a space-time that wrecks conventional forms of remembrance, conventional boundaries of physical experience, and conventional measures of moral assessment and redemption. See esp. Primo Levi, *Survival in Auschwitz*, trans. Stuart Woolf (1958; reprint, New York: Touchstone [Simon and Schuster], 1996); *The Drowned and the Saved*, trans. Raymond Rosenthal (1986; New York: Vintage, 1989); Elie Wiesel, *The Night Trilogy*, trans. Stella Rodway (originally published as *Night*, 1958; New York: Hill and Wang, 1987); Charlotte Delbo, *Days and Memory*, trans. Rosette Lamont (1985; Marlboro, Vt.: Marlboro Press, 1990); and Lawrence Langer, *Holocaust Testimonies: The Ruins of Memory* (New Haven, Conn.: Yale University Press, 1991), a superb analysis, influenced by Delbo's writings, of videotaped oral testimonies by more "ordinary" survivors.

I want to clarify here that in speaking of an extreme moral devastation with profound implications for human relations, including those among survivors, I do *not* wish to align myself with the tendency, evident in the well-known works of Bruno Bettelheim and in the "Survivor Syndrome" literature of the 1950s and 1960s, to interpret survivors through the lenses of infantilization, complicity, and trauma together leading to psychological pathology. I see complex crosscurrents and contradictory human dynamics among survivors and non-survivors in the death camps, in the writings of Levi, Wiesel, and Delbo; and in my own second-generation experience and memories of the Holocaust. My family experience has exposed me to a rather amazing and paradoxical human resiliency in the rebuilt lives of survivors after the war. This resilience renders the Survivor Syndrome literature too limiting and reductionist, despite its genuine insights and despite the tremendously shattering consequences of the Holocaust. For an excellent contextualization and critique that resonates with my own experience, see Helen Epstein, *Children of the Holocaust* (1979; New York: Bantam Books, 1980), 85–94, 177–78.

Although the Holocaust has been a foundational event, almost an archetype of radical evil in Western consciousness of the late twentieth century, subsequent periods of massive political violence and human rights violations, in distinct parts of the world including Latin America, have given rise to additional illuminating reflections on radical evil. For an outstanding recent study of radical evil and retroactive justice anchored in the Argentine experience of violent dictatorship, massive "disappearances," and subsequent democratization in the 1970s and 1980s, see Carlos Santiago Nino, *Radical Evil on Trial* (New Haven, Conn.: Yale University Press, 1996). For a variation on the banality-of-evil thesis based on the life and death of Dan Mitrione, a U.S. policeman who became involved in advising repressive police forces in Brazil and Uruguay in the 1960s, see A. J. Langguth, *Hidden Terrors* (New York: Pantheon, 1978), and 309–13 of the 1979 Pantheon paperback edition for a final unsettling twist. For perceptive reflections on the sadly current field of genocide studies, and a thoughtful critique of languages of numbing, whether by historical perpetrators or scholars, see Herbert Hirsch, *Genocide and the*

Politics of Memory: Studying Death to Preserve Life (Chapel Hill: University of North Carolina Press, 1995).

It is important to note that the term *radical evil* has a genealogy that reaches back to Immanuel Kant. Equally important, however, is that Kant developed the concept in a quite different context—as part of a reflection on the conflict between goodness and the propensity for evil in human nature, and the implications of radical evil for reversing the moral incentives that guide human choice. The historical context was the effort of Kant, along with other Enlightenment philosophers, to reconcile rationalism, faith, and moral reasoning. See Kant, *Religion within the Boundaries of Mere Reason, and Other Writings*, trans. and ed. Allen Wood and George Di Giovanni (1786, 1791–1794; New York: Cambridge University Press, 1998), 45–73, esp. 46, 52–55, 58–61, and the useful introduction by Robert Merrihew Adams, vii–xxxii. Obviously, more recent thought on radical evil and its cousin concept—crimes against humanity —responds to a different historical context and moral concern, created by specific collective experiences of politically organized violence so extreme that they seem to have taken human communities across the outer limits of "normal" moral sensibility and "normal" rules of coexistence.

27 The "policide" concept I advocate here is meant to enrich the vocabulary by which we refer to the killing of collective groups, social arrangements, or ways of life. I see *policide* as part of a family of terms that have proved useful to extend the language of extermination beyond the individualized killings invoked by terms such as *homicide, patricide,* or *tyrannicide.* The experience of World War II and the Holocaust gave rise to *genocide* (from the Latin *genus* for "race" or "stock," and *-cide* as "slayer" or "slaying") as a term to denote a project to destroy physically and directly the life of racial, religious, or national minority groups. Subsequently, *ethnocide* (from the Greek *ethnos* for nation, tribe, or people) proved useful to refer to the systematic destruction of the conditions or ways of life (whether social, economic, cultural, political, or ecological) that made possible the reproduction of group cultures or identities, even if individual members or descendants of the victimized ethnic or cultural group continued to live in considerable numbers.

It is in this sense that I consider *policide* (from the Greek *polis* for "city-state" or "body politic") a useful term to denote a systematic project to destroy an entire way of doing and understanding politics and governance. Although a project of policide includes systematic killing of specific targeted groups (that is, a political genocide directed at the most dangerous, "irredeemable," or activist representatives of the old political order), the larger target is society as a whole. Policide therefore requires building a culture of fear and fragmentation in ways that go far beyond a project of targeted political executions, and the killing process itself includes acts designed to generalize the terror, such as politically "random" or puzzling abductions, and simulated (as well as real) killings and shoot-outs.

Two caveats should be noted. First, the process of adopting new terms is necessarily a contested one; only over time shall it become clear if others find policide a useful concept. For influential and insightful characterization of the Chilean military regime and similar regimes in South America by political scientists and other scholars, and to which I am greatly indebted, see note 28. Second, the question of including political groups within the definition of genocide, or limiting its application to "involuntary" groups such as racial or religious minorities, was itself a point of some controversy in the 1940s. For a succinct account of Raphael Lemkin's original formulation and the international debate and exclusion of political groups, see Hirsch, *Genocide and the Politics of Memory*, 197–206. Cf. Raphael Lemkin, *Axis Rule in Europe* (Washington, D.C.: Carnegie Endowment for World Peace, 1944). For additional reflections on the resonances—real yet imperfect—between genocide and policide, see trilogy Book Three, Afterword to chapter 2.

28 Political scientists and political sociologists have, understandably, devoted great effort to conceptualizing the nature of the "new" authoritarian regimes that swept over South America in the late 1960s and 1970s—as projects not only to destroy once and for all a failed political order but also to construct a new model of governance and economic development, a modernization guided by technocratic principles and founded in authoritarian rule and key alliances between the state and capitalist groups. For the evolution of a pioneering and influential interpretation, see the writings on "bureaucratic-authoritarianism" by Guillermo O'Donnell, *Modernization and Bureaucratic-Authoritarianism: Studies in South American Politics* (Berkeley: University of California Press, 1973); his "Reflections on the Pattern of Change in the Bureaucratic-Authoritarian State," *Latin American Research Review* 13, no. 1 (1978); and his *Bureaucratic-Authoritarianism: Argentina, 1966–1973, in Comparative Perspective* (Berkeley: University of California Press, 1988). See also Juan Linz, "Totalitarian and Authoritarian Regimes," in *Handbook of Political Science,* ed. Fred Greenstein and Nelson Polsby (Reading, Mass.: Addison-Wesley, 1975), 3:175–411; David Collier, ed., *The New Authoritarianism in Latin America* (Princeton, N.J.: Princeton University Press, 1979); and subsequent treatment in works by political scientists on democratic transition: Guillermo O'Donnell, Phillippe Schmitter, and Laurence Whitehead, eds., *Transitions from Authoritarian Rule: Prospects for Democracy,* 4 vols. (Baltimore: Johns Hopkins University Press, 1986), esp. vol. 3, on Latin America; and Scott Mainwaring, Guillermo O'Donnell, and J. Samuel Valenzuela, eds., *Issues in Democratic Consolidation: The New South American Democracies in Comparative Perspective* (Notre Dame, Ind.: University of Notre Dame Press, 1992).

For analysis that simultaneously studies the "reactive" and "foundational" facets of military rule in Chile, and that draws the comparative literature into dialogue with the particularities—among them, emphasis on an aggressive neoliberalism despite its damaging effects on previously protected national industrialists, and personalized concentration of authority in General Augusto Pinochet—that set the Chilean dictatorship somewhat apart from other South American regimes, see Manuel Antonio Garretón, *El proceso político chileno* (Santiago: FLACSO, 1983); and the significantly revised English-language edition, *The Chilean Political Process*, trans. Sharon Kellum with Gilbert W. Merkx (Boston: Unwin Hyman, 1989). For additional insights on the transformational project and evolution of the Chilean regime (including succinct essays by many Chilean scholars including Garretón), two superb anthologies are J. Samuel Valenzuela and Arturo Valenzuela, eds., *Military Rule in Chile: Dictatorship and Oppositions* (Baltimore: Johns Hopkins University Press, 1986); and Paul W. Drake and Iván Jaksic, eds., *The Struggle for Democracy in Chile*, rev. ed. (Lincoln: University of Nebraska Press, 1995).

See also the celebration and critique, respectively, of the transformation of Chilean life and culture by Joaquín Lavín, *Chile: La revolución silenciosa* (Santiago: Zig-Zag, 1987); and Moulián, *Chile Actual*. Despite the contrasts of perspective, and the special brilliance of Moulián's book, both works share a somewhat flat and overstated quality that pushes aside contradictory crosscurrents that render ruptures and transformation both less complete and more complex. For additional critical perspective framed as a reply to Lavín, see also Eugenio Tironi, *Los silencios de la revolución: Chile: la otra cara de la modernización* (Santiago: La Puerta Abierta, 1988). For a good study of how Chilean intellectuals, especially those opposed to the dictatorship, sized up the political and cultural transformation of Chile, and reconsidered political values and strategies, see Jeffrey M. Puryear, *Thinking Politics: Intellectuals and Democracy in Chile, 1973–1988* (Baltimore: Johns Hopkins University Press, 1994).

29   For interdisciplinary analysis of the culture of fear in Chile and similar South American regimes, see the collaborative project of the Social Science Research Council on the theme in the 1980s, published by Juan E. Corradi, Patricia Weiss Fagen, and Manuel Antonio Garretón, eds., *Fear at the Edge: State Terror and Resistance in Latin America* (Berkeley: University of California Press, 1992). For the Chilean case, see the essays by Garretón, Norbert Lechner, Hugo Fruhling, Javier Martínez, Sofia Salimovich, Elizabeth Lira, and Eugenia Weinstein in *Fear at the Edge*, and the interviews in Patricia Politzer's *Miedo en Chile* (Santiago: CESOC, 1985). For details on the specific workings and effects of repression, see Pamela Constable and Arturo Valenzuela, *A Nation of Enemies: Chile under Pinochet* (New York: W. W. Norton, 1991), esp. chaps. 4, 6; Eugenia Ahumada et al., *Chile: La memoria prohibida*, 3 vols. (Santiago: Pehuén, 1989); Eugenio Weinstein et al., *Trauma, duelo y reparación: Una experiencia de trabajo*

psicosocial en Chile (Santiago: FASIC, 1987); and the "inside story" of military rule in *LHORM*.

30 This point will come through at various points in Books Two and Three of this trilogy, but see esp. Book Two, chapter 6; see also note 31.

31 Doña Elena's personal conservatism and strong sense of morality reach back to the 1940s and 1950s, but were fortified by the wider mobilization of "women of the Right" during the highly politicized years of the 1960s and early 1970s. For a pioneering recent study, see Margaret Power, *Right-Wing Women in Chile: Feminine Power and the Struggle Against Allende, 1964–1973* (University Park: Pennsylvania State University Press, 2002).

Afterword to Chapter 1: Childhood Holidays

1 My conversation with Gabriela C. about her childhood took place on 9 August 1996. Because I did not use a tape recorder, I am summarizing her story in my own words, based on my ethnographic field notebook. I have changed a few details to protect her anonymity. For the information on urban life that appears in this chapter, see note 2.

2 On the spatial arrangements of poor people and squatter settlements in greater Santiago in the 1960s and 1970s, and the military's creation of a more segregated class geography by removing the poor from barrio alto zones to Santiago's poverty belts, see Eduardo Morales and Sergio Rojas, "Relocalización socioespacial de la pobreza: Política estatal y presión popular, 1979–1985," in Jorge Chateau et al., *Espacio y poder: Los pobladores* (Santiago: FLACSO, 1987), 75–121 (including maps 1 and 2, between pp. 118 and 119). For the broader picture of urban history, see also the sources cited in chapter 1, note 4, of this book.

3 Maurice Halbwachs, *The Collective Memory*, trans. Francis J. Ditter Jr. and Vida Yazdi Ditter (New York: Harper and Row, 1980). Cf. his *Les cadres sociaux de la mémoire* (Paris: F. Alcan, 1925); and *On Collective Memory*, ed. and trans. Lewis A. Coser (Chicago: University of Chicago Press, 1992). For a perceptive recent reflection that builds on this foundation while placing more emphasis on the individual and the historical researcher, see Susan A. Crane, "Writing the Individual Back into Collective Memory," *American Historical Review* 102, no. 5 (December 1997): 1372–85. That Crane's point in no way undermines the utility of "group memory" analysis comes through strongly in Harold Marcuse, *Legacies of Dachau: The Uses and Abuses of a Concentration Camp, 1933–2001* (New York: Cambridge University Press, 2001).

Chapter 2: Dissident Memory

1 All quotations of Señora Herminda Morales come from my interview with her in the late afternoon and evening of 11 September 1996 in her home in La Legua. I also wish to acknowledge and thank Señora Herminda's family (especially her son Vladimir and her daughter Rosanna) for informal conversation and hospitality.

   As will become obvious, in addition to the interview I have drawn on data in the report of Chile's National Truth and Reconciliation Commission (*ICNVR*), and in the Commission archives and case files (ACNVR, incorporated into the archive of the Corporación Nacional de Reparación y Reconciliación). The ACNVR case files include copies of sworn testimonies given in the 1970s by Señora Herminda, her husband, Ernesto, and her son Vladimir. Finally, I should also note my debt to the Arzobispado de Santiago, Vicaría de la Solidaridad, for the case file report in *DETOES*, 3:722–26.

2 For the official summary, see *ICNVR*: vol. 1, bk. 2:539–40, vol. 2:366, 372. The summation includes a minor error in the age of Ernesto Salamanca at the time of his detention; he was twenty rather than twenty-four years old. The archival documentation is in ACNVR, Carpeta 1842, Ernesto Guillermo Salamanca Morales; Carpeta 1814, Gerardo Ismael Rubilar Morales.

3 For events in La Legua on the eleventh, which stood out precisely because armed resistance in Santiago, outside the area of La Moneda Palace itself, was weak and almost nonexistent, see *ICNVR*, vol. 1, bk. 1:107–8, 436–37; and Raúl Silva Henríquez, *Memorias*, ed. Ascanio Cavallo, 3 vols. (Santiago: Copygraph, 1991), 2:283–84. See also *LHORM*, 34, 35; and *DETDES*, 3:722.

4 ACNVR, Carpeta 1842, Ernesto Guillermo Salamanca Morales. The declaration was given in Santiago on 16 November 1979. For the atmosphere at the stadium, see the memoir-*testimonio* by Adolfo Cozzi, *Estadio Nacional* (Santiago: Editorial Sudamericana, 2000).

5 For the position of the Communist Party, see Silva Henríquez, *Memorias*, 2:275–80. See also Sergio Bitar, *Chile, 1970–1973: Asumir la historia para construir el futuro* (Santiago: Pehuén, 1995), 367–68. On the strategy of hoping for military splits between *golpistas* and Constitucionalistas, and the role of civilian resistance in such a scenario, I am grateful to my conversation with Raúl S., 15 August 1998, who (as a member of the "moderate" faction of MAPU, known at the time as MAPU Obrero-Campesino) was involved at an intermediate level of contingency planning (including military mapping) within his party and within the Unidad Popular. Raúl's comments are consistent with those of Jaime Gazmuri, in Eugenio Ahumada et al., *Chile: La memoria prohibida*, 3 vols. (Santiago: Pehuén, 1989), 126 n. 1. See also the conversation with Allende, 8 September 1973, about a plebiscite and potential splits in the army, recounted in Carlos

Prats González, *Memorias: Testimonio de un soldado* (1985; Santiago: Pehuén, 1996), 509–10; and Carlos Altamirano's retrospective in Patricia Politzer, *Altamirano* (Buenos Aires: Ediciones Grupo Zeta, 1989), 33–35. On the march and confrontation with carabineros in La Legua, see *DETDES*, 3:722. Cf. *ICNVR*, vol. 1, bk. 1: 435–36; and Carmen Castillo, *Un día de octubre en Santiago* (Mexico City: Era, 1982), 23–25. Castillo makes clear that the "worker column" was a group that escaped a shoot-out at the INDUMET metals factory and that had machine guns rescued from the presidential house "Tomás Moro." (For this reason, it was probably the worker column that shot at the Carabinero bus.) Earlier at INDUMET, Communists, Socialists, MIRistas, and workers met to decide how to respond to the coup. According to Castillo, the Communists who were present argued against armed resistance.

6 For a good description of the detentions that filled soccer stadiums, and military barracks, schools, ships, and bases around the country, and the estimate of nearly 45,000 detentions in the first month, see *LHORM*, 34–40.

7 There is some confusion in the witness accounts about 24 January versus 25 January 1974 as the precise date of the unexpected visit. For that reason the summation given by the Rettig Commission (see note 2 in this chapter) gives the date as on or before 25 January.

8 *ICNVR*, vol. 1, bk. 2: 539–40, for quote.

9 ACNVR, Carpeta 1842, Ernesto Guillermo Salamanca Morales.

10 *ICNVR*, vol. 1, bk. 1: 45–46.

11 *DETDES*, 3:723–25. On one interpretive point I disagree with the excellent, rigorously researched account prepared by the Vicaría staff. The account infers that Gerardo and Ernestito were fooled initially by the DINA's ruse. My own reading of the evidence is more ambiguous on this point, because it is so difficult to gauge how quickly and obviously the cover story dropped in the mind of the prisoners and to what extent their occasional presence, as the DINA group went on to arrest ("recruit") other persons from La Legua in subsequent days, occurred because of coercion or because they actually believed the DINA's cover story. Some circumstantial evidence, also inconclusive, suggests to me that Gerardo may have been coerced by being made to feel responsible for the fate of Ernestito. (The DINA group allowed Gerardo to stay one night with his family at San Juan de Lo Gallardo, probably because they still had not managed to locate the prisoners' father and Vladimir. But the group kept Ernestito with them, in effect converting him into a hostage who would keep the older brother quiet.) For an inside view of DINA methods of detention including forced collaboration in identifying others and the use of cover stories too thin or crude to conceal coercion effectively, see Arce, *El infierno*.

12 *ICNVR*, vol. 1, bk. 2: 540 for quote.

13 Hernán Valdés, *Tejas Verdes: Diario de un campo de concentración en Chile* (1974; reprint, Barcelona: Editorial Laia, 1978), passim, with account of torture ses-

sion on 157–78. See also the stunning unburdening by General Oscar Bonilla to Eugenio Velasco after a May 1974 visit to Tejas Verdes, as recounted in Hernán Millas, *La familia militar* (Santiago: Planeta, 1999), 52–53.

A new edition of *Tejas Verdes* was published in Chile by the publishers LOM and CESOC in 1996. The introduction by Manuel Antonio Garretón ("Prólogo: Tejas Verdes y nuestra memoria cultural," 5–16) provides useful additional background on Tejas Verdes and Chilean concentration camps, and a striking personal account (see 10–13) of Garretón's relationship with Valdés before and after 11 September. Valdés, a writer rather than a party-affiliated activist, worked on the editing team of *Cuadernos de la Realidad Nacional,* a major social science journal published by the institute Garretón headed at the Universidad Católica de Chile during the Allende years. Garretón was the "Magus" of the diary—the person Valdés named, when driven to a point of mad desperation, as a conspirator plotting action against the junta. Once Valdés was released and found shelter in an embassy, he warned Garretón, and Garretón, in turn, worked to find Valdés a network of support in Spain.

14   ACNVR, Carpeta 1842, Ernesto Guillermo Salamanca Morales, sworn declarations given by the elder Ernesto and by Vladimir in Santiago on 24 October and on 16 November 1979, respectively. I should clarify here that because of a defect in the notes on Vladimir's declaration that I dictated into a cassette tape, I cannot confirm absolutely that the quotation given is an exact replica from the original declaration. There is a slim possibility that the quotation is based on my notes, albeit verbatim notes that would have reproduced the original language very closely.

15   I have not personally reviewed the case files on Gerardo and Ernestito at the Fundación y Archivo de la Vicaría de la Solidaridad. My research in that archive concentrated on social networks and processes of information gathering, solidarity, and truth telling rather than specific juridical files. However, my research in the archives of the Truth and Reconciliation Commission showed that for these and other cases, the truth commission relied on copies of documents from the Vicaría's juridical files to build an initial foundation of facts and hypotheses. The Vicaría's judicial files typically traced the long struggle to document legally and precisely the circumstances of a disappearance and to document, as well, the frustrating effort to find answers from the state. On the latter point, see esp. ACNVR, Carpeta 1814, Gerardo Ismael Rubilar Morales; and for the Vicaría files on the same point, *DETDES*, 3:726.

16   Elizabeth Jelin and Susana G. Kaufman, "Layers of Memories: Twenty Years After in Argentina," in *The Politics of War Memory and Commemoration,* ed. T. G. Ashplant, Graham Dawson, and Michael Roper (New York: Routledge, 2000), 89–110. A dramatic instance of the ways an earlier "founding moment" of generational memory frames a life comes through in Daniel James, *Doña María's Story: Life History, Memory, and Political Identity* (Durham, N.C.: Duke

University Press, 2000). In the 1980s, the "rescue" of Juan Domingo Perón from prison by mass demonstrations on 17 October 1945 proved fundamental in her memory-identity trajectory, even as the contemporary politics of memory focused enormous energy on deaths and disappearances under the military dictatorship of 1976–83.

17 Even on this point, however, my research with various people underscored a more complex ambivalence—lives of struggle for hope despite an impending despair, in which the same person could enter into and out of cycles of activism that might provide significant solidarity, energy, and resilience, and cycles of withdrawal marked by a sense of utter solitude or despair. Especially helpful in this regard were the discussions held by relatives of the executed and the disappeared, and by survivors of torture, at the Seminario Internacional "Impunidad y sus efectos en los procesos democráticos," Comisión 4, "Métodos de lucha y experiencias de superación de la impunidad," Santiago, 13–15 December 1996.

The comparison between activist and solitary versions of memory as rupture is too flat and simplistic, therefore, if taken as a rigid contrast between different human beings with always fixed adaptations, rather than as an invitation to consider the complex contradictions, cycles, and ruptures that mark varied human responses to trauma.

18 The information on Violeta E. and her family is based on my interviews with Violeta E., 26-VIII-96, 27-VIII-96, and 5-IX-96; an interview with a niece, Nieves R., 5-VII-96; and various informal conversations with Violeta E. and other members of her family in 1996 and 1997. All quotations from Violeta E., with the exception of the last remark, several paragraphs down, on Villa Francia, are from our recorded interviews.

19 I refer to the "Christian Left" in the broad sense rather than to the political party known as the Izquierda Cristiana.

20 The call for citizen informing on suspicious leftists and on the whereabouts of specific dignitaries of the Unidad Popular is now an object of considerable amnesia in middle-class and Center-Right circles. On this point I am grateful to Claudio Rolle for a vivid and illuminating conversation (on 17-VI-97) about family forgetfulness of flyers posted in 1973 that offered money rewards for suspects; cf. José Antonio Viera-Gallo, *11 de septiembre: Testimonio, recuerdos y una reflexión actual* (Santiago: CESOC, 1998), 88–89.

21 For a succinct and well-researched history of the Comité Pro-Paz and its successor, the Vicaría de la Solidaridad, see Pamela Lowden, *Moral Opposition to Authoritarian Rule in Chile, 1973–1990* (New York: St. Martin's Press, 1996). For additional detail, see Ahumada et al., *Chile: La memoria prohibida;* and Consuelo Pérez Mendoza, *Los protagonistas de la prensa alternativa: Vicaría de la Solidaridad y Fundación de Ayuda Social de las Iglesias Cristianas* (Santiago: FAV, 1997). For context on the Catholic Church, the best book is Brian H. Smith, *The*

Church and Politics in Chile: Challenges to Modern Catholicism (Princeton, N.J.: Princeton University Press, 1982), updated in a comparative context in Michael Fleet and Brian H. Smith, *The Catholic Church and Democracy in Chile and Peru* (Notre Dame, Ind.: University of Notre Dame Press, 1997).

22 On the Lonquén case, see, aside from discussion in the sources in note 21, the documents and photos in Máximo Pacheco G., *Lonquén*, 2nd ed. (Santiago: Aconcagua, 1983); and Patricia Verdugo and Claudio Orrego V., *Detenidos-desaparecidos: Una herida abierta*, 2nd ed. (Santiago: Aconcagua, 1983). See also Patricia Verdugo, *Tiempo de días claros: Los desaparecidos* (Santiago: CESOC, 1990), 151–208. Publication of the first editions of the books by Pacheco and by Verdugo and Orrego, dated 1980, was prohibited. Pacheco's first edition circulated as a private club text legally exempted from the censorship restriction; the first edition of the Verdugo and Orrego text (see the preface to the second edition) made its way through a bureaucratic labyrinth only to be declared "lost" in March 1983. Later that year, when pre-review of books for potential censorship was lifted, the second editions of these books were published. The twists and turns of censorship policy are discussed and documented in detail in trilogy Book Two.

23 See Lowden, *Moral Opposition*, 43, 175–76 n. 87; and Ahumada et al., *Chile: La memoria prohibida*, 2:167–209.

24 It should be pointed out, however, that the actual experience of the staff in the Vicaría's Zones Department, responsible for social programs in the poblaciones of Santiago, was complex, in part because the economic and political conditions of late 1970s life rendered much of the populace reluctant to engage in collective mobilization and self-help that went beyond immediate economic needs. For this very reason, reweaving the social fabric of an oppositional culture became an important and complicated task by the early 1980s. For a brief summary of these tensions, see Lowden, *Moral Opposition*, 86–91.

25 See Book Two, chapter 2, of this trilogy, and Lowden, *Moral Opposition*, 94–104, esp. 94–99.

26 The recent memoir of Patricio Aylwin Azócar is organized around this very theme: *El reencuentro de los demócratas: Del golpe al triunfo del No* (Santiago: Ediciones Grupo Zeta, 1998). See also note 27.

27 A good feel for these controversies can be gained by comparing several different Christian Democrat memoirs and accounts: Aylwin, *El reencuentro;* Jorge Lavandero, *El precio de sostener un sueño* (Santiago: LOM, 1997); and Genaro Arriagada, *Por la razón o la fuerza* (Santiago: Editorial Sudamericana, 1998), 169–97, 219–64. For additional context on the political "learning process" and the trajectory of intellectuals and the Left, see Manuel Antonio Garretón, "The Political Opposition and the Party System under the Military Regime," in Paul W. Drake and Iván Jaksic, eds., *The Struggle for Democracy in Chile*, rev. ed. (Lincoln: University of Nebraska Press, 1995), 211–50; Jeffrey M. Puryear,

Thinking Politics: Intellectuals and Democracy in Chile, 1973–1988 (Baltimore: Johns Hopkins University Press, 1994); Katherine Hite, *When the Romance Ended: Leaders of the Chilean Left, 1968–1998* (New York: Columbia University Press, 2000); and Kenneth M. Roberts, *Deepening Democracy? The Modern Left and Social Movements in Chile and Peru* (Stanford, Calif.: Stanford University Press, 1998). Cf. Clodomiro Almeyda M., *Reencuentro con mi vida* (Santiago: Ornitorrinco, 1987); and Politzer, *Altamirano.*

28 This point emerged from a number of interviews and conversations about the 1970s and 1980s, especially if one compares the fear experience of those who were young adults in the 1970s and those who came of age in the protest cycle of the early and mid-1980s. The point was especially driven home in my interviews (13-XII-96 and 24-I-97) with Tonya R., a young mother of working-class background whose husband was a student leader in the 1980s. See trilogy Book Two, Afterword to chapter 4.

29 For comparable discussions in other neighborhoods, and the role of people involved in solidarity pastoral organizations and alternative media groups such as Ictus, I benefited from conversation with Manuel S., 21-III-97. The discussions among intellectuals and political elites included a tradition of weekly breakfast discussions among political leaders of the Right, Center, and Left sponsored by the prominent journalist Emilio Filippi at the offices of the magazine *Hoy* as early as 1983 and subsequently continued at the newspaper *La Epoca* in 1987–88. Interview with Emilio Filippi, 3-IV-97. See also Puryear, *Thinking Politics;* and Aylwin, *El reencuentro.* As the plebiscite approached, one of the great themes of discussion in the Center-Left was establishing the credibility of the plebiscite as a means of deposing a dictatorship. Interview with Ricardo Lagos, 25-VII-97.

30 The tacit avoidance pact was not unusual in family conversation. Interview with Nieves R., 5-VII-96.

31 Interview with Nieves R., 5-VII-96. The Frente Patriótico and its relation to the Communist Party's turn toward a political line that argued the right and necessity of armed insurrection in the 1980s are extremely controversial topics. For a thoughtful discussion that situates the Frente within the larger history of armed conflict and challenges conventional views, see Hernán Vidal, *Frente Patriótico Manuel Rodríguez: El tabú del conflicto armado en Chile* (Santiago: Mosquito Editores, 1995). For the Frente's attempted assassination of Pinochet in 1986, see *LHORM*, 500–8; and Patricia Verdugo and Carmen Hertz, *Operación Siglo XX* (Santiago: Ornitorrinco, 1990).

32 I am grateful to Father José Aldunate for clarifying the interplay and distinctions between testimony as protest about social realities, and testimony as theological meaning and religious function ("signs of the action of God in history"). Interview, 10-I-97.

33 The special affection that Father Bolton felt for Rafael Vergara was underscored

in our interview, 21-X-96. Two weeks before Rafael Vergara was wounded in a shoot-out with police (on 29 March 1985) and subsequently executed, Vergara, then eighteen years old and a MIR militant committed to armed resistance, secretly visited Father Bolton in his shack late at night. He took a bath and shared his mystical experience of a figure who constantly pursued the youth, who could not seem to shake his pursuer. When Father Bolton realized that the figure was Jesus Christ, he recalled asking, "Rafael, are you thinking of becoming a priest?" The youth's reply: "Yes, but not now, I have another task now." Bolton and Vergara then prayed together. Cf. Luis Morales Herrera, *Caminando con la Iglesia de los pobres: Homenaje al P. Roberto Bolton* (Santiago: LOM, 1996), 70–72, 91. On the circumstances of Rafael Vergara's death, see *ICNVR*, vol. I, bk. 2: 640.

34 Interview with Father Roberto Bolton, 21-X-96.

Afterword to Chapter 2: The Lore of Goodness and Remorse

1 A succinct introduction to Chilean regional geography and the Lakes Region may be found in Brian Loveman, *Chile: The Legacy of Hispanic Capitalism*, 2nd ed. (New York: Oxford University Press, 1988), chap. 1. A good photographic introduction, organized by regions, is *Paisaje de Chile* (Santiago: Alguero, n.d.). A tourist guide unusual for its intelligent cultural chattiness and its often spectacular photography is Tony Perrottet, *Insight Guides: Chile* (Boston: Houghton Mifflin, 1995).

2 For a convenient consolidation of figures from the two commission reports and given by region, see CCHDH, *Nunca más en Chile: Síntesis corregida y actualizada del Informe Rettig* (Santiago: LOM, 1999), 231. The totals and percentages given include victims killed by opponents of military rule (152 cases), which raised the total victim count to 3,196; the substantive point about regional distributions would not change if the death-by-opponents category were excluded. For the truth commission reports, see *ICNVR;* and Corporación Nacional de Reparación y Reconciliación, *Informe a su Excelencia el Presidente de la República sobre las actividades desarrolladas al 15 de mayo de 1996* (Santiago: La Nación, 1996). There is a slight discrepancy between the total number of confirmed individualized cases of death or disappearance attributable to human rights violations by the state or other political violence in the latter report (3,197 cases) and in the published 1999 synthesis (3,196 cases).

It should be noted that during the period of more massive killing and permanent disappearances, September 1973 to August 1977, the number of cases attributable to agents of the state or private persons acting on behalf of the state amounted to nearly 94 of every 100 cases (93.6 percent, or 2,422 of 2,587 cases). Deaths in political confrontations by authors who cannot be specifically attributed, but which in most instances involved civilians shot during curfews, probably by agents of the state, accounted for another 5 of every 100 cases (4.9 percent, or 127 of 2,587 cases). Deaths attributable to political violence by those who opposed the military regime accounted for less than 2 of every 100 cases (1.5 percent, or 38 of 2,587 cases). Only in the period between September 1977 and March 1990, when killing by the state became more sporadic and cyclical, and when organized armed resistance to the regime became significant, did the proportions shift notably. Of the 609 confirmed deaths and disappearances in this period, agents of the state or those acting for the state still accounted for the overwhelming majority (79.3 percent, 483 cases), but opposition groups and individuals now accounted for a significant minority (18.7 percent, 114 cases). CCHDH, *Nunca más en Chile*, 229.

3 The best starting point to examine direct and activist involvement of civilians in repression in the South, and historical specificities that figured in the repression, is to read the reports on September through December 1973 for the Eighth through Tenth Regions, in *ICNVR*, vol. 1, bk. 1: 325–424. See also the case reports on the Eighth through Tenth Regions in *DETDES*, 7:2515–636, and 8:2637–3041. These summations and case reports may be supplemented by several studies on the Seventh through Tenth Regions by research teams directed by Dr. Paz Rojas B. and organized by the CODEPU (Comité de Defensa de los Derechos del Pueblo): *Crímenes e impunidad: La experiencia del trabajo médico, psicológico, social y jurídico en la violación del derecho a la vida* (Santiago: CODEPU, 1996); *Chile: Recuerdos de la guerra. Valdivia—Neltume—Chihuío—Liquiñe* (Santiago: CODEPU, 1994); and *Labradores de la esperanza: La región del Maule: Talca—Linares—San Javier—Melozal—Parral—Cauquenes—Chanco—Constitución* (Santiago: CODEPU, 1992). Fundamental is a new regional study, highly original and rigorously argued, that systematically documents and compares the social and psychological consequences of extreme repression for Mapuche and non-Mapuche cases in the Ninth Region. See Roberta Bacic Herzfeld, Teresa Durán Pérez, and Pau Pérez-Sales, *Muerte y desaparición forzada en la Araucanía: Una aproximación étnica* (Santiago: Ediciones Universidad Católica de Temuco and LOM, 1998), 53–61, on relations between carabineros and civilians during the initial repression. The research in progress by Florencia E. Mallon on the Eighth Region will further illuminate the specificities of the South, and I am grateful to her for numerous conversations.

4 Aside from the sources mentioned in note 3, see, for a good introduction to the history of Colonia Dignidad, Gero Gemballa, *Colonia Dignidad* (Santiago: CESOC, 1990).

5 All quotes, unless otherwise specified, are from my interviews with Ramiro I. and Claudia de I., 6-II-97 and 7-II-97. These interviews were supplemented by informal conversations, accompanied by long walks and some social visiting, during several days while I lived as their guest in the Tenth Region, and I am

grateful to them for their hospitality. That the racialized language used below by Claudia de I. to describe rural life and exploitation fits a larger pattern of cultural coding in servile class relations, and need not be taken literally, comes through in Heidi Tinsman, *Partners in Conflict: The Politics of Gender, Sexuality, and Labor in the Chilean Agrarian Reform, 1950–1973* (Durham, N.C.: Duke University Press, 2002), 37–41, 48.

6 On the Angulo and Burdiles cases, see *ICNVR*, vol. 1, bk. 1: 408–9; vol. 2, 25, 63; *DETDES*, 8:2958–61, 2966–68; and ASVS, *¿Dónde están?*, 7 vols. (Santiago: ASVS, 1978–79), 7:1217–18, 1226–27. On the Comisaría de Rahue, see *ICNVR*, vol. 1, bk. 1: esp. 396, and 395, 408–18 passim.

7 ACNVR, Carpeta Carlos Alberto Carrasco Matus. Luis Alejandro Fuentes Díaz was the personal friend with whom Carrasco shared his crisis and who was subsequently imprisoned and exiled; his declaration was given in Stockholm, Sweden, on 5-VII-90, and ratified with minor additions and clarifications, again in Stockholm, on 19-XI-90. The testimony on "Mauro" as having a sweet disposition was given on 18-X-90. Additional information on Mauro, and on Rodolfo Valentín González Pérez, an air force conscript recruited into secret police work who also stood out as "good" to prisoners and was subsequently tortured and disappeared by the DINA, is in *ICNVR*, vol. 1, bk. 2: 589–90; vol. 2, 83, 175; in Arce, *El infierno*, 79–81, 277, 379–80; and in the *testimonio* by Norma Matus de Carrasco, the mother of Carlos Carrasco ("Mauro"), in *Memorias contra el olvido* (Santiago: Amerinda, 1987), 174–206. According to the aunt who raised Valentín as her son, he insisted on helping political prisoners—with food, clothing, and communications to their families—even though his family members tried to persuade him that such acts were too risky. Copy of testimony to International Commission of Jurists, 2-XII-76, in ACNVR, Carpeta Rodolfo Valentín González Pérez.

8 See *DETDES*, 8:2966–68; and ASVS, *¿Dónde están?*, 6:1226–27 (includes more complete version of sarcastic "otro comunista" quote).

9 The striking number of people who turned themselves in, especially in the provinces, is evident if one reads case reports on the disappeared in *DETDES*, and the less detailed summaries in *ICNVR*. For the reality of complex guiltlike feelings among a significant minority of close relatives of the disappeared, and for the importance of those self-doubts that focus specifically on whether a relative did everything possible to prevent either the detention or its eventual consequences, see Bacic Herzfeld, Durán Pérez, and Pérez-Sales, *Muerte y desaparición forzada en la Araucanía*, 231–47, esp. 235, 237–44. While such sentiments were significant in both the Mapuche and non-Mapuche populations, the authors note two additional factors that heightened such reactions among Mapuches—first, the idea that bad fortune derives from a relationship with or intervention by someone who is known to the victim; and, second, the ethnic discrimination that facilitates a sensation of having been timid (or incom-

petent) when the interests of the detained relative required insistent pressure on non-Mapuche authorities. See ibid., 67–71, 242–43. On the vulnerability of mothers of victims to such sensations, see CODEPU, *Crímenes e impunidad*, 95; for the wider context of intrafamilial psychological dynamics and political repression, see the sources in note 13 in this chapter.

10 ACNVR, Carpeta 215, José Guillermo Barrera Barrera; *ICNVR*, vol. 1, bk. 2: 583; vol. 2, 48; and *DETDES*, 3:729–33. On 16 January 2003, Gerardo Aravena Longa, former carabinero lieutenant in Curacaví, was arrested on murder and kidnapping charges in the Barrera—Gárate case: www.elmostrador.cl, 17-I-03.

11 Leopoldo Benavides, Tomás Moulian, and Isabel Torres, "El movimiento sindical textil en Tomé: Un proyecto de historia popular," in ECOCD, Servicio de Documentación ECO: *Educación y Solidaridad* 16 (July 1987): 25–34, 34 for quote.

12 Interview with Marisa T., 8-X-96.

13 Interview with Gastón Gómez Bernales, who served as a staff lawyer of the Rettig Commission and was present at the family's truth commission session, 20-II-97. I also learned much about the capacity of revelation sessions to spark or deepen intrafamilial conflicts in an interview with Paula Serrano, who served as a staff social worker of the Rettig Commission, 21-I-97. One particularly sad case involved a mother who experienced a real-life "Sophie's choice," when she had to give up one child to protect the others. Another involved a young mother who decided she would protect her children from stigma, danger, and insecurity by moving away to relatives rather than pursuing aggressively the fate of a disappeared husband whom she also loved fiercely. To shield the children, she decided, she would tell them that their father had simply abandoned them. When the time arrived to investigate the disappeared, the children's grandmother—obviously complicit in the fiction until that point —told them that the time had arrived to do right by their missing father. She took them with her to her Truth Commission session, and they finally learned the truth about the disappearance and probable torture of a father whom they had once resented. In both cases of revelation, the mothers' already tremendous torment was compounded by the new torments of their children (and, as one might expect, by difficult intrafamilial dynamics). Fuller discussion of family dynamics including remorse sentiment appears in Book Three of this trilogy, chapter 2 and its Afterword.

For an intelligent, therapeutic perspective on children and truth in politically repressive contexts, see Eugenia Weinstein et al., *Trauma, duelo y reparación: Una experiencia de trabajo psicosocial en Chile* (Santiago: FASIC, 1987); also Loreto Alamos et al., *Infancia y represión: Historias para no olvidar. Experiencia clínica con niños y familiares que han vivido la represión política* (Santiago: PIDEE, 1992). For additional context on mental health, therapy, and politics, see Elizabeth Lira et al., *Psicoterapia y represión política* (Mexico City: Siglo Veintiuno,

1984); and Elizabeth Lira and Isabel Piper, eds., *Reparación, derechos humanos y salud mental* (Santiago: ILAS, 1996).

14 Interview with Mónica V., 5-VI-97. Cf. the comments on the connections between recognition of the death of the disappeared and ideas of disloyalty toward the loved one and release of their executors from responsibility, in Juan Manuel Pérez Franco and Gloria Duarte Castro, "Procesos de reorganización vital en familiares de detenidos-desaparecidos," in Alamos et al., *Infancia y represión*, 191–95.

15 Interview with Tonya R., 13-XII-96 and 2-I-97.

16 To avoid confusion of readers because my last name is different from my paternal grandfather's, I ought explain that I have two fathers—my original father, Sam Rosenzweig, now divorced from my mother; and my adoptive father, the late Egon Stern, who married my mother after her divorce and whose last name I received when I was legally adopted. For other examples of the power of "goodness stories" in times of Holocaust destruction, see the story of Lorenzo, the Italian worker who supplied some of his own food ration, a vest, and postal messaging to Primo Levi, in Levi's *Survival in Auschwitz*, trans. Stuart Woolf (1958; New York: Touchstone [Simon and Schuster], 1996), 119–22; and the vignette about Esther, the youngster from Belarus who supplied Charlotte Delbo a toothbrush and garment, in Delbo, *Auschwitz and After*, trans. Rosette C. Lamont (New Haven, Conn.: Yale University Press, 1995), 139–41.

17 See Levi, *Survival in Auschwitz*; Levi, *The Drowned and the Saved*, trans. Raymond Rosenthal (1986; reprint, New York: Vintage, 1989), esp. "The Gray Zone," 36–69; Elie Wiesel, *The Night Trilogy*, trans. Stella Rodway (originally published as *Night*, 1958), 5–119, esp. the depictions of fathers and sons; and Lawrence Langer, *Holocaust Testimonies: The Ruins of Memory* (New Haven, Conn.: Yale University Press, 1991), esp. chaps. 3–5.

18 The examples of ocean outings, tennis shoes, and small reciprocities and encouragement are not literary license but are based on personal knowledge. I personally witnessed the latter two during my field research and received independent confirmation of the ocean outings.

Chapter 3: Indifferent Memory

1 The interview with Gonzalo Vial took place on 10-VI-97. The members of the Truth and Reconciliation Commission divided up the work of producing an initial draft of the report, in accord with their fields of special interest or expertise. Key sections provided historical, legal, and institutional context; other members of the Commission I interviewed (especially José Zalaquett, 23-IV-97) agreed that Vial had written the first draft of the historical background section. For the origins of *Qué Pasa*, I am also indebted to journalist Cristián Zegers,

interview, 19-V-97. Vial's revelation that he participated in the writing of the "White Book" did not come until 1999, after our interview, amidst a controversy among historians about memory and an open letter by Pinochet to Chileans during his detention in London. See Sergio Grez and Gabriel Salazar, eds., *Manifiesto de los historiadores* (Santiago: LOM, 1999); also *La Segunda*, 2-II-99, 12-II-99.

2   In this regard, I respectfully dissent from some aspects of the depiction in Tina Rosenberg, *Children of Cain: Violence and the Violent in Latin America* (1991; New York: Penguin, 1992), 333–87. Her interpretation of a transition to full amnesia sealed by a Faustian bargain is a bit too neat and seamless, although it includes powerful insights and vignettes.

3   For a blistering critique and historical review along these lines, see Tomás Moulian, *Chile Actual: Anatomía de un mito* (Santiago: LOM, 1997). For humorous literary treatment of the culture of forgetting, see Marco Antonio de la Parra's play *La pequeña historia de Chile*, printed with critical responses in *Revista Apuntes* (published by the Escuela de Teatro de la Pontífica Universidad Católica de Chile), 109 (winter 1995): 3–38. A full analysis of the causes of the impasse that took hold in the 1990s, and the resulting temptations of a "will to forget," is in trilogy Book Three.

4   The interview with Colonel Juan F. took place on 7-V-97 and was supplemented by conversations with a mutual friend-and-colleague before and after the interview.

5   For an orientation to the history of the DINA, the MIR, and repression in the South, see, aside from the relevant sections of *INCVR*, several works coordinated by CODEPU, *Chile: Recuerdos de la guerra. Valdivia–Neltume–Chihuío–Liqiñe* (Santiago: CODEPU, 1994); *Labradores de la esperanza: La región del Maule Talca – Linares –San Javier – Melozal – Parral – Cauquenes – Chanco – Constitución* (Santiago: CODEPU, 1992); and *Crímenes e impunidad: La experiencia del trabajo médico, psicológico, social y jurídico en la violación del derecho a la vida* (Santiago: CODEPU, 1996). A profoundly important new study on the ethnic dimension is Roberta Bacic Herzfeld, Teresa Durán Pérez, and Pau Pérez-Sales, *Muerte y desaparición forzada en la Auracanía: Una aproximación étnica* (Temuco and Santiago: Universidad Católica de Temuco and LOM, 1998).

6   For superb analysis of the politics of agrarian reform and revolution in the Aconcagua Valley, particularly its gendered dynamics, see Heidi Tinsman, *Partners in Conflict: The Politics of Gender, Sexuality, and Labor in the Chilean Agrarian Reform, 1950–1973* (Durham, N.C.: Duke University Press, 2002).

7   *ICNVR*, vol. 1, bk. 1: 291.

8   The data that follow on the massacre are based on *ICNVR*, vol. 1, bk. 1: 292; vol. 1, bk. 2: 494–96, 487; vol. 2, 28, 67, 124, 154, 155, 195–96, 224, 234–35; and *DETDES*, 7:2355–63. The latter summation of data in the Vicariate of Solidarity case files is a crucial supplement to the Truth and Reconciliation Commission

report because it includes information on key witnesses and on the more anonymous targets of the roundup and massacre, who could not be included in the Commission's individualized methodology of named victims.

9 *DETDES*, 7:2361.

10 See *ICNVR*, vol. 1, bk. 2: 495–96. It should be noted, as well, that at ages forty-three and forty-six respectively, Gac and Cabezas were also the oldest members of the group of eight—a point that adds to the credibility problems of a story that identifies them as the only successful escapees.

11 *DETDES*, 7:2355–63, esp. 2355–57. It should be noted that there is a slight discrepancy between the date given for Arraño's arrest by the Vicaría report (11 January 1974) and by the Truth and Reconciliation Commission (15 January, in *ICNVR*, vol. 2, 37).

12 *DETDES*, 7:2355–57; *ICNVR*, vol. 2, 37.

13 See Patricia Verdugo, *Los zarpazos del puma* (1989; rev. ed., Santiago: CESOC, 1994); and *ICNVR*, vol. 1, bk. 1: 121–23, and the October 1973 case summaries given for Cauquenes, La Serena, Copiapó, Antofagasta, and Calama. The long epilogue (289–353) in the expanded edition of Verdugo's book recounts her experience of the political and legal conflicts linked to the book through December 1993. The controversies about the Arellano episode actually began in the 1980s and generated considerable press attention, as well as an important dissenting account by General Arellano's son: see Sergio Arellano Iturriaga, *Más allá del abismo: Un testimonio y una perspectiva* (Santiago: Proyección, 1985). Eventually, the Caravan of Death affair provided a legal foundation that ensnared Pinochet in criminal proceedings in Chile (and expanded the number of known executions). See Book Three of this trilogy, chapter 4.

14 It should be noted that multiple purposes were evident in the October hardening—not only a hardening of repression but an assertion of control from Santiago and by Pinochet personally. The October affair "dirtied the hands" of Arellano and was probably part of the systematic process whereby Pinochet marginalized army generals who might otherwise have contended for power. See Pamela Constable and Arturo Valenzuela, *A Nation of Enemies: Chile under Pinochet* (New York: W. W. Norton, 1991), 56–57. Cf. Arellano Iturriaga, *Más allá*; Arturo Valenzuela, "The Military in Power: The Consolidation of One-Man Rule," in *The Struggle for Democracy in Chile, 1982–1990*, ed. Paul W. Drake and Iván Jaksic, rev. ed. (Lincoln: University of Nebraska Press, 1995), 21–72.

15 Interviews with Carlos G., 21-X-96 and 25-X-96, supplemented by numerous conversations. (The reason Carlos G. was willing to talk about these experiences is that the disappearance of a relative whom he loved and admired had caused a crisis—both a crisis of conscience that turned him into a critic of human rights violations, and a crisis of career, because Carlos G.'s kin connection to a leftist eventually tainted him as untrustworthy.) On the "Community of Intelligence," see *ICNVR*, vol. 1, bk. 2: 461. The importance of compartmen-

talization of responsibility came through in several interviews and conversations with members of the military. See also the illuminating discussion of "numbing" and the language of extermination, in Herbert Hirsch, *Genocide and the Politics of Memory: Studying Death to Preserve Life* (Chapel Hill: University of North Carolina Press, 1995), 97–108.

16 Interview with Colonel Eugenio Rivera, 9-IV-97. See also the sources cited in note 13 in this chapter (testimony by Colonel Rivera is cited extensively in Verdugo's book and was confirmed as accurate in my interview with him).

17 Interview with Father Alejandro P., 8-V-97.

18 ACNVR, Carpeta 1905, Manuel Sanhueza Mellado. The testimony of the soldier was dated 10-X-90.

19 Pisagua had been the site of a military concentration camp earlier, in González Videla's 1948 repression of the Communist Party. In the 1970s, it once again became a major detention center; the activities included executions and mass burials in secret pits, discovered and publicized during the first year of democratic government in 1990. For a brief summary, see *ICNVR*, vol. 1, bk. 1: 245–47. On Pisagua's place in Chilean history, lore, poetry, and politics, see Book Two, Afterword to chapter 6, of this trilogy; and during the transition to democracy specifically, trilogy Book Three, chapter 1. The 1974 removal of bodies by the conscript group occurred because of insecurity about the cover-up. The original location and shallowness of some clandestine graves near Pisagua had left them vulnerable to exposure by the eroding action of coastal wind and water.

Afterword to Chapter 3: The Accident

1 Conversation and interview with Mónica V. on 13-I-97 and 5-VI-97, respectively. In January Mónica V. was certain of the identity of the man she saw (described in the chapter text that follows), but by June a tiny bit of doubt had entered her mind (even though the man had turned to stare at her too, and she discerned no sexual undercurrent). I confirmed the basic outlines of the imprisonment, torture, and disappearance that happened to Mónica V. and her husband in key documents—*ICNVR; DETDES;* and Luz Arce, *El infierno.* To protect Mónica V.'s privacy, however, I refrain from citing the relevant page numbers.

The issues of coexistence and accidental encounter have found brilliant literary treatment in Ariel Dorfman's play, *Death and the Maiden* (1991; New York: Penguin ed., 1994), a revised version of which appeared as a movie under the same title (directed by Roman Polanski) in 1994. The differences between the play and movie versions themselves illustrate ambiguities of identification that sometimes arise. It is important to note also two caveats. First, no such doubts exist about the small group of well-known leading perpetrators of torture and other human rights violations—Manuel Contreras is simply the most famous among them. Second, my conversations with victims of human rights violations and their relatives in the provinces make clear that in those settings, the anonymity effect of life in a large city such as Santiago lessens. Victims must find ways to coexist with persons who, while not especially famous or celebrated at the regional or national levels, are known locally to have participated as perpetrators of or accomplices in extreme acts of repression.

Chapter 4: From Loose Memory to Emblematic Memory

1   This chapter's argument is conceptual. Although it builds on the foundation of human stories presented in previous chapters, it is necessarily somewhat schematic; the full analysis, which places "meat" on the "bones" of conceptual argument, unfolds in Books Two and Three of this trilogy. The chapter has benefited from discussions of an earlier version at the conference "Memoria para un nuevo siglo," organized by the History Department of the USACH (University de Santiago de Chile) and by ECO (Educación y Comunicaciones), in Santiago, Chile, 4–6 November 1998; at the weekly history seminar of IDEA (Instituto de Estudios Avanzados), in Santiago, 7 November 1998; and at the workshop Collective Memory of Repression in the Southern Cone in the Context of Democratization Processes, organized by the Social Science Research Council, in Montevideo, Uruguay, 16–17 November 1998. I have also benefited from comments at public lectures, conferences, and workshops on memory-related themes in the United States, South America, and South Africa during 1999–2002. An early version, now significantly revised, appeared in Mario Garcés et al., *Memoria para un nuevo siglo: Chile, miradas a la segunda mitad del Siglo XX* (Santiago: LOM, 2000), 11–33. I am especially grateful to Teresa Valdés for follow-up communications, after the 1998 presentations, that helped me refine the idea of memory as persecution and awakening (which I had glossed unsatisfactorily as "la memoria como prueba").

2   In formulating the conceptual discussion that follows, I have drawn on insights in the large interdisciplinary and artistic literature related to the theme of memory for several world regions. As explained in the introduction of this volume, I ended up preferring to develop a conceptual language of my own ("emblematic memory," "memory knots," etc.) rather than applying ready-made languages or ideas that proved too confining or problematic for the Chilean historical context. (See, e.g., the discussion of Nora in the introduction and also later in this chapter's notes.) Even a cursory acquaintance with the scholarly literature on memory in history, however, confirms my intellectual debt to scholars and interpreters of memory in other times and contexts, and to students of the related theme of oral history.

Here, then, I wish to record some key intellectual debts and, in the process, orient readers who wish a guide to scholarship on memory useful for historians. (Space limits require ruthless selectivity in the following discussion, and I apologize to other authors of fine, insightful works.) The French sociologist Maurice Halbwachs was the scholarly pioneer who demonstrated the social contexts of both individual and collective remembrance; who sought to distinguish between collective memory as transmitted living history by social groups and generations, and history as a learned undertaking with a more universal vocation; and who traced, as well, the spatial framing of group remembrance. See Maurice Halbwachs, *The Collective Memory*, trans. Francis J. Ditter Jr. and Vida Yazdi Ditter (New York: Harper and Row, 1980), esp. 22–87, 128–57; and his *On Collective Memory*, ed. and trans. Lewis A. Coser (Chicago: University of Chicago Press, 1992). Cf. his *Les cadres sociaux de la mémoire* (Paris: F. Alcan, 1925); and *La topographie légendaire des évangiles en terre sainte: Etude de mémoire collective* (Paris: Presses Universitaires de France, 1941). For recent professional scholarship and commentary in an interdisciplinary context, the best starting point is the excellent journal *History and Memory* (1989–), which leans heavily but not exclusively toward Jewish, German, and Holocaust history and raises conceptual issues of broad significance. See also *representations* 26 (Spring 1989): special issue "Memory and Counter-memory,"; ed. Natalie Zemon Davis and Randolph Starn; and the forum "History and Memory," in *American Historical Review* 102, no. 5 (December 1997): 1371–1412. Susan A. Crane's essay, "Writing the Individual Back into Collective Memory," 1372–85, is especially useful for its comparison of three major pioneers—Halbwachs, Nora, and Yosef Yerushalmi—and for its effort to integrate individual and collective approaches.

In recent years, Pierre Nora and the team he assembled for his giant collective project on *Les lieux de mémoire*, 7 vols. (Paris: Gallimard, 1984–92), usefully streamlined and published in English as *Realms of Memory*, ed. Lawrence D. Kritzman, trans. Arthur Goldhammer, 3 vols. (New York: Columbia University Press, 1996–98), have had a major influence on scholarship and require special comment. Nora's project is a magnificent achievement, and his conceptual approach, summarized in "General Introduction: Between Memory and History," in *Realms of Memory*, 1:1–20 (cf. Nora, "Between Memory and History: *Les lieux de mémoire*," in *representations* 26 [spring 1989]: 7–25), is provocative as a starting point for thinking about the "sites" or "realms" that deposit memory and for the argument about the death of living memory and its displacement by history. While Nora and his group are illuminating about many specific themes and useful for general reflection, however, I think the framework is deeply flawed. It sets up too rigid a dichotomy between the ambience of living memory (his *milieux de mémoire*) and the sites that gain meaning as a repository precisely because living memory has died (his *lieux de mémoire*). It also invites such an astounding multiplication of memory sites that the project becomes more an encyclopedia of memory than a useful conceptual guide or methodology for tracing the history of collective memory. For helpful perspective on Nora's project in its French context and on its evolution over time, see Tony Judt, "A la recherche du temps perdu," *New York Review of Books* (3 December 1998): 51–58. See also the critique in Steven Englund, "The Ghost of Nation Past," *Journal of Modern History* 64, no. 2 (June 1992): 299–320. A similar note of caution about the breach between memory and history applies to the important study by Yosef Yerushalmi, *Zakhor: Jewish History and Jewish Memory* (Seattle: University of Washington Press, 1982). For insightful discussion, see Amos Funkenstein, "Collective Memory and Historical Consciousness," *History and Memory* 1, no. 1 (1989): 5–26. Cf. David N. Myers, "Remembering *Zakhor*: A Super-Commentary," *History and Memory* 4, no. 2 (1992): 129–46, with a rejoinder by Funkenstein on 147–48.

Nora's dichotomy is especially problematic for a theme such as memory of recent violent military dictatorships, in countries such as Chile and Argentina, between the 1970s and 1990s. For this specific memory theme, an environment of living remembrance—more accurately, an ambience of contentiousness about memory and forgetting, and of dialogue between personal ("testimonial") remembrance and collective remembrance—has greatly defined the political and cultural experiences of at least two living generations. In addition, contention and political stalemate have led to a relative scarcity of culturally recognized and institutionally funded physical monuments related to memory of the military dictatorships, if the richer European countries and the traumas linked to the Nazi era and World War II (let alone earlier times) are taken as a baseline. Interestingly, Nora himself developed a more subtle interactive vision of "memory" and "history" in his essay on "Generation," in *Realms of Memory*, 1:498–531. It remains to be seen, of course, whether in the twenty-first century there will arise in Chile the kind of generational distancing and cultural semi-oblivion, for the theme of the 1973 crisis and political violence by the military dictatorship, that will eventually render Nora's conceptual scheme sadly pertinent and persuasive. See, e.g., the provocative reflection by Yosef H. Yerushalmi, "Reflexiones sobre el olvido," in Yerushalmi et al., *Usos del olvido: Comunicaciones al Coloquio de Royaumont* (Buenos Aires: Ediciones Nueva Visión, 1989), 13–26.

In the meantime, alternative approaches are salutary, and I have found the following extremely useful. First, for an event-driven analysis of collective memory of a living generational trauma, see Henry Rousso, *The Vichy Syndrome: History and Memory in France since 1944*, trans. Arthur Goldhammer (Cambridge, Mass.: Harvard University Press, 1991). Despite the unfortunate disease metaphor, Rousso shows how dynamics driven by events and scandals, as well as political ambition and cultural invention, shaped changing emblematic memories of trauma and complicity, as well as ongoing passion and cultural convulsion over the theme of Vichy France. For insightful complements, see the site-based studies by Sarah Farmer, *Martyred Village: Commemorating the 1944 Massacre at Oradour-sur-Glane* (Berkeley: University of California Press, 1999); Harold Marcuse, *Legacies of Dachau: The Uses and Abuses of a Concentration Camp, 1933–2001* (New York: Cambridge University Press, 2001); and the thoughtful reflections on the politics of "memory against memory" in Elizabeth Jelin, *Los trabajos de la memoria* (Madrid: Siglo XXI, 2002). For additional reflection on the political dynamics of memory, the German case is revealing, since its Cold War division and Nazi past turned it into a kind of laboratory for examining the politics of public memory. See Jeffrey Herf, *Divided Memory: The Nazi Past in the Two Germanys* (Cambridge, Mass.: Harvard University Press, 1997). Cf. intersections of politics and memory after civil war: for Spain and memory as "political learning," see Paloma Aguilar, *Memory and Amnesia: The Role of the Spanish Civil War in the Transition to Democracy*, trans. Mark Oakley (New York: Berghahn, 2002); and for the U.S. case, see David W. Blight, *Race and Reunion: The Civil War in American Memory* (Cambridge, Mass.: Belknap Press of Harvard University Press, 2001).

Second, for the ways that memory sites and anniversaries stir up and collect multiple conflicting memories, in a sense acting more as catalysts of living memory than as repositories of dead memory, see the superb study by James E. Young, *The Texture of Memory: Holocaust Memorials and Meaning* (New Haven, Conn.: Yale University Press, 1993). Cf. Elizabeth Jelin, ed., *Las conmemoraciones: Las disputas en las fechas "in-felices"* (Madrid: Siglo XXI, 2002). Bear in mind, too, the countermonument aesthetic and "after-image" sensibilities that can eventually emerge, as described in James Young, *At Memory's Edge: After-Images of the Holocaust in Contemporary Art and Architecture* (New Haven, Conn.: Yale University Press, 2000).

Third, for the various generational and experiential "layers" that shape remembrance and forgetting as a process at once subjective and intersubjective, and for the importance of focusing on dates and on ad hoc creations of memory sites through civic action and performance, see Elizabeth Jelin and Susana G. Kaufman's brilliant study "Layers of Memories: Twenty Years After in Argentina," in *The Politics of War Memory and Commemoration*, ed. T. G. Ashplant, Graham Dawson, and Michael Roper (New York: Routledge, 2000), 89–110. For additional reflection on politics, ownership of memory, and public cultural space, see Elizabeth Jelin, "La política de la memoria: El movimiento de derechos humanos y la construcción democrática en la Argentina," in *Juicio, castigos y memorias: Derechos humanos y justicia en la política argentina*, ed. Carlos H. Acuña et al. (Buenos Aires: Ediciones Nueva Visión SAIC, 1995), 101–46, esp. 141–43.

Fourth, for symbolic human referents in the making of collective memory, see the superlative essay by Hortensia Muñoz, "Human Rights and Social Referents: The Construction of New Sensibilities," in *Shining and Other Paths: War and Society in Peru, 1980–1995,* ed. Steve J. Stern (Durham, N.C.: Duke University Press, 1998), 447–69. Fifth, on the "truths" to be found in the personal and emblematic memories recorded by oral historians, even in cases where the narratives present empirical falsehoods, and for much methodological insight into the practice of oral history, see Alessandro Portelli, *The Death of Luigi Trastulli and Other Stories: Form and Meaning in Oral History* (Albany: State University of New York Press, 1991); cf. Daniel James, *Doña María's Story: Life History, Memory, and Political Identity* (Durham, N.C.: Duke University Press, 2000). See also the perceptive distinctions drawn between the memory evident in oral video testimony of Holocaust survivors, where there emerges the sense of a personal disaster without limit and without sense (a sensibility that is one of the hallmarks, I think, of radical evil), and the memory evident in literary testimonial writings, where one finds more of an impulse to mediate ultimate disaster and meaninglessness by attaching the disaster narrative to a survival or transcendence that might offer hope of finding meaning, by Lawrence Langer, *Holocaust Testimonies: The Ruins of Memory* (New Haven, Conn.: Yale University Press, 1991). Cf. the thoughtful reflections on memory of trauma in Saul Friedlander, "Trauma, Transference and 'Working through' in Writing the History of the *Shoah,*" *History and Memory* 4, no. 1 (spring/summer 1992): 39–59; and for interdisciplinary perspectives leaning toward psychiatry and medical anthropology, see Paul Antze and Michael Lambek, eds., *Tense Past: Cultural Essays in Trauma and Memory* (New York: Routledge, 1996).

  As I thought through my materials and found myself developing a conceptual preference for an actor- and event-driven history of memory, for a language of bothersome and living "memory knots" rather than *lieux de mémoire* in a world emptied of *milieux de mémoire,* and for the idea of bridges built between the personal and the emblematic in the process of making collective memory, I developed a special debt to Rousso, Young, Jelin and Kaufman, Muñoz, Portelli, and Langer.

3 As will become clear in Books Two and Three of this trilogy, the examples of varying specific emphasis, and of eventual layering of flat versions of emblematic memory with historical qualifications, are not hypothetical thought exercises but are based on my field conversations and historical research. At the extreme, even prominent proponents of memory as salvation, socially located within or close to military circles, could eventually turn into "dissidents" who believed that the military had stayed in power too long and that its mission had been corrupted by Pinochet. See, e.g., the interviews in Sergio Marras, *Confesiones* (Santiago: Ornitorrinco, 1988); cf. Marras, *Palabra de soldado* (Santiago: Ornitorrinco, 1989).

4 On the performative aspects of social memory, a useful discussion is Paul

Connerton, *How Societies Remember* (New York: Cambridge University Press, 1989), although he does not analyze the fissures, contestations, and multiple levels of analysis including "media spectacle" aspects that would be needed to understand commemorations of controversial memory in contemporary mass society.

5 Field notes of group discussion and informal conversation at meeting organized by the Comando de Exonerados Militares, Santiago, 30-X-96; interviews with Pepe V. (a pseudonym to protect the privacy of the sailor, whose imprisonment and torture under accusation of sedition were publicized in the press in August and September 1973), 25-II-97 and 27-II-97; and interview with Col. Eugenio Rivera, 9-IV-97.

6 This form of countermemory came up repeatedly in my field conversations and interviews and was even evident in agrarian regions far removed from Santiago. Ramiro I. and Claudia de I. (whose story was presented in the Afterword to chapter 2), for example, interpreted the scarcity crisis in these terms.

7 The full historical analysis of this process emerges in Book Two of this trilogy, esp. part I. See also the "memory against memory" reflection in Jelin, *Los trabajos de la memoria*.

8 My discussion of the person whose memory and existence seem to have split into a "deep" life and a "normal" everyday life is greatly indebted to the distinction between deep and ordinary memory developed by Charlotte Delbo (who uses the molting of snakes as a striking metaphor for memory and the skin of memory), in *Days and Memory*, trans. Rosette Lamont (1985; Marlboro, Vt.: Marlboro Press, 1990); and to the brilliant elaborations inspired by Delbo, in Langer, *Holocaust Testimonies*. I also learned from the sensitive treatment of memory and doubling in a cross-generational context in Helen Epstein, *Children of the Holocaust* (1979; New York: Bantam, 1980); Dina Wardi, *Memorial Candles: Children of the Holocaust*, trans. Naomi Goldblum (London and New York: Tavistock, 1992); and from the resonance between these works and my experiences as a child of Holocaust survivors. These works and experiences sensitized me to perceive and respond to the doubling phenomenon that somehow splits life into a deep memory and identity that seem fundamental, and an ordinary memory and identity that can seem superficial and empty.

However, it must be added that my comments on this point are based primarily upon field research. I am especially grateful to Ximena L. for responding directly to a presentation of this point, in the lecture I gave in Santiago on 6-XI-98, with a conversation about her personal and family life (she was four years old when her father was kidnapped and disappeared by the state in 1976); and to Susana Kaufman, for a psychoanalytic perspective that drew on clinical experience, in response to a presentation of these ideas in a workshop held in Montevideo on 16–17 November 1998.

I should also add that although my discussion of the split into double-persons may seem more an "ethnographic" description of persons rather than a description of the meaning framework of memory as unresolved rupture, this distinction is a limited one. Part of the cultural "message" of memory as unresolved rupture is precisely that "normal" people who continue to be functional persons in many everyday respects have suffered a devastating interior wounding, unbearable precisely because the trauma continues to hurt, continues to define their deepest personhood, continues to defy adequate language of expression, and continues to defy resolution and integration within normal everyday life.

9 To avoid confusion, I should note that in earlier presentations I had used a different language to gloss persecution and awakening as an emblematic meaning framework: "la memoria como una prueba" and subsequently "la memoria como una prueba de la consecuencia ética y democrática." These glosses were cruder in analytical terms and also raise subtle linguistic problems. I am grateful to many people (see note 1 in this chapter), especially Teresa Valdés, for discussions that helped me refine the analysis and search for a linguistic gloss that could serve well in both Spanish and English.

10 The heterogeneity of the memory camp aligned with ideas of persecution and awakening will come through more fully in Books Two and Three of this trilogy.

11 Again (as with note 3 in this chapter), I must emphasize that the examples given are not hypothetical thought exercises. They are based on my field conversations and historical research and are more fully analyzed in trilogy Book Three. The most controversial of the examples given here refers to the ambivalent sympathy that respects the pain of those who suffered rupture but also sees them as an annoying problem, because this ambivalence has been a touchy point between relatives of the disappeared and other human rights organizations on the one hand, and various political elites of the ruling Center-Left coalition (the Concertación) on the other. A fellow researcher, Erica Eppinger, who interviewed various political elites of the Concertación about human rights issues, described the body language of such ambivalence as a "rolling of the eyes" that occurs when a politician receives a telephone call from relatives who "had their turn" earlier in the 1990s but whom one must continue to handle with formal courtesy and sympathy (conversation, 22-VIII-96).

Sola Sierra, the leader of the relatives-of-the-disappeared organization (Agrupación de Familiares de Detenidos-Desaparecidos) for many years until her untimely death in 1999, described the ambivalence of Center-Left politicians who seemed to have a hard time saying "no" or avoiding sympathy with the Agrupación's stances in face-to-face encounters, but who therefore seemed always to postpone interviews. Her complaint with such political figures was not that their "heart" was in the wrong place, nor that their diagnosis of political obstacles was fictional, but that they seemed unwilling to fight hard political battles in defense of their ostensible convictions about truth and justice. Conversation with Sola Sierra and Viviana Díaz, 3-IX-96; and interview with Sola Sierra, 26-III-97. For the broad issue of the role of human rights and social movements in Latin American transitions to democracy, and the disappointments and obstacles that emerge beyond the initial moment of transition, see Elizabeth Jelin and Eric Hershberg, eds., *Constructing Democracy: Human Rights, Citizenship, and Society in Latin America* (Boulder, Colo.: Westview Press, 1996).

12 The frictions—a kind of conflictive synergy among actors formally or substantively aligned with the human rights–oriented memory camp—are specifically documented in trilogy Book Three.

13 An important point, but one which I cannot take up in this chapter, is the fact that the history of the Chilean republic has included a series of political ruptures, massacres, and upheavals. In this context, it is useful and revealing to look at the long-term pattern of closing the box and establishing a public policy that interpreted olvido as a positive good. This point has been put forth recently in pioneering studies by Brian Loveman and Elizabeth Lira: *Las suaves cenizas del olvido: Vía chilena de reconciliación política, 1814–1932* (Santiago: LOM-DIBAM, 1999); and *Las ardientes cenizas del olvido: Vía chilena de reconciliación política* (Santiago: LOM-DIBAM, 2000) For possible connections to the theme of tragedy in Chilean culture since colonial times, see the stimulating essay by Maximiliano Salinas C., *La invención de occidente: Origen y persistencia del espíritu de la tragedia en Chile* (Documento de Trabajo 15, Universidad ARCIS, Centro de Investigaciones Sociales, Santiago, September 1997). I will take up the theme of long-term continuity and change in the handling of traumatic collective memory, and the significance of the Loveman-Lira research, in the conclusion to Book Three of this trilogy.

14 For this form of "mindful forgetfulness," as Andrew Wolpert puts it, in a variety of historical contexts, see Wolpert, *Remembering Defeat: Civil War and Civic Memory in Ancient Athens* (Baltimore: Johns Hopkins University Press, 2002); Aguilar, *Memory and Amnesia;* and Yerushalmi, "Reflexiones sobre el olvido," 13–26. Cf. Jelin and Kaufman, "Layers of Memories"; and Micheline Enríquez, "La envoltura de memoria y sus huecos," in *Las envolturas psíquicas,* ed. Didier Anzieu (Buenos Aires: Amorrortu, 1990), 102–25.

15 As is well known, the 1978 amnesty decree did not apply to these two officials, because of their connection to the assassination by car bombing of Socialist leader Orlando Letelier and his colleague Ronni Moffit in Washington, D.C., in 1976. One effect of the tensions that ensued between the Chilean government and the Carter administration was a technical exception to the amnesty for those who might be found guilty in the Letelier-Moffit case. See trilogy Book Two, chapter 4.

16 The problem of arbitrariness versus authenticity in group memory is theoret-

ically complex. Extreme versions of the first, a kind of hyperconstructivist approach, undermine the threads of continuity that constitute a necessary precondition for group consciousness of history and memory. Extreme versions of the second turn a blind eye to the human meaning-work that processes, selects from, and interprets experience from the standpoint of the present, and can thereby foster group or national teleologies based on a hard line of presumed continuity from past to present. For thoughtful yet diverse reflections on these issues, see Barry Schwartz, "The Social Meaning and Context of Commemoration: A Study in Collective Memory," *Social Forces* 61, no. 2 (December 1982): 374–97; Portelli, *Death of Luigi Trastulli*. In the context of the literature on nations and nationalism, see Benedict Anderson, *Imagined Communities: Reflections on the Origin and Spread of Nationalism*, rev. ed. (New York: Verso, 1991); Anthony Smith, "The Nation: Invented, Imagined, Reconstructed?" in *Reimagining the Nation*, ed. Marjorie Ringrose and Adam J. Lerner (Buckingham, England: Open University Press, 1993), 9–28; Florencia E. Mallon, *Peasant and Nation: The Making of Postcolonial Mexico and Peru* (Berkeley: University of California Press, 1995); and Rudy Koshar, *Germany's Transient Pasts: Preservation and National Memory in the Twentieth Century* (Chapel Hill: University of North Carolina Press, 1998).

17 See esp. Anderson, *Imagined Communities*, and the other works cited in note 16.

18 There is, of course, a notable literature on the public cultural domain, its communication aspects, and its implications for citizenship. Much of it has been inspired by Jürgen Habermas. For a good discussion, see Craig Calhoun, ed., *Habermas and the Public Sphere* (Cambridge, Mass.: MIT Press, 1992). Cf. Habermas, *The Structural Transformation of the Public Sphere: An Inquiry into a Category of Bourgeois Society*, trans. Thomas Burger, with Frederick Lawrence (Cambridge, Mass.: MIT Press, 1989).

19 An excellent study of Chile that clearly illustrates the importance of the generational aspect of cultural and political memory related to the 1973 crisis and its aftermath is Katherine Hite, *When the Romance Ended: Leaders of the Chilean Left, 1968–1998* (New York: Columbia University Press, 2000). For a theoretically informed discussion of memory, life course, and generation, anchored in a specific site and traced over a long period, see Marcuse, *Legacies of Dachau*. On generational transmission despite silence in Holocaust survivor families, I draw especially on Epstein, *Children of the Holocaust*, and on personal knowledge.

20 It should be noted, as well, that the longevity of military rule in Chile (1973–90) and the development of new waves of repression in the 1980s meant that the historical turning point of 1973, and the problem of political violence, constituted a fundamental experience for three key generations—the mature adult (middle-aged) and youth generations who experienced the late 1960s and early 1970s directly, and the youth generation that came of age in the 1980s, an era

whose protest cycles and political mobilizations were inseparable from contentiousness about memory and truth. For many members of these generations, the memory question is a legacy of the heart that cannot be shunted aside easily, even if one wants to do so.

21 See the discussion of Violeta E.'s memory and Lonquén in chapter 2 of this book. For a full discussion of Lonquén and its impact, see Book Two, chapter 4 of this trilogy.

22 See the case of Doña Elena F., chapter 1 in this book. She had moved from a stance of sheer denial of the truth of massive human rights violations in the 1970s to a "social cost" thesis in the 1990s. And for the emergence of a new framework (memory as a closed box) under pressure, see the "Politics and Chronology" section in this chapter, and for full analysis, trilogy Book Two, chapter 4.

23 The point of the "culture of fear" instituted by the military regimes in the Southern Cone of Latin America was precisely to stifle projection of alternative subjectivities and memories, including memories related to politics past and present, into the public domain. See Juan E. Corradi, Patricia Weiss Fagen, and Manuel Antonio Garretón, eds., *Fear at the Edge: State Terror and Resistance in Latin America* (Berkeley: University of California Press, 1992). Cf. Patricia Politzer, *Miedo en Chile* (Santiago: CESOC, 1985); and the wrenching confession, by Argentine parents of a *desaparecida*, that fear had for years prevented them from acting on a letter from their pregnant disappeared daughter, in Eric Stener Carlson, *I Remember Julia: Voices of the Disappeared* (Philadelphia: Temple University Press, 1996), 110. For more on psychological ramifications, see Elizabeth Lira, ed., *Psicología y violencia en América Latina* (Santiago: ILAS, 1994); Eugenia Weinstein et al., *Trauma, duelo y reparación: Una experiencia de trabajo psicosocial en Chile* (Santiago: FASIC, 1987); and Roberta Bacic Herzfeld, Teresa Durán Pérez, and Pau Pérez-Sales, *Muerte y desaparición forzada en la Araucanía: Una aproximación étnica* (Temuca and Santiago: Ediciones Universidad Católica de Temuco and LOM, 1998).

24 I wish to underscore my conceptual debt, in this discussion, to Muñoz, "Human Rights and Social Referents."

25 In the chapter text that follows, I present the connections between specific individuals and symbols. The richer version of this argument and its evidentiary base occurs in trilogy Book Two, esp. part I.

26 For a recent pioneering study of women on the Right and the crisis culminating in 1973, see Margaret Power, *Right-Wing Women in Chile: Feminine Power and the Struggle Against Allende, 1964–1973* (University Park: Pennsylvania State University Press, 2002); and for gender and symbolism in official discourse after 1973, see Giselle Munizaga, *El discurso público de Pinochet: Un análisis semiológico* (Buenos Aires: CLACSO, 1983). Cf. the works on women's experience and symbolism cited in note 27.

27 Out of respect for human suffering as well as historical truth, I need to acknowledge here that although the afflicted female relative has been the key social referent, male relatives have also suffered greatly from the killings, disappearances, or torture inflicted by the state on family members. In the organized solidarity associations (agrupaciones) of victims' relatives, who pressured the state and society to remember and take responsibility for repression of their loved ones, men have also been present among active members, albeit as a minority. In addition, on occasion individual men could become powerful symbols of agonized concern for loved ones. For example, one of the most galvanizing and moving symbols of the early 1980s was Sebastián de Acevedo. His desperation about the fate of his children, arrested on 8 November 1983 by the intelligence police (known then as the CNI, the organism that replaced the DINA in 1977) and whose torture he feared, led Acevedo to set himself on fire in front of the Cathedral on the central plaza of Concepción three days later. The antitorture group briefly joined by Violeta (see chapter 2 in this book) renamed itself to honor Acevedo's memory, and his immolation generated a great deal of publicity in some media. See, e.g., *La Tercera*, 12–13–14-XI-83; *El Sur* (Concepción), 12-XI-83; and the transcripts of news programs on Acevedo, Radio Cooperativa, Radio Chilena, and Radio Portales, in FAV, Recortes sobre Caso Acevedo. A review of *El Mercurio* and *La Segunda* during 12–13–14–15-XI-83 shows, as one might expect, that other prominent media tried to postpone publicity, and, when news reporting became inevitable, to provide low-profile reports while stigmatizing the children or deflecting attention from the torture issue.

Notwithstanding these caveats, afflicted female relatives were the key symbolic referent linked to memory as unresolved rupture. See, e.g., the photographs of hunger strikes and civil disobedience actions during 1977–79, collected in AFDD, *Un camino de imágenes: 20 años de historia . . .* (Santiago: AFDD, 1997), 26–27, 30–32, 34–35, 39–42 (cf. 90). It is helpful to juxtapose the symbolism with studies of the range of women's experiences under military rule: see Teresa Valdés and Marisa Weinstein, *Mujeres que sueñan: Las organizaciones de pobladoras en Chile: 1973–1989* (Santiago: FLACSO, 1993); Edda Gaviola, Eliana Largo, and Sandra Palestro, *Una historia necesaria: Mujeres en Chile: 1973–1990* (Santiago: Akí and Aora, 1994); and María Elena Valenzuela, "The Evolving Roles of Women under Military Rule," in Paul W. Drake and Iván Jaksic, eds., *The Struggle for Democracy in Chile*, rev. ed. (Lincoln: University of Nebraska Press, 1995), 161–87.

28 For representations and testimonials of the rage of youth, see Patricia Politzer, *La ira de Pedro y los otros* (Santiago: Planeta, 1988). For women awakened, see Valdés and Weinstein, *Mujeres que sueñan;* and Gaviola, Largo, and Palestro, *Una historia necesaria.* For political leaders and their rediscovery of one another and the value of democracy, see Patricio Aylwin Azócar, *El reencuentro de los demócratas: Del golpe al triunfo del No* (Santiago: Ediciones Grupo Zeta, 1998).

29 For the practical foundations of this symbolism, see Pamela Lowden, *Moral Opposition to Authoritarian Rule in Chile, 1973–1990* (New York: St. Martin's Press, 1996). The symbolism of religious conscience in the service of dissident memory met with resistance by the state and officialist media, which cast the Pro-Peace Committee and Vicaría de la Solidaridad as "subversive" organizations. This characterization helped justify press neglect of alternative information. For example, I asked the prominent conservative journalist Cristián Zegers—a cofounder of *Qué Pasa* magazine in the Allende era, a rising star and the eventual subdirector of *El Mercurio* in the early military years, and the director of the newspaper *La Segunda* in the 1980s—why he and other mainstream reporters had not taken seriously disturbing information gathered by the Vicaría and the Santiago Church before the Lonquén lime ovens case broke at the end of 1978. Zegers stated that in the early years he simply did not consider the Santiago Church and the Vicaría a credible source: the Vicaría staff had drawn on defeated Marxists and leftist lawyers, and he considered official sources neutral and credible. This is a rather stunning statement—a confession of a fundamental lack of curiosity by a journalist whose professional raison d'être was, presumably, curiosity. It says much about the political bitterness and stigmas (as well as fears) that shaped journalism in the 1970s. Interview, Cristián Zegers, 19-V-97.

30 See Book Two, chapter 4, of this trilogy, for the political pressures, events, and discourses linking the amnesty decree, soldiers, and memory as a closed box.

31 On learning processes and human rights, I am indebted to the particularly sensitive explication (for the case of Peru) in Muñoz, "Human Rights and Social Referents."

32 It is provocative to recall, when considering the importance of interrupting a more unthinking or habitual life to establish "memory" during and after times of evil, that Hannah Arendt came to consider "thoughtlessness" as integral to the paradoxical link she eventually drew between radical evil and the banality of evil. On this point, and on the unresolved tensions in Arendt's thought between the concepts of radical evil and the banality of evil, see *History and Memory* 8, no. 2 (autumn/winter 1996): thematic issue "Hannah Arendt and *Eichmann in Jerusalem*," esp. the essays by Adi Ophir, "Between Eichmann and Kant: Thinking on Evil After Arendt," 81–136; Seyla Benhabib, "Identity, Perspective and Narrative in Hannah Arendt's *Eichmann in Jerusalem*," 35–59, esp. 44–48; and José Brunner, "Eichmann, Arendt and Freud in Jerusalem: On the Evils of Narcissism and the Pleasures of Thoughtlessness," 61–88.

33 A bodily metaphor is especially appropriate, I think. The human body was the material and psychological focus of torture practices designed to destroy the subjective world of the tortured, and to impress upon the victims that the outer world could neither hear nor respond to their plight. For discussion, see Elaine Scarry, *The Body in Pain: The Making and Unmaking of the World* (New York:

Oxford University Press, 1985). In addition, basic bodily functions became a source of mental and physical anxiety for political prisoners; see Hernán Valdés, *Tejas Verdes: Diario de un campo de concentración en Chile* (1974; Barcelona, Editorial Laia, 1978). Finally, and as we shall see in detail in trilogy Books Two and Three, finding and burying the bodies of the missing became a huge symbolic aspect of memory struggles.

34 See Pierre Bourdieu, *Outline of a Theory of Practice*, trans. Richard Nice (New York: Cambridge University Press, 1977), who theorizes the habitus as a system of socially patterned dispositions that structure individual improvisation and practices "without presupposing a conscious aiming at ends" (72). For a superb critical discussion that sets Bourdieu within a wider web of intellectuals who provide insight on practical and discursive consciousness, see Steven Feierman, *Peasant Intellectuals: Anthropology and History in Tanzania* (Madison: University of Wisconsin Press, 1990), chap. 1. For the related problem of numbing and euphemistic languages that can foster "thoughtless" practice of evil, see Herbert Hirsch, *Genocide and the Politics of Memory: Studying Death to Preserve Life* (Chapel Hill: University of North Carolina Press, 1995), esp. 97–108. For a chilling South American case study, see Marguerite Feitlowitz, *A Lexicon of Terror: Argentina and the Legacies of Torture* (New York: Oxford University Press, 1998).

35 My thinking on the way that memory knots stir up multiple memories and human performances that insist on memory has been greatly influenced by Young, *Texture of Memory*. Cf. Jelin and Kaufman, "Layers of Memories."

36 The detailed empirical foundation of the paragraphs that follow will become evident in Books Two and Three of this trilogy.

37 The events and anniversaries mentioned in the previous two paragraphs—and the performances and responses they elicited—are analyzed extensively in trilogy Book Two. For the 11 September anniversary, see also the important study by Azun Candina Polomer, "El día interminable: Memoria e instalación del 11 de septiembre de 1973 en Chile (1974–1999)," in Jelin, *Las conmemoraciones*, 9–51. For the specific emergence of International Women's Day as a galvanizing anniversary on a par with May Day, see FAV, "Informe Confidencial, Marzo 1980," 13; and Taller de Lavandería, Taller de Acción Cultural (TAC), *Lavando la esperanza* (Santiago: TAC, 1984), 49, 155.

38 See Book Two, chapter 4, of this trilogy, for the detailed history of the Lonquén struggles, the concerns in the military junta about the galvanizing effect (both cultural and political) of Lonquén, and the eventual property transfer and dynamiting of the mining ovens.

39 The political aspect of memory of great traumatic upheaval comes through in a wide variety of historical cases. Germany in the twentieth century offers an especially useful example, since its Cold War division into two polities allows one to see clearly how political factors channel dominant memory mythologies

of the Nazi era. See Herf, *Divided Memory*. For other continental European cases related to the same era, see Rousso, *Vichy Syndrome;* Farmer, *Martyred Village;* and Aguilar, *Memory and Amnesia*. For the reworking of violent upheaval and civil war into mythologies profoundly influenced by politics, see also the case of the U.S. Civil War, as analyzed in Blight, *Race and Reunion*.

40 An excellent starting point for understanding the connections between repressive dynamics and an emerging Christian moral language of dissent in the 1970s is Lowden, *Moral Opposition*. For additional context, see also Patricio Orellana and Elizabeth Q. Hutchison, *El movimiento de derechos humanos en Chile, 1973–1990* (Santiago: CEPLA [Centro de Estudios Políticos Latinoamericanos Simón Bolívar], 1991); and Eugenio Ahumada et al., *Chile: La memoria prohibida*, 3 vols. (Santiago: Pehuén, 1989).

41 The chronology presented in the text that follows is distilled from the detailed analysis presented in trilogy Books Two and Three.

42 On the importance of tracing specific word usage, see, for the Argentine case, Feitlowitz, *Lexicon of Terror*. On the emergence of "memory" as a more explicit language or code word in Chile, see Book Two of this trilogy, chapters 4, 5.

43 The existential aspect of memory is not limited to relatives of disappeared or executed victims, survivors of political imprisonment, and activists involved in quotidian human rights work. For a vivid example by a Christian Democratic political leader, see Jorge Lavandero, *El precio de sostener un sueño* (Santiago: LOM, 1997), 19–23 (esp. 21–22), 26–27.

44 See notes 19–20 in this chapter; Jelin and Kaufman, "Layers of Memories"; and Jelin, *Los trabajos de la memoria*, 117–33, esp. 125–26. For a classic reflection on history, politics, and the making of generational consciousness, see Karl Mannheim, *Ideology and Utopia: An Introduction to the Sociology of Knowledge* (San Diego: Harcourt, Brace, Jovanovich, 1985).

45 See Halbwachs, *Les cadres sociaux* (cf. *On Collective Memory*), and his treatment of dreams as a limiting case to the general framework.

46 For a theoretically powerful examination of the ways subnational groups organize hegemonic and counterhegemonic processes, at a grassroots level and in dialogue with the national state, to define community voice and symbolism and thereby shape the "nation," its community of citizens with rights, and its symbols and mythologies, see Mallon, *Peasant and Nation*. For a useful complement and contrast, see Anderson, *Imagined Communities*.

Afterword to Chapter 4: Memory Tomb of the Unknown Soldier

1 Interview with Cristián U., 2-X-96, supplemented by informal conversations before and after the interview. All quotations that follow are from the interview.

2 In deference to Cristián and his fears, I have disguised the real name of the

conscript. The pseudonym "Lara," however, lends itself to the kind of diminutive used by the conscript's army comrades.

3 For troop levels in Chile in 1973, see Institute for Strategic Studies (London), *The Military Balance 1973–1974* (London: Chatto and Windus for ISS, 1974), 61. Total force levels, excluding 200,000 army reserves, amounted to about 90,000: army, 32,000; navy, 18,000; air Force, 10,000; and carabineros (para-military police), 30,000. Breakout figures for army conscripts are not available until 1976 (when the total army level had increased to 45,000 and the conscript force numbered 20,000). Based on the pattern over time—a difficulty in increasing the conscript force level (stuck at 20,000 during 1976–79) even as total army force level rose to 50,000 by 1979—an "about half" estimate for conscripts in 1973 is reasonable. See Augusto Varas, *Los militares en el poder: Régimen y gobierno militar en Chile, 1973–1986* (Santiago: Pehuén, 1987), 93–94 (Cuadro 4.4).

4 See José Toribio Merino C., *Bitácora de un almirante: Memorias* (Santiago: Editorial Andrés Bello, 1998), esp. 209–16, 226–28; Carlos Prats González, *Memorias: Testimonio de un soldado* (1985; reprint, Santiago: Pehuén, 1996), esp. 502–4; *Chile Hoy*, 30-VIII-73, p. 6 (interview entitled "Torturas en la Armada"); and *El Mercurio*, 10-IX-73 and 11-IX-73 ("Altamirano reconoció" and editorial "Discurso del Senador Altamirano," respectively). Cf. *El Siglo*, 10-IX-73. I am also grateful to my interview with Pepe V., one of the sailors accused of sedition, 25 and 27-II-97, for insight on this point.

5 *ICNVR*, vol. 1, bk. 1: 248, vol. 2, bk. 3: 277; APJCC, videotape interview of Ana Sáez by Juan Cifuentes Campos, ca. 5/97 (from a series of videotape interviews with members of the AFDD). See also Jorge Lavandero, *El precio de sostener un sueño* (Santiago: LOM, 1997), 47.

6 I am grateful to Elizabeth Lira, an experienced psychologist, activist, and scholar of human rights, for an illuminating conversation which clarified that speculations about additives to food to manipulate the soldiers' state of mind were not unusual. She also observed that some credible people in the human rights community had concluded that the idea could not be ruled out.

7 Cristián's struggle to find the right language and approach—and his initial jump to a discussion of God—may be fruitfully compared to the illuminating discussion of how a person may struggle to find the right "mode" for difficult or traumatic memory themes, as described in Daniel James, *Doña María's Story: Life History, Memory, and Political Identity* (Durham, N.C.: Duke University Press, 2000), 186–212. Cf. Alessandro Portelli, *The Death of Luigi Trastulli and Other Stories: Form and Meaning in Oral History* (Albany: State University of New York Press, 1991), esp. 1–26.

8 For an insightful analysis and diagnosis of "irruptions" as an aspect of a problematic elite pact or negotiated transition to democracy, see Alexander Wilde, "Irruptions of Memory: Expressive Politics in Chile's Transition to Democracy," *Journal of Latin American Studies* 31, no. 2 (May 1999): 473–500. Cf. the

analysis of the culture of prudence and convulsion in trilogy Book Three, chapter 3.

Conclusion: Memories and Silences of the Heart

1 The detailed analysis and documentation of the events mentioned here and of the array of issues yielding a certain "circle of impasse" appear in Book Three of this trilogy.

2 The chronology presented here is discussed in more detail in chapter 4 of this volume, but for full documentation and analysis, see Book Two of this trilogy, part I.

3 Although scholarship on the history of memory is a dynamic and burgeoning field, counterpart scholarship on the making of silence is less well developed. Problems of silence, as in this book, often arise as an integral aspect—an underside of myth making or memory making—in case studies; see, e.g., Jan T. Gross, *Neighbors: The Destruction of the Jewish Community in Jedwabne, Poland* (Princeton, N.J.: Princeton University Press, 2001), esp. 126–31; Sarah Farmer, *Martyred Village: Commemorating the 1944 Massacre at Oradour-sur-Glane* (Berkeley: University of California Press, 1999). For a pioneering anthology on silence as a problem in historical anthropology, analyzed in relation with commemoration, official history making, and earlier reflections on voice and power in the production of historical knowledge, see Gerald Sider and Gavin Smith, eds., *Between History and Histories: The Making of Silences and Commemorations* (Toronto: University of Toronto Press, 1997); also Michel-Rolph Trouillot, *Silencing the Past: Power and the Production of History* (Boston: Beacon Press, 1995).

For excellent recent reflection on silence with both European and South American cases in mind, see Elizabeth Jelin, *Los trabajos de la memoria* (Madrid: Siglo XXI, 2002), 29–32, 132–33. For a subtle reading of Chilean culture, fear, and disenchantment in relation to memory and silence, see Norbert Lechner, *Las sombras del mañana: La dimensión subjetiva de la política* (Santiago: LOM, 2002), esp. 61–82 (essay in collaboration with Pedro Güell). For revealing studies, oriented toward communication theory and ranging from linguistics to music and art, see Adam Jaworski, ed., *Silence: Interdisciplinary Perspectives* (Berlin: Mouton de Gruyter, 1997). Jaworski et al. show the fruitfulness of analyzing silence as communication event or metaphor rather than "absence of sound" (3). For insight on related issues of "lies and secrets" from the standpoint of historical analysis, see *History and Theory* 39, no. 4 (December 2000), special number on " 'Not Telling': Secrecy, Lies, and History," esp. Luise White, "Telling More: Lies, Secrets, and History," 11–22. Cf. White, *Speaking with Vampires: Rumor and History in Colonial Africa* (Berkeley: University of California Press, 2000). I am grateful to Thongchai Winichakul for orienting me toward some of this scholarship and his important new project, "Moments of Silence: The Ambivalent Memories of the October 1976 Massacre in Bangkok."

4 Ariel Dorfman, "Sol de Piedra"/"Sun Stone," in *In Case of Fire in a Foreign Land: New and Collected Poems from Two Languages* (Durham, N.C.: Duke University Press, 2002), 72–73. For the prison guard story, see Afterword to chap. 2; for the soldier, Marisa T., interview, 8-X-96.

5 The fuller analysis and documentation of this point will emerge in Books Two and Three, especially Book Three, of this trilogy.

Essay on Sources

This essay provides a guide to the research sources I used for "The Memory Box of Pinochet's Chile." Since I conducted integrated research for the entire trilogy, and since each book is influenced by research findings of the others, it makes little sense to provide a distinct essay on sources for each book. As a courtesy to readers, this essay is reproduced in each volume.

The first research phase involved a year of intense field and archival investigations in Chile, from July 1996 to August 1997. The second phase involved supplementary research via five shorter visits to Chile during 1998 to 2002, and library, microfilm, and Internet work (mainly media tracking) in the United States. I read newly published books through 2001, the close of the period under study, as comprehensively as possible. After 2001, I continued to read widely, albeit less comprehensively, among new publications while completing the first draft of all three volumes. I also continued to track relevant media developments or findings.

I relied on three streams of sources: (1) written documents—archival, published, and, more recently, electronic—that constitute the traditional heart of historical research; (2) audio and visual traces of the past and its memory struggles, in television and video archives, photojournalism, radio transcripts, and sound recordings; and (3) oral history including formal, semistructured interviews, less formal interviews and exchanges, and field notes from participant-observation experiences and focus groups. Participant-observation experiences also included visits to physical sites or ruins.

Below I divide the research sources somewhat differently, in order to consider traditional and nontraditional "media" sources in a more integrated fashion.

Readers should note that—with the exception of media—I do not offer a guide below to the vast published literature. The latter includes primary sources, especially an extensive *testimonio* and memoir literature; secondary sources on twentieth-century Chilean history; and rich comparative and theoretical literatures on memory in history. I have used these illuminating literatures extensively, but they are cited systematically in the notes, which often include commentaries for interested readers. To review these works again here would needlessly lengthen this essay, whose focus is on primary sources beyond the book publications available in major university libraries in the United States.

Before proceeding, however, I should note three aspects of the published literature that may be useful for other researchers. First, as is apparent in the notes, the testimonio and memoir genre is rich because it embraces social actors from a wide variety of social strata. They range from political and cultural elites with varied ideologies and experiences along Chile's Left-Center-Right spectrum, and in institutional niches (the Catholic Church, the military) more ambiguously related to specific political parties or identities; to grassroots actors from varied social worlds and experiences, that is, priests as well as Catholic lay activists, shantytown women indirectly affected by repression as well as direct victim-survivors and their relatives, former political prisoners as well as former agents of repression and prisoners coerced into collaboration. Second, two documentary publications require special mention, not only because of the quality of their data, but also because they serve as useful complementary guides for research in archives: Arzobispado de Santiago, Vicaría de la Solidaridad (hereinafter ASVS), *Detenidos desaparecidos: Documento de trabajo,* 8 vols. (Santiago: ASVS, 1993), which provides meticulous accounts of key data (events of repression, witness testimonies, judicial trajectory) in the Vicariate of Solidarity's individual case files on disappeared persons, on a case-by-case basis for the entire country; and Comisión Nacional de Verdad y Reconciliación, *Informe de la Comisión Nacional de Verdad y Reconciliación,* 2 vols. in 3 books (Santiago: Ministerio Secretaría General de Gobierno, 1991), which was the report of the Truth and Reconciliation Commission organized in 1990 by the newly elected administration of Patricio Aylwin Azócar. The 1991 Truth Commission report also presented a case-by-case analysis of individual victims, set within a reliable larger narrative on patterns. Below (and in the notes) these sources are cited as *DETDES* and *ICNVR,* respectively.

Finally, one must underscore that in research on contemporary and recent history of contentious memory, the conventional line between "primary" and "secondary" sources blurs and sometimes disintegrates altogether. A book by a reporter about historical events that occurred well before the date of publication, for example, can become a crucial "primary" source or document because of the politicocultural responses it generates. In addition, the role of investigatory journalism, and the prominence of testimonio-style witnessing in the culture and politics of persuasion, mean that books that might at first sight seem a secondary source account may turn out to include substantial primary source material (interviews, testimonios, documents). An excellent example of both phenomena—strong responses that turn a book into a document of its era, narratives that mix primary and secondary source features—is the pioneering 1989 study of the Caravan of Death episode of 1973 by journalist Patricia Verdugo, *Los zarpazos del puma* (1989; rev. ed., Santiago: CESOC, 1994). For context, see Book Three of this trilogy, esp. chapter 1.

The abbreviations used below after the first mention of archives, documentation centers, and library collections correspond to those provided in the abbreviation list that precedes the notes. To ease identification of distinct archives or sources (and comparison with the abbreviation list), I italicize their first mention here.

A. Archives, Documentation Centers, and Library Collections

The archives and collections mentioned in this section exclude repositories that pertain exclusively to the "Media" section below.

A1. Church and State Archives

Given the history of memory struggles and the role of the Santiago Catholic Church, the fundamental institutional starting point for research is *Fundación de Documentación y Archivo de la Vicaría de la Solidaridad, Arzobispado de Santiago* (FAV). The FAV is the most comprehensive and well-organized human rights and memory archive in Chile (and arguably, in the entire Southern Cone region of South America). Particularly useful for tracking human rights and memory themes over time is the Informe Confidencial series, whose inside-information aspect sometimes has the flavor of an intelligence service outside the formal state. The FAV's Caja A.I. and Caja A.T. series are also invaluable because they reproduce documents by theme and by organization. Much of the work and documents of other important human rights groups—among them AFDD (Agrupación de Familiares de Detenidos-Desaparecidos), FASIC (Fundación de Ayuda Social de las Iglesias Cristianas), and Comisión Chilena de Derechos Humanos—are tracked and reproduced in these FAV series. Also collected are documents from the predecessor organization to the Vicariate of Solidarity, the Pro-Peace Committee (COPACHI). The FAV Recortes files contain amazingly comprehensive press clippings files (including radio and television transcripts), organized by theme and running back in time to 1973. They thereby facilitate media research. In the 1990s, the tracking function also came to include a useful computerized Banco de Datos (database) on human rights and judicial themes. The judicial case files are extensive (but often restricted) and are well summarized, for disappearance cases, in the *DETDES*. The excellent library contains a full run of *Solidaridad,* as well as other magazines and books.

State archives usefully complement the FAV holdings. Among the most important for me were case files from the 1990–91 Truth and Reconciliation Commission: *Archivo de la Comisión Nacional de Verdad y Reconciliación* (ACNVR). The case files from the original archive were not held separately but incorporated into the case files of the state's follow-up organism, Archivo de la Corporación Nacional de Reparación y Reconciliación, but for sake of clarity I cite only case files from the original ACNVR. Theoretically, this archive is to be incorporated into Chile's national archive system and made available to researchers. The de facto reality has been that the materials are considered very sensitive and the archive remains under control of the Ministry of the Interior. I was fortunate to secure access for a limited period (ca. six weeks) that enabled me to review and analyze the Commission's work through a sample of thirty case files. These were mainly Santiago Metropolitan Region cases, organized by two fundamental criteria: (1) several cases each chosen from the various political back-grounds in play (victims with militance in each of the distinct parties subjected to targeted repression, and also victims without identifiable militance), and (2) cases with cross-record linkage potential, based on my prior research. I supplemented these cases with several cases of special human or research interest (e.g., cases of the DINA [secret police] turning against its own agents or collaborators). The *ICNVR* was a crucial companion guide for this research.

I also made use of *Archivo Siglo XX del Archivo Nacional* (ASXX), which has volumes of papers on deposit from various ministries. Although the purge of sensitive papers by the outgoing military regime has hampered the ASXX collection on sensitive topics—it does not hold, for example, Ministry of the Interior documents from the 1970s—the state had many ministries, and the purge was far from complete. I focused especially on the Reservados volumes of the Education Ministry from the early-to-mid 1970s; they documented the pressure and means used to rid educational institutions of dissidents and "subversives," and they also reproduced copies of external documents—such as directives and reports from Pinochet and the DINA, and early minutes of junta sessions—that might have been more effectively purged or withheld in other branches of the state.

Courtesy of Florencia Mallon, I also consulted photocopied material from *Archivo Intendencia Cautín* in Temuco (AICT). This archive was subsequently incorporated into Archivo Regional de Araucanía, Temuco. The AICT provides unusual access to regional documents and correspondence with authorities tracing grassroots support for and concern about the incoming military regime.

A2. Nongovernmental Organizations (NGOs) and Social Actors

The FAV archive documents a good deal of memory-related work and struggles by many NGOs (not simply the Vicaría de la Solidaridad) and by social actors inside and outside the state. Nonetheless, numerous other NGO and social actor holdings also proved important in the research.

For transnational solidarity activities related to Chile's memory struggles, and synergies with struggles within Chile, a superb starting point is *Fundación Salvador Allende, Centro de Documentación* (FSA). Particularly valuable is its *Archivo Sergio Insunza* (FSA, ASI), a major archive built up in exile by Allende's last minister of justice, Sergio Insunza. As a former member of the Unidad Popular and in his work with the International Commission of Democratic Jurists, Insunza participated ac-tively in European solidarity networks that crossed Cold War boundaries. His papers include witness-survivor testimonies, and mock trials of the junta held in various parts of the world; public declarations and pamphlets; confidential correspondence and communications among Democratic Jurist and Unidad Popular networks, and more generally between activists, diplomats, officials, and United Nations organ-isms; and extensive press clippings files organized by theme. The FSA also has, in addition to documents from Allende's life and presidency, collections of interest to memory work after 1973: messages and memorabilia left at Allende's tomb, the politics of street naming and monument projects to honor Allende's memory within and beyond Chile. With the assistance of Claudio Barrientos, a graduate student at the University of Wisconsin, Madison, the cataloging system of the FSA, ASI changed and became more rationalized after I did my work. My citation method corresponds to the older system, but the new system is sufficiently meticulous to enable one to find the cited documents.

For transnational solidarity, the strength of the FSA, ASI lies in its coverage of Europe and Latin America. For the U.S. side of the story, good complementary holdings are at *State Historical Society of Wisconsin Archives* (SHSWA), particularly its Community Action on Latin America Records, 1971–91, which documents grassroots activities in Madison, Wisconsin, and links out to other U.S.-based solidarity organizations and to U.S. congressional activity; and the survivor-witness testimony in the Adam Schesch Papers, 1965–74, which includes an important press conference reel (2 October 1973) about Schesch's imprisonment at the National Stadium in September 1973. As of 2004, researchers also have permission to utilize the SHSWA's Institute for Policy Studies Records, 1961–92, the important solidarity and think-tank NGO where Orlando Letelier worked before his assassination in Washington, D.C., in 1976.

Various Chilean NGOs have documentation centers whose holdings include a variety of published and unpublished sources including NGO bulletins related to their memory work. I benefited from documents, bulletins, and publications at the following: *Archivo, Corporación Parque Por La Paz Villa Grimaldi* (ACPPVG) documents the successful struggle in the 1990s to stop a project to obliterate the former torture-and-disappearance center Villa Grimaldi and transform it into a Peace Park. *Agrupación de Familiares de Detenidos-Desaparecidos, Centro de Documentación* (AFDDCD) focuses on the truth, justice, and memory struggles of relatives of the disappeared. *Comité de Defensa de los Derechos del Pueblo, Centro de Documentación* (CODEPUCD) is the working library of a human rights NGO important since the 1980s, with notable emphasis on torture and a policy explicitly embracing defense of the human rights of armed opponents of dictatorship. *Educación y Comunicaciones, Centro de Documentación* (ECOCD) documents ECO's trajectory in organizing grassroots history and memory of the labor movement, and in recovering popular memory and histories of struggle in local grassroots contexts. *Fundación para la Protección de la Infancia Dañada por los Estados de Emergencia, Centro de Documentación* (PIDEECD) is the working library of the PIDEE, an NGO that pioneered work on family and youth mental health issues related to repression. *Ictus, Centro de Documentación* (ICTUSCD) consists of a vast video repository with related print documents and bulletins on the cultural work of Ictus (originally an experimental theater group), whose staff and actors became heavily engaged with the world of alternative video-forums in the 1980s. I should clarify that in the case of the AFDDCD and

ACPPVG, I did not work directly in the repositories but rather was kindly given copies of bulletins and documents held by these organizations; as of 2002, a major reorganizing effort has been under way to reorder the AFDDCD holdings in a new building and to establish a computerized catalog or database.

Personal archives were also valuable for documenting some kinds of grassroots social activities: *Archivo Personal de Alicia Frohmann* (APAF), for ephemera related to underground bulletin work during the state of siege of 1984–85 and for initiatives by young historians in the 1980s; *Archivo Personal de Eugenia Rodríguez* (APER), for pro-junta clippings, magazines, and ephemera, and publications and activities of the Secretaría de la Mujer; *Archivo Personal de Juan Campos Cifuentes* (APJCC), for documents and videos related to the work of relatives of the disappeared, and a run of Carabinero- and military-related documents; *Archivo Personal de Teresa Valdés* (APTV), the invaluable archive tracing the work of the women's human rights group Mujeres Por La Vida.

A3. Additional Special Libraries, Collections, and Ephemera

I benefited from several libraries and collections, in addition to the vast FAV library and the specialized documentation centers mentioned above. The *Biblioteca Nacional* (BN) has an invaluable repository of Chilean newspapers. I used it for targeted research, examining key dates (usually, a two-week period whose center point was the key date), to supplement gaps that remained after using thematically organized clipping files in repositories such as the FAV and FSA. Comprehensive reviews of major weekly magazines also helped me identify less obvious dates (events or anniversaries) that might need further newspaper examination at the BN, and sensitized me to ways memory played out during noncharged as well as charged seasons and moments. The *Biblioteca de* FLACSO (BF) includes an excellent collection of books and magazines related to memory and human rights issues, and it also has a fine collection of polling surveys by various organizations, including FLACSO (Facultad Latinoamericana de Ciencias Sociales–Chile). Its *Archivo Eduardo Hamuy* (BF, AEH) also offers a database that documents polling research performed by Eduardo Hamuy. The *Princeton University Library Pamphlet Collection, Chile* (PUC) is a treasure, in part because it includes so much ephemera related to social movements and politics under military rule (as well as more standard material, such as newspaper and magazine runs). I relied on microfilm copies (available from Scholarly Resources, Inc., by agreement with Princeton University Library) of both the "Main" and "Supplement" collections.

B. Media Sources: Print, Audio and Visual, and Electronic

Research on the recent history of memory struggles requires considerable attention to media, not only as a basic source for historical events (the traditional "first draft of history" role of journalists) but also as an object of analysis in its own right. The sources below are listed with both functions in mind, and therefore they include not only listings of media as historical sources but archives or collections oriented to analysis of media.

B1. Print Media

The list below combines newspapers and magazines. An asterisk (*) after the listing marks those media reviewed systematically, as distinguished from those used sporadically for specialized themes or purposes—for example, documentation of the publicity given to the alleged Plan Z conspiracy or of events and reactions related to the London arrest of Pinochet. When no city or country is listed in parentheses, the place of publication is Santiago and the publication is normally considered "national." City citations in parentheses refer to "de provincia" periodicals within Chile; country citations in parentheses mark foreign media. For some media, I relied in part on electronic (online) editions after 1997. In those cases, I have also supplied the online Web page location used. In a few instances, the medium is exclusively online. I note this by listing such media in quote marks rather than italics (i.e., "El Mostrador" rather than *El Mostrador*).

I must underscore my appreciation for the extensive and well-organized clippings files at the FAV. Without that foundation (and the complementary clippings files at the FSA, ASI), I could not have reviewed as many media as systematically, nor pulled into my radar complementary media for specific cases or events, nor developed an efficient targeted methodology (see section A3 above) for media work at the BN and other collections.

To ease location and render common Spanish and English usages compatible, I retain *El* and *The* in the alphabetical list below. The only exceptions are *New York Times, Ultimas Noticias,* and *Washington Post,* which bow to contemporary conventions.

When a magazine or newspaper uses a week as its date of publication, I generally use the first day listed as the "date of publication" in the notes. For example, a magazine dated 3 to 10 September 1978 would simply be listed as 3-IX-78.

Readers should note that a number of the publications cited no longer exist. Some date to the Allende era and were closed by the dictatorship but were important for research on efforts to establish a memory script for a "coup foretold." Others played significant roles under dictatorship or during times of democratic transition but eventually succumbed to the difficulties of a concentrated and changing media market in the 1990s.

Amiga
Análisis*
Apsi*
Cal y Canto
Caras
Cauce*
Chile-America* (Italy)
Chile Hoy*
Clarín (Argentina; also
    www.clarin.com.ar)
Clarín (Santiago)
Concordia de Arica (Arica)
Cosas*
Crónica (Concepción)
El Correo (Valdivia)
El Cronista
El Día (La Serena)
El Diario
El Diario Austral (Temuco)
El Mercurio* (also at www.emol.com,
    formerly www.elmercurio.cl)
El Mercurio (Antofagasta)
El Mercurio (Valparaíso)
El Mercurio de Calama (Calama)
"El Mostrador"*: www.elmostrador.cl
El Mundo (Spain; also www.el-
    mundo.es)
El Observador (Quillota)
El País (Spain; also www.elpais.es)
El Rodriguista
El Siglo*
El Sur (Concepción)
El Tarapacá (Iquique)
Ercilla*
Estrategia
Fortín Mapocho
Hoy*
"Inter-Press Service" (international):
    www.ips.org
La Bicicleta
La Cuarta

La Epoca* (also www.laepoca.cl)
La Estrella (Valparaíso)
La Estrella de Iquique (Iquique)
La Estrella del Norte (Antofagasta)
La Firme
La Funa*
La Nación
La Opinión (Argentina)
La Patria
La Prensa (Iquique)
La Prensa (Nicaragua)
La Prensa (Tocopilla)
La Prensa (Vallenar)
La Prensa de Santiago
La Segunda*
La Tercera* (also www.tercera.cl,
    formerly www.latercera.cl)
Latin American Weekly Report* (U.K.)
Mensaje
Miami Herald (U.S.)
NACLA Report on the Americas (U.S.)
New York Times* (U.S.; also
    www.nytimes.com)
Pluma y Pincel
Prensa
Prensa Libre (Guatemala)
"Primera Línea": www.primeralinea.cl
Proa (San Antonio)
Punto Final*
Puro Chile
Qué Pasa*
Realidad
Revista Carabineros de Chile*
Rocinante
"Santiago Times":
    www.santiagotimes.cl (also link at
    www.derechoschile.com; formerly
    "CHIP News," www.chip.cl)
Solidaridad*
SurDA
The Clinic*

The Economist (U.K.)
The Guardian (U.K.; also
   http://reports.guardian.co.uk)
The Nation (U.S.)
The New Republic (U.S.)

The New Yorker (U.S.)
Ultimas Noticias
Vea
Washington Post (U.S.)

B2. Audio and Visual Sources

Photojournalism played a significant role in memory struggles and is a marvelous point of entry into the 1973–2001 period. The print media listed above, of course, make ample use of photojournalism. The Web sites listed below (section B3) also provide visual documentation. I complemented these with photojournalism collections by professional photographers. The *Archivo Gráfico Personal de Helen Hughes* (AGPHH) has the work of gifted photographer Helen Hughes, who has lived in Chile since 1977 and worked actively with the Vicaría de la Solidaridad and human rights networks. The archive graciously allowed me to use selections from her photo collection in this trilogy. Her annotations to photos in her personal archive add valuable insight and context for work in visual sources. The *Archivo Gráfico Personal de Miguel Angel Larrea* (AGPMAL) is a fine personal collection by a working photojournalist and provides an excellent sense of the images important in oppositional journalism in the 1980s. The *Archivo Gráfico del Arzobispado de Santiago* (AGAS) complements the AGPHH and AGPMAL nicely, because it includes images that date back to the 1970s and that were important for the work of the Vicaría de la Solidaridad and in the early activities of relatives of the disappeared.

Radio, television, and alternative audiovisual networks (grassroots screenings and discussion forums) all proved important media streams and focal points of memory struggles. For radio, which was especially important in the 1970s, the FAV archive has transcripts of relevant news and commentary within its clippings files and bulletins on human rights and memory controversies. The coverage embraces pro-official, church-oriented, and dissent-oriented radio: *Radio Agricultura, Radio Balmaceda, Radio Chilena, Radio Cooperativa, Radio Minería, Radio Nacional, Radio Portales*. I complemented the FAV transcripts with documents from personal collections: Radio Agricultura recordings, from the APER; and clandestine radio broadcasts by the Frente Patriótico Manuel Rodríguez, from the APMM (*Archivo Personal de "MM,"* whose name is withheld to preserve anonymity).

Sound as a medium of communication and memory struggles also circulated outside the sphere of radio and outside the genre of news-talk (i.e., news reports, commentary, and interviews). Particularly important as "alternative sound" was music (see trilogy Book Two, Afterwords to chapters 3, 7). Under the dictatorship, this included private cassettes circulating the repressed "New Song" music of the 1960s and early 1970s, such as the work of Violeta Parra, Víctor Jara, and Patricio

Manns or of groups such as Inti-Illimani and Quilapayún. It also included newer music produced under conditions of dictatorship, by such groups as Congreso, Illapu, Los Prisioneros, and Sol y Lluvia. Since the democratic transition in the early 1990s, such music has become readily available for purchase in new compact disc editions, circulates publicly, and feeds into ongoing memory work or struggles. For musical documentation, I relied on the personal collection Florencia Mallon and I have built up over the years, in dialogue with data from interviews and documents.

An additional source of alternative sound was cassettes of audio documents and testimonies that circulated extensively in the mid-1980s and which aired sounds then considered taboo on radio—for example, Allende's last speech and intercepts of communications between Pinochet, Gustavo Leigh, and other high military officials on 11 September 1973. The most important production was "Chile: Entre el dolor y la esperanza" (1986), directed by journalists Mónica González and Patricia Verdugo, in the series *El Sonido de la Historia* and kindly copied for me by a person in exile. Here, too, I relied on my personal collection.

My research on television and on alternative audiovisual media drew on several sources. Most important were *Televisión Nacional, Centro de Documentación* (TVNCD), *Archivo Audiovisual de la Vicaría de Pastoral Social (Santiago)* (AAVPS), and the ICTUSCD. At the TVNCD, the working video and documentary center of Televisión Nacional, I was able to review news reporting in the 1980s, as well as specific media events and spectacles in the 1980s and 1990s—including the television strips (*franjas*) by both sides in the 1988 plebiscite, and news interviews and programs (especially the *Informe Especial* news magazine) that sparked attention and controversy during the 1990s.

The purging of archives conducted by the outgoing military regime made 1970s programming more scarce at the TVNCD. Fortunately, the 1970s transcripts included in the clippings files and bulletin reports at the FAV included news and commentary at Televisión Nacional (Canal 7) and at Televisión de la Universidad Católica de Chile (Canal 13).

Both the AAVPS and ICTUSCD were crucial for understanding the world of alternative audiovisual media. The AAVPS not only contained video copies of key public events (such as President Patricio Aylwin's televised 1991 speech to the nation about the report of the Truth and Reconciliation Commission), thereby allowing me to concentrate on other matters during my limited access time at the TVNCD. It also contained a run of the forty-six highly professional and counterofficial news programs in the *Teleanálisis* series of 1984–89, barred from television but distributed in videos for viewing and discussion forums in shantytowns and popular settings, with church and NGO assistance. The ICTUSCD collection rounded out the street world of alternative audiovisual media programming via its marvelous holdings of videos (movies, documentaries, and theater, produced by Ictus and other alternative media groups) used in popular screening-forum events in the 1980s, and via its records on the distribution and popularity of specific works.

Additional viewing of significant audiovisual productions, some from the world of public programming and some from the semiunderground world of communications, came from various sources. I was assisted in this way by the ECOCD, FSA, APAF, APJCC, APTV, and *Archivo Personal de Sol Serrano* (APSS).

Finally, I should mention personal archives that offered important insight on television and audiovisual communications. *Archivo Personal de Diego Portales Cifuentes* (APDPC) allowed me access to published and unpublished reports by the NGO media group ILET, Instituto Latinoamericano de Estudios Transnacionales. The ILET was crucial in the emergence of sophisticated audiovisual analysis and experience in Chile in the years leading up to the 1988 plebiscite. Similarly, *Archivo Personal de María Eugenia Hirmas* (APMEH) offered copies of her extensive and astute media analyses, including her influential and insightful studies of television publicity and propaganda related to the 1988 plebiscite. An interview with María Elena Hermosilla, 14-III-97, also offered sharp analysis of the world of alternative communications and pointed me toward promising leads and personal archives.

B3. Electronic Sources

The Internet and World Wide Web emerged as a world media phenomenon during the last four years covered by this study (1998–2001) and had implications for the course of memory struggles. The theme receives explicit attention in Book Three of this trilogy. For my purposes, the most important research implication was the ability to track from abroad media reports and spectacles in online editions of newspapers, which also came to include links to documents or exposés of interest. Since 1998, the leaders in newspapers with links to memory archives and documents have been "El Mostrador" (www.elmostrador.cl) and *La Tercera* (www.tercera.cl), which may be usefully supplemented by "Santiago Times" (www.santiagotimes.cl). In the pre-1998 phase of Internet adoption in Chile (see trilogy Book Three, chapter 4), the now defunct *La Epoca* (www.laepoca.cl) also played a pioneering role.

Beyond electronic newspapers and their links to archives of back articles and thematically organized documents, other World Wide Web sites have organized memory-related information, documents, forums, and testimonios. In other words, they have become memory "players" in ongoing struggles. A note of caution is in order. Web site addresses change and evolve. A few sites have shut down—either because the flux of business and markets rendered them untenable, as in the case of *La Epoca,* or because questions of politics, legality, or timeliness undermined them, as in the case of Despierta Chile, organized by former secret police agents and sympathizers to publish "confessions" by tortured prisoners.

The list below is organized by World Wide Web address, with parenthetical notes to identify the organizing group and to add, if needed, a brief annotation. The list is necessarily selective, reflects only sites I consulted and found useful, and offers a spread of memory frameworks and political perspectives. Rather than provide lengthy extensions in the address, I generally provide the point of entry, since links to the Chile-related memory sectors of the site are easy to find.

Unless otherwise noted, all addresses below begin with the conventional *www.* prefix. I simply provide the remainder of the address.

amnesty.org (Amnesty International)
cerc.cl (Centro de Estudios de la Realidad Contemporánea; polling)
chipsites.com (Chile Information Project)
codepu.cl (CODEPU; human rights NGO in Chile)
derechoschile.com (Derechos Chile; fairly comprehensive map of memory and human rights issues and history in Chile)
derechos.org/nizkor (Equipo Nizkor; human rights, Latin America)
despiertachile.netfirms.com (Despierta Chile; former secret police)
ejercito.cl (Chilean Army)
foia.state.gov (U.S. State Department)
fundacionpinochet.cl (Fundación Presidente Augusto Pinochet Ugarte)
geocities.com, at /Athens/Delphi/9574/grimaldi.htm (Villa Grimaldi Peace Park; also, http://members.xoom.com/grimaldi)
gn.apc.org/warresisters (War Resisters International, U.K.)
guillo.cl (Guillo Bastías; brilliant political cartoons)
hrw.org (Human Rights Watch)
manuelcontreras.com (Manuel Contreras; former head of the DINA)
memoriaviva.com (Memoria Viva; memory and human rights, organized by Chilean exiles in the U.K.; related international tree-planting project at ecomemoria.com)
mesadedialogo.cl (Mesa de Diálogo sobre Derechos Humanos; 1999–2000 dialogue initiative encompassing military and civilians)
nsarchive.org (National Security Archive; NGO, systematic work with U.S. government documents and Freedom of Information Act, major link to Chile documents via Clinton administration's Declassification Project and Freedom of Information Act; also at gwu.edu/~nsarchiv)

C. Oral History Sources

In addition to written documents and audio and visual traces of the past, I used oral sources. Below I first consider the basic purpose and parameters of the oral research, then turn to more subtle issues of method, relationships with informants, and representation.

The fundamental purpose of my oral research was to explore in depth the ways people from diverse memory camps and walks of life defined meaning and memory of the 1973 crisis and the violence of military rule, both in terms of their own lives and in terms of the wider society. Of course, I also used many oral interviews to help me hypothesize or reconstruct empirical historical facts that could be corroborated or cross-checked with other sources, and to ask informants, in turn, to react to hypotheses and findings based on my work in written or other sources. My main quest, however, was to establish relationships, interviews, and participant-observation experiences—in the spirit of an ethnographer or a journalist involved in field immersion—that might enable me to achieve an in-depth human exploration of memory and meaning in Chilean society.

For purposes of historical analysis, the oral research served two objectives: understanding the human faces of memory and meaning as of the mid-to-late 1990s, especially among ordinary rather than well-known Chileans; and integration of what I learned via oral research and field immersion in the mid-to-late 1990s moment into the analysis of memory creation and struggle over time, as a process traced through historical records from the 1970s through the 1990s.

Several consequences followed for my oral research strategy. First, I gave priority to semistructured life history interviews, not to the design of formal questionnaires for statistically valid analysis or representative population samples modeled in the manner of social science opinion surveys. I relied on survey data by Chilean pollsters and social scientists—they are of good quality from the mid-to-late 1980s on—to help me understand wider public opinion contexts and to serve as a check against misleading findings through historical and oral research. The semistructured life history interviews walked us through the interviewees' personal background and history, as well as key events or turning points significant for collective memory—while remaining sufficiently open-ended to let the interviews move toward the experiences my collaborators thought meaningful and important.

At its best, the method in semistructured yet open-ended interviews is a bit like playing jazz with a partner. One must be attentive and sensitive to the places one's partner wants to go and must therefore improvise. One needs to "listen and learn" rather than stick to a rigid scripting. One welcomes and adjusts to the unexpected flow or riff. At the same time, one bears in mind a leitmotif—the basic research questions and a sequence of themes for discussion—and therefore finds the moment when one can fruitfully return or build a conversational bridge to still unaddressed and pertinent questions or topics. See also section C2 below for the importance of deliberate insertion of "off-balance" moments in the interview process.

Second, I sought to develop a multilayered rather than monodimensional approach to "interview" research. Because I sought depth, I wanted not only to compare oral research with findings from other source streams (especially written documents but also visual, audio, and audiovisual) but also to develop different kinds of oral experiences and evidence. I complemented the formal semistructured life history with less formal—more "spontaneous" and opportunistic—interviews and exchanges and kept track of these exchanges in a field notebook. I supplemented the one-on-one approach with focus-group meetings. I valued participant-observation experiences such as joining in a workshop, a demonstration, or a commemoration, and again kept track of what I learned or observed in a field notebook. I kept relationships going by returning transcripts to persons interviewed, soliciting reactions to the transcript, and in some instances following up with additional interviews. In cases where "key informants" emerged—people who offered exceptionally rich possibilities for in-depth reflection—I supplemented my information not only with cross-record research in written sources but also ethnographic work and conversation with friends or relatives of the informant who could help me diversify and contextualize my understanding of the person and my interviews. (I do not include such conversations in the "interview count" given below.)

Third, while I made no pretense of building a scientifically valid cross-section of society as my interviewee universe, I *did* actively seek out persons from a wide variety of memory camps, social backgrounds, and political perspectives. After all, my purpose was to understand how memory struggles and issues played out in society as a whole, not simply in one or another memory camp of a divided society. My informal working goal was to assure that I had achieved "good" in-depth interview experiences with at least several examples of almost every relevant social perspective I could imagine—by social class, political alignment, memory camp, degree of direct connection to repression, and the like. Thus I ended up interviewing persons from very different walks of life and experiences of military rule. I interviewed women from working-class poblaciones, from middle-class neighborhoods, and from elegant upscale sectors. As to social status and class, there were low-status laborers, such as electricians, carpenters, and security guards; middle-class or lower middle-class workers, such as secretaries, schoolteachers, and librarians; professionals, such as journalists, lawyers, and therapists; and persons of high wealth or power, such as financiers, journalism directors, and political leaders. Most important for my purposes, I interviewed persons across the social boundaries that have historically defied "memory conversation" within Chile—across the various memory camps I discovered in my research; across the social roles of victim, perpetrator, and bystander; and across identities as civilian or military.

Even within a superficially homogeneous social type, I sought diversity. My "priests," for example, included a cerebral intellectual who offered inspiring theological insight, in addition to experience in the world of human rights; a street priest living in a shack in a población, and whose insights into everyday life added texture to research on memory events and controversies in the población; and a former military chaplain who went on to serve a church in an upscale neighborhood and who drew me into the world of conservative Catholic Church outlooks and experiences. Similarly, my "military and police folk" included not only former officers but also former conscripts, not only defenders and participants in military rule but also those purged or marginalized as dissenters and unreliables. Among victim-survivors, I sought out not only the persistent activist who stays involved with a group such as the relatives of the disappeared through thick and thin, but also the person who had become discouraged and dropped out, or dropped in and out.

Fourth, my interest in understanding "ordinary" Chileans meant that with some exceptions, I gave priority to gaining access to lesser-known or unknown individuals, rather than celebrities or public figures whose memory voices and views were available in a host of other sources—and who were not likely to deviate in interviews from already-established positions or to move into the personal. The exceptions were that for specific organizations or groups who played large roles in memory struggles or the politics of truth, I did seek out leaders and public figures. For example, I interviewed three members (the late Jaime Castillo, and Gonzalo Vial and José Zalaquett) of Chile's Truth and Reconciliation Commission and former president Patricio Aylwin, who staked his presidency and its legitimacy on the work of the Commission, and I also interviewed well-known journalists (Emilio Filippi, Patricia Politzer, Patricia Verdugo, Cristián Zegers). But even in such cases, I also sought out the lesser-known faces—not simply the Truth Commission's voting members but the staff that laid the groundwork for meetings with relatives of victims, gathered and analyzed records, implemented the approach framed by the Commission, and prepared summary memos and files for the deliberations by Truth Commission members. Even when focusing on persons who worked with human rights organizations such as the Vicaría de la Solidaridad, I granted strong priority to learning the perspective of a secretary, a social worker, or a photojournalist.

From my own point of view, the biggest weakness of the oral research was concentration of the interview work on Greater Santiago and on urban rather than rural experiences. Fortunately, regionally based research by superb scholars such as Claudio Barrientos, Lessie Jo Frazier, Florencia Mallon, and Heidi Tinsman have done much to compensate for this weakness.

I used three methods to identify and connect to potential interviewees: social contacts, social location, and proactive opportunism. (1) To build an initial network of collaborators ("interviewees"), I mobilized the full range of my social contacts to connect with distinct sorts of people. My Chilean colleagues and human rights contacts played important roles in opening up the world of human rights networks, grassroots social organizations, and professionals such as journalists. My wonderful extended Chilean family of *tías, tíos,* and *primos* helped me connect to more conservative and traditionalist slices of Chilean society. As my web of contacts expanded, I used the snowball method—asking people to help me identify other promising persons—to expand my map of possibilities and establish initially elusive contacts, such as former soldiers. (2) I also benefited from social location. Precisely since certain places and activities draw persons involved in one or another sort of memory work or struggle, my research itself provided possibilities for expanding social networks and connections. For example, everyday research at the FAV archive created opportunities to meet people such as former political prisoner and memory activist Pedro Matta, who also showed up at the FAV day after day, eventually became a close friend, and opened up new layers of oral, written, and field site research possibilities. Similarly, attending a forum (organized by my social science colleagues and friends at FLACSO) of pobladora women provided opportunities to meet and learn from poor women in a working-class neighborhood. (3) Proactive opportunism is perhaps the most difficult method to explain to the uninitiated. It involves a state of hyperalertness—like a journalist obsessively pursuing and sniffing out a story—that enables one to notice and "seize" any opening that emerges at any moment and to create verbal lures to observe reactions and actively create openings. For example, running away from tear gas in a demonstration commemorating 11 September 1973 created a bond and an opportunity to ask about the life of a Chilean exile recently returned from Canada. Consider a more subtle example. My trips to the "Israeli Stadium" for exercise and family activity prompted a person to ask how Jews relate to Israel. I channeled the conversation toward the idea of diasporas and mentioned that Chileans would of course understand the diaspora concept, since so many ended up wandering to so many places in the world. Then I watched for body language, verbal reaction, possible engagement.

These methods yielded ninety-three interviewees, whom I prefer to think of as collaborators in a conversation. Among these collaborators, fifty-four participated in formal semistructured interviews, virtually all of them tape-recorded. (A few declined to speak with a tape recorder on.) In almost every case, the interview lasted at least an hour and a half; in some cases, the taped conversations lasted more than four hours and actually involved several interview sessions. In almost all instances, I also learned from my collaborators via informal interviews and exchanges, both before and after the formal interviews. The thirty-nine remaining collaborations followed more "opportunistic" interview formats or informal exchanges. To help readers distinguish between the semistructured formal interviews (almost always taped) and more opportunistic or informal conversations (usually recorded or summarized in field notebooks), I gloss the former as *interview* and the latter as *conversation* in the notes. By Chilean cultural standards, however, almost all such exchanges would be considered "interviews."

The focus group–style discussions that supplemented the one-on-one approach took place in five forums. In some, "memory" was the central issue for explicit discussion; in others, memory was an informing issue, an aspect of experience or identity that came up and conditioned discussion formally organized around a distinct topic. The groups and topics assembled in the forums, all in 1996–97, were the following: shantytown women discussing their needs and experiences as women and as poor people; a testimonio-style workshop of human rights survivors and activists discussing memory, truth, and justice strategies in dialogue with personal experience; shantytown men and women discussing educational and economic needs; military veterans, purged for their Constitutionalist rather than pro-coup inclinations in 1973, discussing the possibility of securing dignity and reparation within democracy; and members of the organization of relatives of the disappeared discussing the problem of legal impunity after an initial panel presentation by invited human rights lawyers and political figures.

To preserve privacy, and also to make clear for non-Chileans the distinction between public figures and "ordinary" Chileans, I use the following naming convention in the text. For public figures, I use the authentic first and last names. For nonpublic figures, I respect privacy by using a pseudonym given as a first name and the initial of a last name. In a few instances, when a person expressed special concern about identification, I also introduced small changes (for example, occupation) that would not affect the larger analysis. An exception to this naming convention is that some "ordinary" persons had reason to prefer use of their true names, regardless of the implications for privacy. For example, for a person such as Herminda Morales, a mother of disappeared sons who waged a long struggle against official lies, to use a pseudonym would play into the hands of the culture of secrecy and misinformation against which she battled. An additional exception occurs when some ordinary persons became transformed for a time, for reasons beyond their control, into figures linked to public events, as in the case of Paulina Waugh (see trilogy Book Two), the owner of a fire-bombed art gallery.

C2. Methods, Relationships, and Representation

Some aspects of method, particularly the nature of oral "truths" and one's relationships with "informants," raise subtle issues that have become an object of scholarly discussion and debate. Here I wish to offer my approach to these questions.

As noted above, I emphasized the semistructured, yet open-ended interviewing method that places a premium on "listening" and "conversation," a collaboration akin to a jazz performance. My option for this approach—rather than, say, the prescripted survey with multiple choice answers that lends itself to statistical analysis, or the "hunt for facts" interview that prioritizes isolating and discarding the fallacies of memory—aligns me with the approach to oral truths and method outlined by historians such as Alessandro Portelli. See *The Death of Luigi Trastulli and Other Stories: Form and Meaning in Oral History* (Albany: State University of New York Press, 1991). As Portelli brilliantly demonstrates, if one "accepts" one's collaborator and the idea that oral research connects most fundamentally to meaning, one can discover truths elusive in other sources. One need not take the interviewee's narrative of facts at face value—on the contrary, one must subject all sources, written or oral, to critical appraisal and corroboration. But in oral research and especially for study of memory in history, the gap between the verifiable empirical historical record of events and the ways they are remembered and interpreted itself turns into empirical information, becoming a source of "truth" for investigation. As Portelli puts it, "the diversity of oral history consists in the fact that 'wrong' statements are still psychologically 'true'" (51).

Three subtle issues of method and representation arise within this approach and require comment. First, building a conversational collaboration requires finding a basis for mutual acceptance. As a practical matter, I used any true facet of my own background, interests, personality, and social experiences that might help me connect with people and build a relationship of credibility or confidence. Of course, with some individuals I was more successful than with others, and in some social contexts I found the process easier than in others. The fact that I am a second-generation Holocaust survivor, and that this aspect of my family history has shaped me to the core of my soul—my sense of self, my social sympathies, my anxieties and ideals—made me feel most at ease with persecuted people who had passed through intense life-and-death experiences. I did not use my Holocaust background crudely or wave a banner of horror (tender loyalties to my own relatives and their memory preclude such vulgar instrumentalism), but it is also true that in some instances, my Holocaust background provided a bridge of credibility, empathy, and intuitions useful in conversation. In the end, and although this may sound strange to others, I am most "at home" with people who have experienced or witnessed social injustice or violent persecution.

In other contexts, other facets of my background helped me find bridges of intuition, connection, or acceptance for a conversational collaboration. In the world of human rights professionals, my background as an intellectual who leans Left and supports human rights solidarity provided a way to connect. With elders, the manners I learned from my parents helped. With conservatives, the value I place on family, the genuine affection and the social embeddedness I experienced with my Chilean family, and my general ability to embrace individuals unlike myself all helped me find ways to connect and accept. (My ability to enjoy people quite different from me may derive partly from the fact that I have long been an outgoing social climber from modest origins—a tailor's son and a first-generation college student at an Ivy League university—as well as a "stranger" from a Holocaust refugee family. I am long used to being both an "outsider" and a social traveler who enjoys navigating, connecting with, and learning from people of radically different backgrounds.) Perhaps most important, when personal connection proved elusive, was sheer intellectual curiosity. I have long taken intellectual delight in discovering the "logic" of other people's thought and experiences, and as a foreigner I could ask innocent or delicate questions—in a sense, seek cultural mentoring—without necessarily giving offense.

A second subtle issue involves striking a balance between "listening" with an open mind for the authentic truth embedded in a person's story or memory, and using one's critical faculties to "push" for more or to "test and critique" the narrative.

Notwithstanding the collaborative aspect of the conversation, there also emerges, to a greater or lesser degree, a potential tug-of-war. One wants to hear and understand people's stories in their integrity, but at times one also wants to move discourses away from the preferred narrative, toward unintended or taboo areas. I took care in my interviews to insert the occasional decentering or uncomfortable question (for example, "when did you come to accept the death of your disappeared loved one?"), or to engage in some "arguing back" with the logic of the narrative ("but some people might say . . ." or "I saw some documents that said . . ."), or to organize a follow-up interview or conversation that pursued a new line of discussion. The goal here was not to obstruct the interviewee or to prevent us from getting back, after a detour, to the story the person wanted to tell but to achieve greater depth and to find the balance between "listening" and "probing."

For similar reasons (and as mentioned above), I found it helpful to do complementary research on key informants who offered exceptional possibilities for in-depth reflection. I supplemented the oral information they provided with cross-record research in written sources, and with ethnographic work and conversation with friends or relatives who might help me diversify and contextualize my understanding of the person and the interviews.

A third difficult issue when making use of oral sources is representation. Since the late 1980s, scholarly controversies about ethnographic authority in anthropological writings, and about the uses and misuses of testimonial writings, have drawn great attention to issues of truth and representation in oral history and anthropology. A salient issue is how to represent relationships between researchers and "informants." See James Clifford, *The Predicament of Culture: Twentieth-Century Ethnography, Literature, and Art* (Cambridge, Mass.: Harvard University Press, 1988); Georg M. Gugelberger, ed., *The Real Thing: Testimonial Discourse and Latin America* (Durham, N.C.: Duke University Press, 1996); and the recent Rigoberta Menchú controversy, in David Stoll, *Rigoberta Menchú and the Story of All Poor Guatemalans* (Boulder, Colo.: Westview Press, 1999), and Arturo Arias, ed., *The Rigoberta Menchú Controversy* (Minneapolis: University of Minnesota Press, 2001).

The most satisfying response to the problem of representation occurs through the genre of life history writing. The scholar or collaborating partners can pursue in depth a person's life experience, the analysis of interview transcripts, and the dynamics of the relationship between scholar and "informant." The genre can lend itself to thoughtful sections or essays, separate from the life history narrative or transcripts, explicitly analyzing the relationship of "author" and "subject" and its representation, as well as the nature of the "truths" available in the interview transcripts. The Latin American history field has recently witnessed two superb examples of this response: Daniel James, *Doña María's Story: Life History, Memory, and Political Identity* (Durham, N.C.: Duke University Press, 2000); and Rosa Isolde Reuque Paillalef, with Florencia E. Mallon, ed. and trans., *When a Flower Is Reborn: The Life and Times of a Mapuche Feminist* (Durham, N.C.: Duke University Press, 2002).

As Mallon has pointed out, moreover, the life history genre has a long and distinguished tradition—it reaches back to the 1950s fieldwork of Oscar Lewis and Sidney Mintz—in Latin American anthropology.

The new life history studies have been instructive and have informed the critical eye I bring to my interview sources. For my purposes, however, these wonderful studies have not solved the problem of representation. Several obstacles arise. First, the goal of this project is to understand and trace systematically the making of memory struggles. It is not primarily an oral history. It requires mobilizing such a huge array of sources from multiple genres—written, audio and visual, and oral— that a life history approach inviting explicit extended reflections on relationships and representation related to particular oral sources and interviews is not practical. Just as some research topics require that a social historian glean historical truths from thousands of critically analyzed documents, rather than focusing especially (as a literary scholar might) on a singularly rich text, so it is that I would find it reductionist and misleading to home in on a single life for this project.

Second, I have a "Holocaust problem." To enter into extended in-depth reflections about myself and my relationships in the text—beyond the reflections in this essay on sources—would risk violating the integrity of my collaborators and the Chilean story. My own family story is so dramatic and relates so tightly to one of the overwhelming symbols of our times that to dwell on it at length, in a study about Chile, seems ethically and professionally irresponsible. To do so would risk turning the searing Chilean experience into a kind of one-dimensional foil, rather than a human story worth analyzing in its own right. The "memory box of Pinochet's Chile" would subtly morph into the story of "a Holocaust Jew in Pinochet's Chile." There may be another time and another venue for a more extended personal reflection, but not in this trilogy.

Third, precisely because Pinochet's Chile is an example of "radical evil," it issues a challenge to representation far more extreme and intractable than the issues that attach to oral history as such. In this sense the difficulties of representation that bedevil this book belong to a stream of scholarly and philosophical reflections on representation provoked by the Holocaust and other examples of radical evil in world history. The design of this trilogy—the use of an introductory volume focused on human stories, the use of Afterwords that extend and sometimes unsettle the main chapters that immediately precede them, the sobering "futility of history" reflection in the Afterword (to chapter 2 of Book Three of this trilogy) that follows analysis of the Truth and Reconciliation Commission—prioritizes this larger issue of representation. The big issue is, How do we represent, historicize, and analyze social relations and atrocities so extreme they defy our imagination, our assumption of moral order, and our notion of humanity?

Rather than including in the text extended reflections on oral sources and my relationships with them, I have resorted to a more subtle compromise and approach. In Book One, the introductory volume emphasizing human portraits of a society caught in memory impasse, and the book most "literary" or ethnographic in texture, I allow my role in interviews and conversations to emerge here and there, as an organic part of the story. In chapter 2 and its Afterword, I also allow glimpses of the dialogue between my family's Holocaust background and the professional research experience in Chile. In all three books, when relevant for the analysis I allow skepticism about specific informant stories or memories to become part of my own narrative strategy. An obvious example occurs in the story of Colonel Juan (Book One, chapter 3). A more subtle example occurs when I critique activist memories that draw too strong and linear a line between "ant's work" activism prior to 1983 and the eruption of major street protests during 1983–86 (Book Two, chapter 5).

In all three books as well, I have used the notes as a vehicle for commentary as well as documentation. This allows room for more extended critical appraisal of specific methodological problems or historical sources, whether written or oral.

Index

Aeschlimann, Werner Arias, 34

Agrarian reform: in Brazil, xxiv; Christian Democrats and, 17–18; expropriation of land, 13, 14–15, 21; Frei and, 13, 14; in Peru, 161 n. 6; Tomic and, 17–18

Agrupación de Familiares de Detenidos-Desaparecidos (AFDD), 48, 132, 163 n. 11, 204 n. 11, 208 n. 27. *See also* Disappeared persons; Morales, Señora Herminda

Aguirre Cerda, Pedro, 8, 9

Aldunate, José, 189 n. 32

Alessandri, Jorge, 9–10, 11, 12–13, 18–19

Allende Gossens, Salvador: Christian Democrats and, 21, 23, 43; Communist Party and, 43–44; democracy and, xxvi, 19, 20; economic populism of, 22–23; food shortages, 23; FRAP (Popular Action Front), 9–10, 11; government experiment of, 19–20, 172 n. 15; as minority president, 21, 22, 26; MIR (Movimiento de Izquierda Revolucionaria) and, 24, 175 n. 20; personal charm (muñeca) of, 20, 27, 171 n. 13; popular opinion of, 24–25, 83, 88, 176–77 n. 23; presidential elections (1958, 1970), 9–10, 18–19, 168 n. 5; social platform of, 9, 18, 19–20, 83; Soviet Union and, xxvi, 172–74 n. 16; ultra (maximalist) factions and, 23, 24, 174 n. 18; Unidad Popular and, 18, 19, 23, 174 n. 18; U.S.

opposition to, xxvi, 19, 22; violence and, 26, 175 n. 22; women voters and, 9, 83, 168 n. 5. *See also* Coup d'état (September 1973); Frei Montalva, Eduardo; Pinochet, Augusto; September 11, 1973

Altamirano, Carlos, 23

Amnesty decree (1978), 109, 112, 118–19, 127, 144, 148, 205 n. 15

Angulo, Lucio, 74, 75–76, 77–78, 80, 86–87

Arellano Stark, Sergio, 97, 99, 196 nn. 13–14

Arendt, Hannah, 31, 178 n. 26, 209 n. 32

Argentina, xxv, 123, 127, 178–80 n. 26

Ariztía, Fernando, 56, 57

Arraño Sancho, Levy Segundo, 96, 97

Assassinations: authentication of, 115; Letelier-Moffitt murders, 122, 127, 205 n. 15; in Lonquén, 58, 115, 123, 124, 148–49, 188 n. 11; "Plan Z," 105; of Carlos Prats, 122; of René Schneider, 19, 24. *See also* Violence

Aylwin Azócar, Patricio, 47, 62–64, 172 n. 15

Barrera, José Guillermo Barrera, 81–82

Benedetti, Mario, xxxi, 163 n. 11

Bettelheim, Bruno, 178–80 n. 26

Bolton, Roberto, 65–66, 67, 189 n. 33

Borremans, Luis, 42

Bourdieu, Pierre, 121, 210 n. 34

Burdiles, René, 74, 76, 80

Cabezas Pares, Rubén Guillermo, 96
Calama massacre, 99
Caravan of Death, 97–98, 99, 196 n. 13
Carlos G., 98, 196 n. 15
Carrasco Matus, Carlos Alberto
  (Mauro), 79–80, 192 n. 7
Catholic Church: on Communism, 99–
  100; dissident memory and, 126;
  moral conscience and, 32–33, 118,
  209 n. 29; priests in, 56, 57, 65–66,
  67, 99, 189 n. 33, 228–29; in San-
  tiago, 115, 125, 126, 129; social doc-
  trine of, 8, 16; testimony, 66. *See also*
  Vicariate of Solidarity (Vicaría de la
  Solidaridad)
Center-Left coalition: Agrupación de
  Familiares de Detenidos-
  Desaparecidos (AFDD) and, 204 n. 11;
  Allende and, 18; Patricio Aylwin
  Azócar, 47, 62–64; Concertación,
  63–64, 110, 204 n. 11; democracy
  and, 118; human rights and, 118, 128;
  politics of memory, 90
Center-Right coalition, 88, 90, 187
  n. 20
Chile: agrarian reform in, 13, 14–15, 17–
  18, 21; as civilized society, xxiv, xxvii,
  xxviii, 56, 138–39, 161 n. 4, 162 nn.
  8–9; democracy in, xxvi, xxviii, 16–
  17, 19, 110–11, 118; "German problem" in, xxvii, 162 n. 9; industrialization in, 10; inversion of responsibility
  by, 85–86; modernization in, 10, 127;
  neoliberalism in, xxvi, 127; United
  States and, xxvi, 9, 11, 13, 19, 22, 25,
  169 n. 8, 172–74 n. 16. *See also*
  Allende Gossens, Salvador; Coup
  d'état (September 1973); Frei Montalva, Eduardo; Pinochet, Augusto;
  September 11, 1973
Chilean Senate Human Rights Commission, 158–61 n. 3

Christian Democrats: Allende and, 21,
  23, 43, 64; capitalism and, 8; Communism and, 8; democratization, 13;
  Leighton and, 122; MAPU (Movimiento de Accíon Popular Unitaria),
  17, 54; middle class and, 51; presidential elections (1958, 1964), 10; radical
  agrarian reform, 17–18; shantytown
  constituencies of, 13; social reform,
  13; Radomiro Tomic, 17–18; Unidad
  Popular and, 18. *See also* Frei Montalva, Eduardo
Church, Frank, 169 n. 8
CIA (Central Intelligence Agency), 11,
  22, 25, 169 n. 8
Civil disobedience: children of activists
  in, 62; coup d'état (September 1973),
  44, 184 n. 5; hunger strikes as, 122,
  126, 129; in La Legua, 42, 44, 184 n.
  3; Movimiento contra la Tortura
  "Sebastían Acevedo," 61, 208 n. 27;
  street actions, 61
Communist Party: Allende and, 43–44;
  Catholic Church and, 99–100; coup
  d'état (September 1973) and, 43–44,
  184 n. 5; La Juventud Comunista, 39–
  40; in La Legua, 39; Law for the Permanent Defense of Democracy, 9;
  legality of, 8, 9; MIR (Movimiento de
  Izquierda Revolucionaria) and, 17;
  moderate Left line of, 43; Popular
  Front coalition, 8; in Santiago, 43;
  urban migration and, 167 n. 4
Concertación, 63–64, 110, 204 n. 11
Contreras, Manuel, 45, 46, 112–13, 144,
  205 n. 15
Corporation of Repair and Reconciliation, 158–61 n. 3
Coup d'état (September 1973): arrests,
  44, 184 n. 6; Communist Party and,
  43–44, 184 n. 5; deaths as social cost
  of, 29–30, 91, 108, 146, 148; denun-

238 Index

ciations after, 55–56, 187 n. 20; food shortages, 55, 107, 117; neighborhood tensions, 54–55; as pronouncement (pronunciamiento), 29, 30, 117; support for, 27, 33–34, 88–89, 121, 144; test of personal values during, 59–60; "White Book," 88, 194 n. 1. *See also* Military; Soldiers; Torture; Violence

Cuban Revolution, xxiv, xxvi, 16, 17, 22

Culture of memory impasse, xxx–xxxi, 128, 163 n. 11

CUT (Central Unica de Trabajadores), 40

Cuthbert, Sofía, 122

De Acevedo, Sebastián, 61, 208 n. 27

Death, as social cost of war, 29–30, 91, 108, 146, 148

Delbo, Charlotte, 194 n. 16, 203 n. 8

Democracy, xxvi, xxviii, 16–17, 19, 110–13, 118, 138–39

DINA (Dirección de Inteligencia Nacional): agents of, 45–46, 102–3, 197 n. 1; Caravan of Death and, 97–98; Carlos Alberto Carrasco Matus (Mauro) and, 79–80, 192 n. 7; CNI and, 208 n. 27; Colonia Dignidad (German immigrant community), 73; Manuel Contreras and, 45, 46, 112–13, 144, 205 n. 15; disappearances from alleged Left fratricide (July 1975), 123; goodness lore in, 79, 192 n. 7; identification of victims, 79, 150; La Legua "recruitment" in, 44–45, 185 n. 6, 185 n. 11; Londres 38 and, 45, 47; memorial for victims of, 163 n. 11; MIR leaders and, 175 n. 20; at Tejas Verdes, 44–45, 185 n. 6; victims' confrontation with agents of, 102–3, 197 n. 1; violence of, 45–46, 92, 122

Disappeared persons: accepting death of, 83–85, 194 n. 14; Agrupación de Familiares de Detenidos-Desaparecidos (AFDD), 48, 132, 163 n. 11, 204 n. 11, 208 n. 27; break-ins (allanamientos), 42, 135–37, 138, 139–40; children of, 84, 193 n. 13, 203 n. 8; corpses of, 58, 100–101, 188 n. 11, 197 n. 19; documentation of, xxiii–xxiv, 44, 158–61 n. 3, 190 n. 2; family responsibility and, 82–86; fathers of, 208 n. 27; government denial of, 109; Charles Horman, 172–74 n. 16; hunger strike for, 122, 126, 129; in Lake Region, 72, 74–78, 80, 86–87; Lonquén massacre, 58, 115, 123, 124, 148–49, 188 n. 11, 209 n. 29; Morales brothers (Ernesto and Gerardo) as, 41, 42, 43, 44, 50, 52, 53, 132, 146–47; National Arrests Secretariat (SENDET), 47; Pro-Peace Committee (Comité Pro-Paz) and, 47, 57, 59, 115, 125, 209 n. 29; Quillota massacre and, 94–97, 158–61 n. 3; as repression technique, xxiv, 158–61 n. 3; soldiers as, 139; stigmatization of, 89–90, 91, 92, 117–18, 208 n. 27; use of term, 128; voluntary presentation to authorities, 76, 80–82, 95, 96, 139, 151, 192 n. 9. *See also* Human rights; Memory headings; Morales, Ernesto "Ernestito"; Morales, Gerardo; Rupture, memory as; Torture; Truth and Reconciliation Commission (1990–91); Vicariate of Solidarity (Vicaría de la Solidaridad); Violence

Doña Elena F.: on Allende presidency, 15, 29; Catholic charity of, 32–33; Christian Democrats and, 18; on Frei presidency, 11, 13–15; on fundos expropriation (tomas), 14–15, 27–28; on human rights violations, 29–30, 148, 207 n. 22; memory as salvation, 8, 108, 121, 145, 146; on military rule,

Doña Elena F. (*cont.*)
27, 29–30; National Women's Secretariat and, 121; Pinochet's election, 7–8; rescue "just in time," 143; on September 11, 1973, 27, 33–34, 121, 144; social values of, 12, 32–33, 117, 145, 165–67 n. 3, 183 n. 31
Dorfman, Ariel, 151, 197–98 n. 1
Durán, Margarita, 45
Duran Pérez, Teresa, 158–61 n. 3

El Mercurio, 121, 209 n. 29
Emblematic memory: authenticity of, 115; bridges to, 120, 130, 131; echo effect in, 113, 114, 116, 119, 120; flexibility in, 115–16, 207 n. 22; generational aspects of, 114; goodness lore and, 131, 132, 151; as human activity, 114, 119, 151–52; as interactive performance, 106, 115; loose memory and, 104, 106, 116, 120, 130–31; memory as rupture, 108–9, 203 n. 8; memory lore, 68–69, 113–14; personal memory and, 106, 130–31; in public domain, 106, 113, 116; social referents, 116–17, 141; spokespersons (portavoces) for, 119; of subcultures, 132–33; truth in, 113. *See also* Memory as a closed box; Memory knots; Persecution and awakening, memory as; Remorse lore; Rupture, memory as; Salvation, memory as
Eppinger, Erica, 204 n. 11
Espinoza Bravo, Pedro, 112, 205 n. 15

Fear: identification of subversives, 55–56, 185 n. 11, 187 n. 20; in 1980s, 63, 189 n. 28; self-censorship and, 116; of soldiers, 137; in testimony, 158–61 n. 3; of torture, 46
Fernández, Sergio, 127
Food shortages, 23, 55, 107, 117
Forgetting: amnesia, 89, 195 n. 2;

amnesty decree (1978), 109, 112, 118–19, 127, 144, 148, 205 n. 15; Center-Right coalition, 90; forgetting (olvido), xxviii–xxix, 89, 112, 162 n. 9; informants and, 55, 187 n. 20; mindful forgetfulness, 112, 205 n. 14; social process of, 131; will to forget, 89–90
FRAP (Popular Action Front), 9–10, 11
Frei Montalva, Eduardo, 8; agrarian reform and, 13, 14; CIA (Central Intelligence Agency) and, 11, 22, 169 n. 8; fundos expropriation (toma), 13, 14–15, 21; optimism in, 83; presidential elections and, 10, 11–12, 169 n. 8; social reforms of, 13, 15; trade unions and, 15; U.S. copper mines nationalized, 13; women voters and, 168 n. 5
Frente Patriótico Manuel Rodríguez, 64, 189 n. 31
Frenz, Helmut, 59
Fresno, Anita, 122
Fuenzalida, Victor Enrique Fuenzalida, 95
Fundos (landed estates), 12, 13, 14–15

Gabriela C., 150
Gac Espinoza, Pablo, 95, 96
García Márquez, Gabriel, 172 n. 15
García Ramírez, Mireya, 163 n. 11
Germany: Colonia Dignidad (German immigrant community in Chile), 73; "German problem" in Chile, xxvii; political aspects of memory in, 210 n. 39. *See also* Holocaust
González Videla, Gabriel, 8, 9
Goodness lore, 131, 132, 151; Lucio Angulo, 77–78, 86–87; Carlos Alberto Carrasco Matus (Mauro), 79–80, 192 n. 7; in Holocaust, 86; Ramiro I., 77–79; of victims of persecution, 41, 69–71

Grass roots activism, 17, 55, 63, 83
Gremialista movement, 25
Group memory, 205 n. 16
Guevara, Ernesto "Che," 17
Guzmán, Juan, 158–61 n. 3

Halbwachs, Maurice, 37, 130, 198–202 n. 2
Hersh, Seymour M., 172–74 n. 16
Herzfeld, Roberta Bacic, 158–61 n. 3
Holocaust: author's family background and, 65, 86, 194 n. 16, 203 n. 8, 232, 234; Chile and, xxvii; collective memory in, 114; goodness lore in, 86, 194 n. 16; intergenerational transmission and, 114; radical evil of, 31, 32, 178–80 n. 26, 198–202 n. 2, 209 n. 32, 234; silence and, 114, 213 n. 3; sources on, 198–202 n. 2; Survivor Syndrome, 178–80 n. 26
Horman, Charles, 172–74 n. 16
Human rights: Christian faith and, 65–66, 118; collaborations for, 126, 129; exile and, 158–61 n. 3; goodness as emblematic memory, 69–70; indifference to, 88, 90, 92–93, 101, 146; inversion of responsibility for, 85–86; Pro-Peace Committee (Comité Pro-Paz) and, 47, 57, 59, 115, 125, 209 n. 29; trials, 112; victims' confrontation of perpetrators, 102–3, 197 n. 1. See also Vicariate of Solidarity (Vicaría de la Solidaridad)
Hurtado Martínez, Manuel Hernán, 95

Ibáñez del Campo, Carlos, 9
Ictus, 61, 189 n. 29
Identification of subversives, 55–56, 77–78, 79, 150, 185 n. 11, 187 n. 20
International Women's Day, 123
ITT (International Telephone and Telegraph), 20

James, Daniel, 186 n. 16, 233

Jelin, Elizabeth, 48, 198–202 n. 2
Juan F. (Colonel): body language of, 92–93, 149; ceremonies of commemoration, 122; code of silence, 122; counseling of soldiers, 99, 100, 101; on human rights, 91, 92–93, 101, 122, 149; memories of, 90–91, 132–33; on patriotism, 91–92; on political violence, 92–93; Quillota massacre and, 101, 149

Kant, Immanuel, 178–80 n. 26
Kaufman, Susana, 48, 198–202 n. 2, 203 n. 8
Kennecott Copper Corporation, 20
Kennedy, John F., 11
Kissinger, Henry, xxvi, 22, 172–74 n. 16

Lakes Region: agrarian reform and, 72; Lucio Angulo in, 74, 75–76, 77–78, 80, 86–87; René Burdiles in, 74, 76, 80; disappearances from, 72–73, 190 n. 2, 191 n. 3; poverty in, 73–74; Puerto Octay, 74, 76, 151. See also Ramiro I.
La Legua: Communist Party in, 39; coup d'état (September 1973), 44; DINA "recruitment" in, 44–45, 185 n. 6, 185 n. 11; housing in, 40; police break-ins (allanamientos), 42; resistance in, 42, 44, 184 n. 3; self-defense in, 44. See also Morales, Señora Herminda
Land ownership: agrarian cooperative settlements (asentamientos), 13; agrarian reform (1967), 13; inquilinos, 12, 13; landed estates (fundos), 12, 13, 14–15; land expropriation (toma), 13, 14–15, 21, 22
La Segunda, 209 n. 29
Lavandero, Jorge, 158–61 n. 3
Left: coalition politics of, 9; dictatorship (1973–76) as rescue from, 126; disap-

Left (*cont.*)

peared persons and, 55; expropriation of U.S. copper mines, 9; FRAP (Popular Action Front), 9–10; informants and, 55, 187 n. 20; military government in Peru and, 161 n. 6; multiparty democracy, 17; "Plan Z," 105; political discussion groups, 55, 63; post–September 11 indictments of, 55–56, 187 n. 20; Radical Christian activism and, 17; social welfare initiatives of, 9; state repression in 1970s, 125; urban shantytowns (callampas) and, 9, 167 n. 4

Leigh, Gustavo, 127

Leighton, Bernard, 122

Letelier, Orlando, 122, 127, 205 n. 15

Lira, Elizabeth, 212 n. 6

Lonquén massacre, 58, 115, 123, 124, 148–49, 188 n. 11, 209 n. 29

Loo Prado, Julio Arturo, 95

Loose memory, 104, 106, 116, 120, 130–31

Mallon, Florencia, 211 n. 46, 233

Mapuche Indians, 191 n. 3, 192 n. 9

MAPU (Movimiento de Accíon Popular Unitaria), 17, 54, 74–75, 96, 184 n. 5

María Verónica, Señora, 80, 81

Marisa T., on Frei-Allende period, 83

Massacres: at Calama, 99; at Lonquén, 58, 115, 123, 124, 148–49, 188 n. 11, 209 n. 29; at Quillota, 94–97, 101, 158–61 n. 3, 196 n. 14

Media, 28, 61, 88, 121, 175 n. 22, 177 n. 22, 194 n. 1, 208 n. 27, 209 n. 29

Memory: amnesia, 89, 187 n. 20; body language and, 41–42, 58, 88, 92–93, 149, 204 n. 11; of the Center, 64; childhood and, 36–38; of Christian Democrats, 64; collective, 37, 113, 114, 119, 145; culture of memory impasse, xxx–xxxi, 128, 163 n. 11; existential

aspects of, 129; of Frei-Allende period, 64; generational, 48–49, 114, 186 n. 16, 206 n. 20; history and, xxix–xxx, 162 n. 10, 198–202 n. 2; impasse of, xxx–xxxi, 128, 163 n. 11; Lonquén case and, 58, 115, 148–49, 188 n. 11; loose, 104, 106, 116, 120, 130–31; politics and, 124–28, 210 n. 39; privacy and, 89; society building and, 102; of trauma, 105; vocabulary of, 127–28. *See also* Emblematic memory; Persecution and awakening, memory as; Rupture, memory as; Salvation, memory as

Memory as a closed box: amnesty decree (1978), 109, 112, 118–19, 127, 144, 148, 205 n. 15; Christian responsibility and, 125; good manners and, 12, 88, 89, 101; indifference and, 88, 90, 92–93, 101, 146; language of, 127–28; policide, 31–32, 92–93, 101, 178–80 n. 26, 180 n. 27; sacralization of memory, 127–28; silence and, 111–12, 114, 122, 133, 149–50, 213 n. 3; soldiers and, 101, 119, 132–33, 141–42, 146; truth and, 127. *See also* Forgetting

Memory knots: activism and, 120–21, 126–27, 209 n. 32; dissidence and, 126; habitual life and, 120–21, 147, 209 n. 32; heroic memory, 121; human actors in, 151–52; public commemorations, 121–23; sites of humanity, 121; social body and, 121, 209 n. 33

Military: break-ins (allanamientos), 42, 92; Caravan of Death, 97, 196 n. 13; chaplains in, 99; compartmentalization of responsibility, 98–99; exonerados (dismissed officers), 106; human rights trials, 112; "Plan Z" assassinations, 105; professionalism of, 99, 106–7, 137; rescue "just in time," 143; soldiers' morale, 99, 100, 101. *See also* Soldiers

MIR (Movimiento de Izquierda Revolucionaria), 17, 24, 26, 72, 92, 175 n. 20

Moffitt, Ronni, 122, 127, 205 n. 15

Mónica V., 84–85, 194 n. 14

Moral conscience: bearing witness, 103, 129; Christianity and, 32–33, 61, 118, 125, 146, 209 n. 29; human rights activism, 57, 61, 118; personal awakening to, 109–10; radical evil, 31, 32, 87, 178–80 n. 26, 209 n. 32, 234; religious conscience as social referent, 118, 209 n. 29; of survival, 137

Morales, Ernesto, 39–40, 43, 46, 49

Morales, Ernesto "Ernestito": civil resistance in La Legua, 44; Communist Party and, 41, 43; DINA "recruitment" of, 44–45, 185 n. 6; goodness lore of, 41, 132; photographs of, 50, 52, 146–47; Tejas Verdes prison, 44

Morales, Gerardo: arrest of, 42, 43; civil resistance in La Legua, 44; Communist Party and, 43; DINA "recruitment" of, 44–45, 185 n. 6; goodness lore of, 41, 132; photographs of, 50, 53, 146–47; Tejas Verdes prison, 44; trade union activism, 40

Morales, Señora Herminda: bearing witness, 50–52, 129; Communist Party and, 39, 40; facial expressions as open wound, 42; on loyalty, 49, 50; memory as rupture, 47, 48–50, 117, 145–46, 187 n. 17; resilience of, 49–50; search for missing sons, 47–48, 126; strategies of struggle, 48–50, 121–22, 148, 187 n. 17; in Tejas Verdes, 43; Truth and Reconciliation Commission testimony, 47–48; urban migration and, 39–40

Morales, Vladimir, 42–43, 44, 46

Myth of democratic resilience, xxviii

Myth of exceptionalism, xxviii, 162 nn. 8–9

Nash Sáez, Michel Salim, 139

National Arrests Secretariat (SENDET), 47

National Corporation of Reparation and Reconciliation, 72

National Party, 25

National Stadium, 42, 43, 158–61 n. 3

National Women's Secretariat, 121

Nixon, Richard, xxvi, 19, 22, 161 n. 6, 169 n. 8

Nora, Pierre, xxix, 4, 198–202 n. 2

O'Donnell, Guillermo, xxii, 157 n. 1, 181 n. 28

Oral research, 227; Alessandro Portelli and, 178 n. 25, 198–202 n. 2, 205 n. 16, 231; representation and, 233–35

Paraguay, xxv

Peasant Trade Union "Liberator," 74–75

Pérez Sales, Pau, 158–61 n. 3

Persecution and awakening, memory as: Centrists and, 64; Christian responsibility and, 125; cultural sensitization to human rights, 129; human rights work and, 58–62, 110, 118, 145, 209 n. 29; moral conscience, 125; popular Catholicism and, 66; Ramiro I., 75–76; street protests, 118; women pobladoras, 118; young adults, 118

Pinochet, Augusto: amnesty decree (1978), 109, 112, 118–19, 127, 144, 148, 205 n. 15; anti-Communism, xxvi; arrest of, 1; authoritarian regimes, 31, 181–82 n. 28; Caravan of Death and, 97–98, 99, 196 n. 13; denial of persecution, 109; Fernández, Sergio, 127; human rights and, xxvi–xxvii, 88; plebiscite (1988), 128; as savior, 105; support for, 88;

Pinochet, Augusto (*cont.*)
United States and, xxvi. *See also* Disappeared persons; Military
Pisagua, 100–101, 197 n. 19
"Plan Z," 105
Policide, 31–32, 92–93, 101, 178–80 n. 26, 180 n. 27
Political discussion groups, 55, 63
Popular Unity. *See* Unidad Popular (UP)
Portelli, Alessandro, 178 n. 25, 198–202 n. 2, 205 n. 16, 231
Prats, Carlos, 122
Pro-Peace Committee (Comité Pro-Paz), 47, 57, 59, 115, 125, 209 n. 29
Public space: commemorations in, 106, 121–24, 148–49, 198–202 n. 2; emblematic memories and, 106, 113, 116; memory knots, 121–23; sacralization of space, 123–24
Puerto Octay, 74, 76, 151

Qué Pasa (magazine), 88, 194 n. 1, 209 n. 29
Quillota: army takeover at, 94; Caravan of Death compared, 97–98; massacre at, 94–97, 101, 158–61 n. 3; SIM (Servicio Inteligencia Militar), 98; soldiers in, 101; voluntary presentation to authorities, 95, 96, 139

Radical Christian activism, 17
Radical evil, 31, 32, 87, 178–80 n. 26, 209 n. 32, 234
Radical Party: FRAP (Popular Action Front) and, 11; Popular Front coalition, 8; presidential election (1958), 10
Radio Agricultura, 11, 34, 121
Ramiro I.: idealism of, 110; isolation of, 75, 76, 110, 145; memory as persecution and awakening, 110; Peasant Trade Union "Liberator," 74–75; rural persecution of, 145; social ethic

and, 87; survival of, 77–78, 86–87; as teacher, 73, 74; on worker exploitation, 73–74
Remorse lore: disappeared persons and, 83–85, 194 n. 14; guilt in, 69, 82–86; mothers and, 43, 80, 81, 84, 193 n. 13; power of, 70–71, 131; textile workers in Tomé, 82; voluntary presentation to authorities and, 76, 80–82, 139, 151, 192 n. 9
Rettig, Raúl, 47, 158–61 n. 3
Rettig Commission. *See* Truth and Reconciliation Commission (1990–91)
Right: Allende's revolution and, 21–22; Partido Nacional, 18; Patria y Libertad, 26, 40, 41; presidential elections (1964), 11; Sociedad Nacional de Agricultura, 11; SOFOFA (Society for Industrial Development), 24–25
Rivera, Eugenio, 99
Rolle, Claudio, 187 n. 20
Rosenberg, Tina, 162 n. 9, 195 n. 2
Rousso, Henry, 198–202 n. 2
Rupture, memory as: ambivalence and, 67, 110–11, 204 n. 11; authenticity of, 115; Christian responsibility and, 125; conscript soldiers and, 141–42, 212 n. 8; cultural sensitization to human rights, 129; denial of violence and, 30–31, 108–9, 115–16; everyday life and, 109, 137–38, 142, 203 n. 8; goodness lore, 131, 132; historicity and, 114; memory lore, 69; Herminda Morales and, 47, 48–50, 117, 145–46, 187 n. 17; national imaginary and, 132, 211 n. 46; photographs and, 50, 52, 53, 67; Ramiro I. and, 77–78; strategies of struggle and, 48–50, 148, 187 n. 17

Sáenz, Orlando, 24, 26
Salvation, memory as: denial of persecutions, 115–16; dictatorship of 1973–76 and, 125–26; flexibility in,

115–16, 207 n. 22; Gabriela C. and, 150; radical evil and, 31, 32, 178–80 n. 26, 234; September 11, 1973, in, 105, 107, 108, 117; symbolic referents for, 117; treason vs., 106–7; truth and, 30–31

Santiago, 110; Communist Party in, 43; population of, 10; resistance in, 184 n. 3; social class in, 36, 183 n. 2

Santiago Nino, Carlos, 31, 178 n. 26

Schesch, Adam, 158–61 n. 3

Schneider, René, 19, 24

September 11, 1973: Allende's last radio address, 115, 206 n. 20; commemorations of, 122; Communist Party, 43–44, 184 n. 5; democracy after, 138–39; emblematic memory on, 111; La Moneda bombing, 114–15, 206 n. 20; memory as salvation, 105, 107, 108, 117; as pronunciamiento, 29, 30, 117; voluntary submission to arrest after, 80–81, 139, 151, 192 n. 9

Shantytowns: in Brazil, 161 n. 5; housing in, 40; La Legua, 39, 40, 42, 44–45, 184 n. 3, 185 n. 6, 185 n. 11; poblaciones, 33, 39, 55–56, 83, 167 n. 4; police break-ins (allanamientos), 42, 135–37, 138, 139–40; social welfare programs in (Frei), 13; urban callampas, 9, 167 n. 4; urban migration and, 10, 11, 39–40, 167 n. 4

Sierra, Sola, 204 n. 11

Sikkink, Kathryn, xxvi–xxvii

Silence, 111–12, 114, 122, 133, 149–50, 213 n. 3

Silva Henríquez, Raúl, 56

SIM (Servicio Inteligencia Militar), 98

Socialist Party: armed struggle, 18; MIR (Movimiento de Izquierda Revolucionaria) and, 17; Popular Front coalition, 8. See also Unidad Popular (UP)

Social referents: conscript soldiers as, 141–42; religious conscience as, 118, 209 n. 29; women as, 117–18, 141, 208 n. 27

Social voice, 151–52

SOFOFA (Society for Industrial Development), 24–25, 26

Soldiers: backgrounds of, 138; bodies disinterred by, 100–101, 197 n. 19; break-ins (allanamientos), 42, 135–37, 138, 139–40; chaplains and, 99–100; compartmentalization of responsibility by, 98–99, 196 n. 15; as disappeared persons, 139; drugging of, 140, 212 n. 6; exonerados (dismissed officers), 106; goodness lore of, 79–80, 192 n. 7; memory and, 90–91, 132–33, 141–42, 212 n. 8; in the navy, 138; night patrols, 139–40; Quillota massacre, 94–97, 101, 158–61 n. 3, 196 n. 14; as social referents, 141–42; trauma and, 98–99, 100–101, 137, 140–41, 212 n. 7; youth of, 135

Soviet Union, xxvi, 22, 172–74 n. 16

Stroessner, Alfredo, xxv

Survivor Syndrome, 178–80 n. 26

Tejas Verdes camp: Manuel Contreras and, 45, 112; DINA in, 44–45, 185 n. 6; living conditions at, 46; torture at, 46, 185 n. 13

Tenth Region. See Lakes Region

Tomic, Radomiro, 17–18, 19

Tonya R., 85

Torture: beatings, 42–43, 46; compartmentalization of responsibility for, 98–99, 196 n.15; demonstrations against, 61–62, 122, 129; goodness lore and, 69–70, 79, 192 n. 7; government denial of, 109; human body and, 209 n. 33; interrogations, 46; Londres 38, 45, 47; mentality of desperation, 44; psychological torture, 46, 56; Rahue station (Lakes Region),

Torture (*cont.*)
75–76, 80; statistics, 158–61 n. 3; at
Tejas Verdes, 46. *See also* Truth and
Reconciliation Commission (1990–
91); Violence
Trade unionism, 15, 39–40, 40, 74–75
Truckers' strike (October 1972), 25, 91
Truth and Reconciliation Commission
(1990–91): Patricio Aylwin Azócar
and, 47; criticism of, 91; on DINA disappearances, 46; founding of, 47;
goodness lore and, 84, 193 n. 13; initial report of, 89, 194 n. 1; intrafamilial conflicts and, 84, 193 n. 13;
Lake Region disappearances, 72;
Morales brothers' disappearance, 42,
44, 46, 47, 186 n. 15; Herminda
Morales's testimony to, 47–48;
Quillota massacre, 94–97, 101, 158–
61 n. 3; on Rahue station (Lakes
Region), 75–76, 80; on regular-army
soldiers' participation in torture, 100;
statistics on death and disappearances, 158–61 n. 3; Gonzalo Vial on,
89, 194 n. 1; witness-survivors, 102–
3, 197 n. 1

Ultra (maximalist) factions, 23, 24, 174
n. 18
Unidad Popular (UP): Allende and, 18,
19, 23, 43–44, 174 n. 18; Christian
Democrats and, 18; CIA opposition to,
25; Communist Party, 18, 19, 23, 174
n. 18; informants on, 55, 187 n. 20;
MAPU and, 17; memory as salvation,
108; MIR and, 24; Patria y Libertad
and, 40; textile workers in Tomé
on, 82
United States: Allende presidency and,
xxvi, 19, 22; Alliance for Progress
(Kennedy), xxvi, 11; CIA (Central
Intelligence Agency), 11, 22, 25, 169
n. 8; copper mines and, 9, 13; demo-

cratic social reform in Chile, xxvi; Frei
Montalva administration, 13;
Kissinger and, xxvi, 1, 22, 172–74 n.
16; Letelier-Moffitt murders, 127, 205
n. 15; Nixon, xxvi, 19, 22, 161 n. 6,
169 n. 8

Valdés, Hernán, 46, 185 n. 13
Valparaíso, Community of Intelligence,
98
Velasco Alvarado, Juan, 161 n. 6
Verdugo, Patricia, 97, 196 n. 13
Vergara, Rafael, 66, 67, 189 n. 33
Vial, Gonzalo, 88
Vicariate of Solidarity (Vicaría de la Soli-
daridad): authentication of persecution, 115; credibility of, 209 n. 29; disappearance statistics, 47, 158–61 n. 3,
186 n. 15; lawyers and, 126; Herminda Morales's search for missing
sons, 126; Pro-Peace Committee
(Comité Pro-Paz) and, 47, 57, 59, 115,
125, 209 n. 29; on Quillota massacre,
95–96, 158–61 n. 3; Solidaridad, 122;
Violeta E. and, 58–59, 121
Violence: Allende and, 26, 175 n. 22;
Calama massacre, 99; Caravan of
Death, 97–98, 99, 196 n. 13; denial
of, 30–31, 108–9, 115–16; everday life
after, 102–3, 109, 137–38, 203 n. 8;
fear, 46, 55–56, 63, 116, 137, 158–61
n. 3, 185 n. 11, 187 n. 20, 189 n. 28;
identification of subversives and, 55–
56, 77–78, 79, 150, 185 n. 11, 187 n.
20; indifference to, 92–93, 101;
Lonquén massacre, 58, 115, 123, 124,
148–49, 188 n. 11, 209 n. 29; multi-
generational impact of, 114, 206 n.
20; Operation Condor, xxv; Patria y
Libertad, 26, 41; policide, 31–32, 92–
93, 101, 178–80 n. 26, 180 n. 27;
Quillota massacre, 94–97, 101, 158–
61 n. 3, 196 n. 14; radical evil, 31, 32,

178–80 n. 26; truckers' strike (October 1972), 25

Violeta E.: Christian Democrats and, 51, 54; Christianity of, 65–67, 146; civil disobedience, 61–62; denunciation of, 55; family political party loyalties, 54, 64–65; human rights work, 57–62; husband's persecution, 55–57, 69; Ictus, 61, 189 n. 29; on Lonquén massacre, 58; memory as persecution and awakening for, 58–62, 110, 118, 145, 209 n. 29; middle-class life of, 51–52; Movimiento contra la Tortura "Sebastián Acevedo" (antitorture group) and, 61, 208 n. 27; political discussion groups, 55, 63; Pro-Peace Committee (Comité Pro-Paz), 57; social programs in poblaciones and, 60, 188 n. 24; test of personal values, 59–61, 146, 147; Vicariate of Solidarity (Catholic Church) and, 58–59, 121

Voluntary presentation to authorities, 76, 80–82, 95, 96, 139, 151, 192 n. 9

Winn, Peter, 23

Wolpert, Andrew, 205 n. 14

Women: activism for, 83; Allende opposed by, 117; Gabriela C., 150; human rights work, 57–62, 118; International Women's Day, 123; memory of salvation, 117; political mobilization, 118; remorse lore, 43, 80, 81, 84, 193 n. 13; search for disappeared relatives, 47–48; as social referents, 117–18, 141, 208 n. 27; suffrage, 168 n. 5; in trade unions, 40; Ximena L., 203 n. 8. *See also* Disappeared persons; Doña Elena F.; Morales, Señora Herminda; Violeta E.; Young adults

Ximena L., 203 n. 8

Young, James, 3–4, 164 n. 2, 198–202 n. 2

Young adults: Allende regime and, 36; children of disappeared persons, 84, 193 n. 13, 203 n. 8; on Cuban Revolution, 16; on democracy, 118; DINA "recruitment" of, 44–45, 185 n. 6, 185 n. 11; goodness lore of, 132; La Juventud Comunista (Communist Party), 39–41, 43; memory as persecution and awakening, 118; MIR (Movimiento de Izquierda Revolucionaria), 17, 24, 26, 72, 92, 175 n. 20; in 1980s, 63, 189 n. 28; parents' political views and, 62, 64–65; Pinochet era's impact on, 2

Zalaquett, José, 59, 158–61 n. 3

Zegers, Cristián, 194 n. 1, 209 n. 29

STEVE J. STERN

is a professor of history at the University of Wisconsin, Madison.

His most recent books include *Battling for Hearts and Minds: Memory Struggles*

in Pinochet's Chile, 1973–1988 (2006) and *Shining and Other Paths:*

War and Society in Peru, 1980–1995 (1998),

both published by Duke University Press.

The Library of Congress has cataloged the hardcover edition as follows:

Remembering Pinochet's Chile : on the eve of London, 1998 / Steve J. Stern.
p. cm. — (Latin America otherwise) (The memory box of Pinochet's Chile ; 1)
Includes bibliographical references and index.
ISBN 0-8223-3354-6 (cloth : alk. paper)
1. Chile—History—1973–1988. 2. Chile—History—Coup d'état,
1973—Psychological aspects. 3. Memory. 4. Autobiographical memory.
I. Title. II. Series.
F3100.S825 2004
983.06'5—dc22   2004001308

ISBN-13: 978-0-8223-3816-1 (pbk. : alk. paper)
ISBN-10: 0-8223-3816-5 (pbk. : alk. paper)